Marilyn Monroe
A Life of the Actress

Studies in Cinema, No. 39

Diane M. Kirkpatrick, Series Editor

Professor, History of Art
The University of Michigan

Other Titles in This Series

Marilyn Monroe
A Life of the Actress

by
Carl E. Rollyson Jr.

U·M·I Research Press

Ann Arbor, Michigan

Produced and distributed by
UMI Research Press
an imprint of
University Microfilms, Inc.
Ann Arbor, Michigan 48106

Library of Congress Cataloging in Publication Data

Rollyson, Carl E. (Carl Edmund)
  Marilyn Monroe : a life of the actress.

  (Studies in cinema ; no. 39)
  Filmography: p.
  Bibliography: p.
  Includes index.
  1. Monroe, Marilyn, 1926-1962.   2. Moving-picture
actors and actresses—United States—Biography.
I. Title. II. Series.
PN2287.M69R65 1986   791.43′028′0924 [B]   86-11322
ISBN 0-8357-1771-2 (alk. paper)

To Lisa

Contents

Figures

Acknowledgments

Several interviews were extremely valuable for the insights Monroe's friends and business associates were able to supply on the shaping of the actress's life and on her attitude toward her art. Bruce Minnix, my good friend and professional colleague, helped to arrange the initial interviews with Ralph Roberts and Steffi Sidney, the daughter of Hollywood columnist, Sidney Skolsky. Sidney made a significant contribution to this biography by shrewdly commenting on an early draft and by questioning some of the "facts" included in other books on Monroe. Because her father was ailing and no longer able to grant interviews, she relayed a few of my questions to him and discussed her own perceptions of a Monroe who delighted in carefully crafting her career in an almost conspiratorial way that often included Skolsky as her confidant. For example, when Ben Hecht had a draft of *My Story* ready for Monroe to check, she read passages from it over the phone to Skolsky to ask his opinion on how they sounded. Although Skolsky wrote a great deal about the actress, he revealed very little about those things she confided to him in strictest confidence. As a result, even his daughter cannot say for sure how much she believes in the stories her father and Monroe concocted together. And Monroe, precisely because she closely held on to parts of herself that were not for distribution, becomes that much more of a complex figure.

Ralph Roberts kindly reviewed what had been written about him in other sources and responded readily to questions about the actress's development of her talent. He conveyed a solid impression of her working life as an actress and of her fervent desire to educate herself. Our discussions of the Method led him to recommend an interview with Ellen Burstyn, who generously shared with me her experience as a movie actress. She encouraged the approach taken in chapter 7, suggested ways in which Stanislavsky would be particularly relevant to Monroe, and helped to work out an approach to life and art partly based on our discussion of Audrey Flack's painting of Monroe.

A long conversation with Audrey Flack suggested that what she had painted was what I wanted to write. For over three years she has been a constant source of support, corresponding with me regularly, commenting on drafts of the biography, and introducing it to friends and associates. Similarly, Norman Rosten consented to several interviews in person, on the phone, and in numerous letters. He has patiently responded to my pleas for advice and has shrewdly assessed several chapters of this book. I am grateful, as well, to his wife Hedda, who took the time to go over her memories of Monroe, especially those concerning *The Prince and the Showgirl*.

Rupert Allan's recollections of Monroe's career, early and late, have proved indispensable. Allan first knew her in his capacity as a writer for *Look*. Then he worked as her press representative. Through it all he remained her close friend. He checked several sections of my manuscript and answered numerous questions in person and on the phone. Stanley Flink, like Allan, first met Monroe when he was working as a writer—in Flink's case, for *Life*. As Richard Meryman suggested to me, Flink's memory of Monroe's early career remains vivid. Her wit and enormous vitality in her first Hollywood years are still reflected in Flink's amusing stories.

Meryman generously made available several hours of his tape-recorded *Life* interview with Monroe, for he wanted to demonstrate how strongly one could get caught up in the verve of her style, in the incredible energy of her laugh. John Springer, the actress's press representative on the East Coast during the last three years of her life, was also very helpful in characterizing the kind of professional life Monroe pursued in New York. Like Meryman and Rupert Allan, he assisted me in getting in touch with others who could confirm her intelligence as an artist.

Susan Strasberg made astute comments on my manuscript that led to further revisions and gave a sharper sense of her mother's part in Monroe's preparations for the screen than were to be found elsewhere. Her father was not available for an interview, but Fred Guiles supplied a tape-recording of his sessions with Lee Strasberg as well as other material that has made a crucial difference in the writing of this biography. Both Guiles and Maurice Zolotow read my early drafts and answered many questions. Without them, several important leads would have been missed.

Milton Greene was available for a brief interview, and he clarified several points about the actress's working life and discussed her attitude toward *My Story*. It was a flawed autobiography, she thought, but worth preserving. Almost everything she ever did, Greene noted, was tinged with her regret over not having been able to do it better. A long telephone interview with Rose Steinberg Wapner yielded insights on Monroe's movie set behavior, and a short one with Patricia Newcomb clarified aspects of the actress's professional plans in her last year. I regret that several other important sources were not available to be interviewed.

Several librarians were instrumental in finding obscure sources and in suggesting fruitful areas of research: Mary Corliss in the Film Stills department of the Museum of Modern Art, Maxine Fleckner and her assistant Nancy Cieki of the Wisconsin Center for Film & Theatre Research, Geraldine Duclow in the Theatre Collection of The Free Library of Philadelphia, and Nancy Goldman of the Pacific Film Archive. For their patient and prompt handling of my requests, I wish to thank the staffs of the Los Angeles Police Department and District Attorney's office; the Theatre Arts Library, University of California, Los Angeles; the Doheny Library, University of Southern California; the Margaret Herrick Library of the Academy of Motion Picture Arts and Sciences; the American Film Institute in Hollywood and in Washington, D.C.; the New York Public Library at Lincoln Center; the Library of Congress; the Columbus Public Library; the Cincinnati Public Library; and the Detroit Public Library. The Museum of Modern Art, Robert Rosen of the University of California, Los Angeles, the Library of Congress, and Films Incorporated all provided opportunities to screen Monroe's films. Although I was not able to visit the Film & Theatre Collection, Humanities Research Center, University of Texas at Austin, Edwin Neal kindly made available information on the library's considerable holdings of Monroe material, and Robert W. Daum and Paul M. Bailey arranged for a copy of Natasha Lytess's memoirs to be sent to me.

Several friends, relatives, and acquaintances were invaluable in keeping track of the enormous output of Monroe items, and my bibliography reflects the attention of the following people: Bridget Allen, George and Barbara Barnett, Judy Bischoff, Kristin Brady, JoAnna Dutka, Avrum Fenson, Mary Lee Field, Joan Fiscella, Cyril Forbes, Ken and Geraldine Grunow, Mike Harmel, Charles Harte, Paul and Jeanne Hauben, Judy Hodge, Gloria House, Mary Hrabik-Samal, M. Thomas Inge, David Jacobs, Ella Johnson, Julie Klein, Patty Mallon, Jim Michels, Bette Z. Olson, Paul Orlov, Lisa Paddock, Hope Palmer, Amy Perrone, Noel Polk, Bob Reinhard, Seymour Riklin, Virginia Rock, Bernie Rodgers, Betty Rollyson, Beulah Rollyson, Frances Saunders, Bette Savage, Roslyn Schindler, Vickie Siegal, Andy Silber, Hugh Stilley, June Taboroff, Brian Tremain, Tomasz Warchol, Rea Wilmshurst, Saul Wineman, Pat and Bob Young, and Bill Zick. For their encouragement and advice, I thank T.H. Adamowski, Shaye Areheart, Michael Daher,

Susan Feinberg, Scott Feltman, Brad Field, Joe Gomez, Barry and Sondra Gross, Barbara Lounsberry, Penelope Majeske, Michael and Jane Millgate, David Saunders, and Pat Trickey.

Bob Reinhard, Paul Orlov, David Jacobs, Joan Fiscella, Jim Michels, Joe Gomez, Anthony Summers, and Joyce Engelson all made searching comments about the various drafts of the biography. Some of the drafts were presented at the American Literature Symposium, II, University of Warsaw (1980), a Popular Culture of the South meeting (1981), joint meetings of the Popular Culture and American Culture Associations (1982, 1984), the Feminist Research in the Eighties Conference at Northern Illinois University (1982), a Midwest Modern Language Association meeting (1982), and a Modern Language Association convention (1983).

Rea Wilmshurst typed a draft of the manuscript and through careful editing saved me from committing many embarrassing errors. I owe the biggest debt of all, however, to my wife, Dr. Lisa Paddock. Every page of this book reflects her precise editing; every passage is richer for her helping me to imagine it.

Introduction

Nearly every year since her death in 1962 new biographies and reminiscences of Marilyn Monroe have appeared. There are already more books written on her than on any other movie star. She has become a great image, a legend, and a reference point in discussions of Hollywood, of the star system, and of sex symbols. Surprisingly little attention has been focused on her artistry or on what it meant to her to act in front of cameras for photographs and films. Although there is no dispute about her pervasive screen impact, there is no agreement on the size of her talent. Indeed, most accounts of her career do not even seem curious about how the actress prepared for her roles.

Joan Mellen offers keen insights on a few of Monroe's films, but her critical remarks are not integrated well with her narrative of the actress's life and career. Norman Mailer is superb on the psychology of performing, but he virtually skips the films—except for *The Misfits*—and never assesses with any rigor the development of Monroe's talent. Maurice Zolotow provides some excellent descriptions of her movie set behavior and of her performances, and Edwin Hoyt is indispensable for his interviews with Monroe's professional associates. Fred Guiles—in addition to providing the best detailed biography of Monroe—documents her absorption in the Method. Yet none of these valuable sources treats movies as events in the biography of a working actress, events that might fill in the gaps in her identity. For Marilyn Monroe, films and photographs were structures for the invisible shaping of her fragile psyche.

This book is about the interpenetration of life and art, a subject approached by other biographies of sex stars but never consistently pursued. Most histories of love goddesses fasten on changing fashions, on Hollywood as an industry producing alluring women for a society that avidly dwells on sexual display. In *Popcorn Venus*, for example, Marjorie Rosen handles Monroe as a figure of the fifties appealing to a taste for big-busted child women. In *From Reverence to Rape*, Molly

Haskell is more attuned to Monroe's unique style, but the survey format of her book allows scant room for pondering the evolution of an individual actress's method.

Situating Monroe within the tradition of sex queens reveals that as an actress in photographs, in films, and in much of her life off camera she was able to transcend that tradition and acquire a significance unrivaled by her predecessors or contemporaries. As a result, she has stimulated the imaginations of writers and artists like Edith Sitwell, Gloria Steinem, Norman Mailer, Ken Russell, and Audrey Flack as well as the commentary of journalists, show business biographers, and reviewers usually concerned with movie stars.

In the typology of Hollywood blondes, Marilyn Monroe has always been directly tied to Jean Harlow (1911–37). Sidney Skolsky, Monroe's close friend and Hollywood columnist and producer, planned to star her in a film about Harlow. Richard Avedon photographed Monroe for *Life* magazine impersonating her prototype. During the filming of *Let's Make Love* Monroe and Simone Signoret reveled in stories about Harlow told by their hairdresser, who was once in Harlow's employ. Without a doubt, Monroe identified with a woman who was often ridiculed by her contemporaries as an actress, but whose films reveal a self-confidence closely connected to the pleasure she takes in her own sexuality. Harlow can be crude and sloppy and at the same time generate sympathy because she has been exploited and brutalized. She is a victim and a survivor, which is exactly how Monroe often defined herself on screen and off. Much of Harlow's publicized private life paralleled her screen biography, and her early death at the age of twenty-six must have haunted Monroe as a ghastly example of the short-lived careers that most sex sirens have had in Hollywood.

As a rule, however, Monroe does not copy Harlow. On screen she has almost none of her exemplar's tough talking manner that apparently emanates from a conception of self more sharply defined than Monroe was ever to demonstrate as an actress. At twenty-six, Monroe was just on the verge of exploring her first major role, whereas Harlow's career was over and her life was already turning into a legend. In Monroe there is a prolonged period of adolescence, of searching for an identity, that Harlow somehow hurtles over by the age of nineteen when she performs in the Howard Hughes production of *Hell's Angels* (1930). In her five films with Clark Gable, Harlow is at her free spirited best, suggesting a healthy nonchalance about her sexuality that Monroe emulates, in a much softer style, in *The Seven Year Itch*. In that film her character, "The Girl," is not fully conscious of her sexual power, and it is hard to imagine

Harlow playing a dumb blonde with nearly so much obliviousness to her appeal.

More than Harlow, Monroe brought her life and loves to public attention. Even more than Rita Hayworth's romance with Prince Aly Khan, Monroe's marriages to Joe DiMaggio and Arthur Miller carried her beyond the bounds of Hollywood hyperbole and made of her a democratic symbol of the times. She approved of Carl Sandburg's emphasis on "the people," adopted Abraham Lincoln as her hero, and saw herself quite consciously as a product of the masses, who would publicly stand by the Lincolnesque Miller when he testified before the House Un-American Activities Committee.

Monroe prepared for her "Happy Birthday" song to John F. Kennedy in Madison Square Garden as carefully as she would for her screen roles. This was a president that Norman Mailer in 1960 described as a "great box office actor." Monroe adored Kennedy as a populist symbol expressive of the country's great possibilities that attracted immigrants like her former father-in-law, Isadore Miller, whom she made a point of introducing to the president. Rumors of her affairs with John and Robert Kennedy circulated during the last year of her life and have subsequently seen print in numerous articles and books. From the worlds of sport and the theater to politics, her mates have contributed to the mystique of a woman who so often complained about the narrowness of her film roles.

Monroe is most like Clara Bow (1905–65), a type of the American working girl on the make, using herself as a sexual advertisement. Bow clearly anticipated Monroe by energetically crafting herself as a sex symbol and then by making her public acutely aware of the heavy burden of always having to be sexy. Both women went through reclusive periods, gaining considerable weight, and succumbing to a melancholy that centered on a bewildered sense of having been hurt irreparably by the popular images of their availability they had worked so hard to create.

Lana Turner (b. 1921), Betty Grable (1916–73), and Jayne Mansfield (1934–67) do not rank very high in importance when compared to Monroe. Turner, the "Sweater Girl," shows minimal skill in most of her screen roles, although her indolent way of sauntering into some of her parts is one of the quintessential qualities of the self-assured sex queen. Betty Grable is almost too cheerful, too everyday in spite of the lavish cinematography Hollywood expended on her legs, to suggest the higher plane of sexuality on which love goddesses reign. Even at her nicest, the sex symbol has to be provocative and suggestive, and Grable is always a little too definite. She has none of the haze of innuendo that surrounds Monroe. Similarly, there is something too obvious about Mansfield, too clearly manufactured for the jokes about her body that are legion in movies like *The Girl Can't Help It* (1956).

Of course, Monroe is also the target of vulgar joking in her movies, but she has a way of enlivening her playing of stereotypes that is quite beyond Mansfield's reach. Perhaps this is why audiences that include people of all ages find Monroe's movies so entertaining. Children, for example, recognize in her the consummate player they all strive to become. In *Gentlemen Prefer Blondes*, Monroe often appears as a little girl all dolled up to look like an adult glamor queen. Not only does she speak in a babyish voice, she also responds to adults with childlike wonder. She is confused about things adults are supposed to know. She speaks of traveling to "Europe, France." She tries to put a diamond tiara around her neck because she thinks it is a necklace. In an effort to sound like an adult she assumes a faked, formalized style of speech, substituting "I" in a sentence where "me" is appropriate. She often does not know what is appropriate because she is a child who has to be parented by Jane Russell. And in one scene she is forced to make-believe with the assistance of a young boy, whose deep voice and quick thinking turn him into an adult who must extricate her from a childish mistake by helping her to pretend she is gazing out of a porthole, when actually she is stuck trying to escape from a man's room. Monroe is funny and adorable in all of these scenes because she is playing, imitating grownups. What could be more fascinating for children to watch?

On the other hand, Monroe is cagey and cunning (a wise child?) in ways that surprise the adults in the movie. She knows how to threaten a waiter to get herself seated next to someone she hopes is the richest man aboard ship. She is better prepared than her girlfriend to drug the man who has incriminating photographs of her, and she outwits her fiancé's wise old father's attempts to prevent his son's marriage. The old man exclaims, "Say, they told me you were stupid!" "I can be smart when it's important, but most men don't like it," she replies, raising questions about the devious ways she uses her intelligence. In some respects, she seems far more worldly than Russell, even though Russell is the tough talking "woman" in the film. When Monroe baby-talks to her boyfriend, she is more than just a conniving child, for she also cradles and mothers him, smoothing his lapels, his brow, his lips by way of reassurance. Clearly, in such scenes she is a seductive adult pretending to be a child.

Rita Hayworth (b. 1918), especially in *Gilda* (1946), manages to combine almost as many of the characteristics of the sex symbol as Monroe does. Hayworth is at once sexy and innocent, vulnerable and a woman of the world. She appears untrustworthy, yet she is loyal to her lover. She is more of an adult than Monroe usually plays, and she is also more assured than most of Monroe's characters. But even in her musical comedies, Hayworth's sexuality does not come off as spectacularly as Monroe's, which always lends itself to huge productions. In *Gentlemen Prefer Blondes*, for example, the film's plot simply stops for the "Diamonds Are a Girl's Best Friend" interval, which is designed to do only one thing: reinforce the stereotype of the sex goddess.

That stereotype, however, has in the figure of Monroe taken on an extraordinarily suggestive power—as Ken Russell's film, *Tommy* (1977), proves. Tommy, who is blind, deaf, and dumb, is taken by his mother to a pop culture shrine, a cathedral where the walls are covered with huge film stills of Monroe from *Niagara* and *There's No Business Like Show Business* and with photographs from all periods of her career. Monroe's acolytes carry star-shaped wands upon which are impressed circular pictures of her. With these portable icons, the acolytes touch a group of supplicants in what amounts to a form of anointment. This scene is accompanied by the lyrics "see me, feel me, touch me, heal me" as a colossal Monroe—based on the famous skirt-blowing scene in *The Seven Year Itch*—is carried into the church and attended by more acolytes, all of whom are ghoulishly masked as Monroe. While the scene recalls images of a Marilyn Monroe absolutely delighted with the circulation of air, of life, around her thighs, the beautifully uplifted skirts of *The Seven Year Itch* are frozen in *Tommy* in the cheap perversity of worshipping a plaster-of-Paris dime store mannequin.

The pasty statue on the pedestal is carried through the church to where various cripples hope to be healed by tapping into Monroe's vibrancy. Eventually the statue is placed on a circular mirror-topped platform, and the cripples pass by not only to touch but to look into the mirror that reflects Monroe's legs all the way up to her panties. Several shots of her mirrored thighs are intercut with the sequence of supplicants. The elevation of this goddess, like much cheap magic, is done with mirrors, with reflecting surfaces that have no depth, no resonance; they represent, instead, only the shadow play of self-realization, the suggestion of a complete identity that bemuses the insubstantial, cryptic individual, the crippled self. In other words, the cripples seek to embrace a wholeness that is sustained only in the presentation of Monroe's image. When Tommy's mother forces him to make contact with the Monroe statue, there is a struggle that eventuates in his crashing against it and smashing it into fragments. The sight of Monroe's shattered figure seems to mock the vision of renewal mirrored in the full revelation of her healthy thighs.

Tommy's ambivalent portrayal of stardom is comparable to a complex attitude toward stereotyping that makes Monroe as actress and mythic figure stand out from her sex symbol counterparts. No film actress has ever been better at playing a type, and mythic figures thrive on an exact, vibrant repetition of a role, so that the community (in this case, a movie audience) can follow along in an almost ritualistic pattern. The actress's individuality is not emphasized, except in the sense that she is better at exemplifying the type than any of her competitors. She then functions as the matrix, the source from which the stereotype seems to have originated. On a movie set, each part of a role can be gone over for as long as it takes until the right copy of the type has been achieved. Monroe was meticulous about just this kind of repetition, and insisted on take after take, to the chagrin of her fellow actors.

Monroe knew, however, that repetition robbed her of the diversity that is essential to the growth of a complex personality and of a sophisticated talent. She faced a dilemma that all popular culture symbols have to solve: how to stay within type but produce enough variation to remain intriguing. At the same time, she contemplated the prospect of shattering the stereotype altogether, so that she could come entirely into her own as a person and a character actress. As a person, an actress, and a mythic figure she had different kinds of work to do, but each kind called upon what the actress knew best: role making. Thus Monroe's life and career have to be seen in terms of her constant inventiveness, of her attempts at artistry in all things.

Norman Mailer's biography comes close to perceiving the creative dynamic of Monroe's life, of her urge to become the artist of her own self-transformation, but only in Audrey Flack's painting, *Marilyn* (1977), is it possible to begin seeing how the myth of the artist's self is demonstrated in the actress's work. The texture of Flack's eight-foot-square canvas is dense with the symbols of self-transformation: mirrors, perfume, and various implements of makeup—like the lipstick, the powder puff, and the makeup jars in Monroe's hair. Concomitantly, the burning candle, the timepiece, the hourglass, and the calendar mark the awareness that human identity is confined to a short span—as Elton John's recording of "Candle in the Wind," which Flack played constantly while painting, emphasizes.

Marilyn narrates Monroe's brief life in the sense that she faces us as an image Flack has painted from a 1950 photograph which captures, as Flack rightly observes, a state of transition in which Norma Jeane blends into Marilyn. Her expression is enthusiastic, but this is truer of the original photograph than of the painting, for Flack has lined Monroe's brow with a slight trace of pain. The calendar is turned to August, the month of Monroe's suicide, and the black end of the paintbrush points to the day she died. The flower, the fruits, the luxuriance of the drapery,

Figure 1. Audrey Flack, *Marilyn* (Vanitas), 1977
Oil over acrylic on canvas, 96″ × 96″.
*(Courtesy Louis K. Meisel Gallery/Audrey Flack;
Photograph by Bruce G. Jones)*

the bold colors—especially the reds—evoke memories of the color schemes of Monroe's movies and of her photographs, especially the nude calendar shot of 1949. But these are Flack's colors as well, colors that dominate many of her other paintings and that are especially prominent in her *Vanitas* series, of which *Marilyn* is a part. The point of *Vanitas*, Flack explains, is to "encourage the viewer to think about the meaning and purpose of life." The meaning of Flack's life is also indicated by her inclusion of a photograph of herself as a child and by the paintbrush with its drops of paint on the paperback text of Mailer's biography of Monroe, a biography that gives Monroe credit for painting herself into an instrument of her own will.

Flack shows that there is a natural progression from Mailer's text (which is about Monroe's childhood discovery of makeup), to the photograph of Monroe (which represents what the actress has made of herself for the camera), to the whole painting's vision of the need for self-definition, the need for one artist to inspire another artist to inspire another artist, and so on. By depicting Monroe's reflection in a domestic context—in a dressing table mirror—Flack forces us to probe our own desire for recognition, so that we can see ourselves in a larger world. Monroe's distorted image (notice how her face takes on the oval shape of the mirror) makes manifest the ways in which the self's own shape is twisted, magnified, elongated, and blurred in the process of reproduction. Although this painting is very specifically about one woman's replicated life, it can also be read as the story of the underlying motivations that drive all people to be creative, to fashion the largest possible sense of themselves. Through this work of art Monroe's life becomes a paradigm of all lives, and Monroe, to use Mailer's phrase, becomes "the magnified mirror of ourselves."

1

Childhood (1926–1938)

On the outside of the world

On February 11, 1924, Gladys Pearl Baker married Martin E. Mortensen. She already had two children (who were not living with her) by a previous marriage to John Newton Baker, from whom she was divorced. She was a quiet woman who worked as a film cutter at one of the studios in Hollywood. Gladys kept to herself most of the time, and friends and family never seem to have fathomed what went wrong in her second marriage to Mortensen, a union that lasted only sixteen months. Although they were not divorced until June 1, 1927, Gladys left him two years earlier on May 25, 1925. When her daughter, Norma Jeane, was born on June 1, 1926, the birth certificate listed her last name as Mortensen, although Mortensen almost certainly was not her father.

Gladys never told Norma Jeane who her father was, although the mother confided to her daughter a few things about him, including a story about his death in an auto accident that the child refused to believe. Many years later when Norma Jeane became the starlet, Marilyn Monroe, she learned that her father was Stanley Gifford, one of her mother's coworkers in the film industry. He refused to acknowledge her efforts to contact him, and she took his rejection bitterly. It gave her one more reason to think of herself as a "waif."

Norma Jeane never had anything resembling a normal relationship with her mother. Just twelve days after the child's birth, Gladys took her to Wayne and Ida Bolender's home in Hawthorne, California. They were neighbors who would look after the baby for more than six years while Gladys worked. Gladys must have doubted her capacity to handle a child full time because even when she was not working she seemed more like an aloof visitor to the Bolender home than a mother who missed her child. She did not respond to her daughter's use of the word "mama." Instead, as Monroe later remembered it, her mother stared at her and gave no sign of affection. She did not even hold her daughter, and she barely spoke to the expectant little girl. On visits with Gladys, Norma Jeane was frightened and spent most of her time in the bedroom closet hidden among her clothes. Gladys cautioned Norma Jeane not to make "so much noise," as if the child were an intruder. Even the sound of Norma Jeane turning the pages of a book made her mother nervous. In sum, the child had few opportunities to behave in a free, spontaneous, and autonomous fashion.

Norma Jeane looked for a way to fill the void in her visits with her mother. She noticed on the wall of Gladys's room a photograph of a rather jaunty looking man with a lively smile and a Clark Gable mustache, and she was thrilled to learn from her mother that this robust figure was her father. No more was said about the photograph, but Norma Jeane dreamed about it constantly, probably because it exemplified the exuberance of spirit stilled within her.

In October of 1933, Gladys felt confident enough to move with her six-year-old daughter into a white frame bungalow. The mother evidently promised that now Norma Jeane could look forward to a warmer home life, including piano lessons. Indeed, the child would be the center of attention as the mother sat near a fireplace on a loveseat listening to her play. All of these idyllic visions abruptly vanished when Gladys was committed to Norwalk State Hospital in January of 1934 and diagnosed as a paranoid schizophrenic. Just five years earlier, Gladys's mother, Della Monroe, had died in the same hospital during treatment for "manic depressive psychosis."

Norma Jeane spent several months with an English couple, movie extras who had rented part of the bungalow from Gladys. Then Grace McKee, Gladys's friend and coworker, was named the child's guardian. But McKee kept her ward with her for only a brief period, and Norma Jeane found herself in her first foster home with the Giffens family before being sent to an orphanage on September 13, 1935, where she spent nearly two years. When she left the institution in June of 1937, she stayed temporarily with two foster families before settling again with Grace in January or February of 1938.

In her years as a starlet, Marilyn Monroe would exaggerate the number of foster homes she was transferred to and the drudgery of washing dishes in an orphanage, fabricate a rape story, embellish various versions of an incident involving her grandmother Della's attempt to smother her, and dwell on several traumatic events worthy of inclusion in a Dickensian novel. Most of her shocking tales had some basis in her feeling that she had been deprived and violated at a very early age. The normal pattern of growth had been disrupted, and she had trouble making the usual connections between herself and the world that children from stable families take for granted.

Norma Jeane had to discover some way of building and controlling her self-image in a world that could easily wipe away her attachments to it. She turned to daydreaming and to the movies as a means of self-fortification, for she was a child who "often felt lonely and wanted to die." As Monroe later put it, fantasizing exercised her imagination: "in a daydream you jump over facts as easily as a cat jumps over a fence." Daydreams provided her with an effortless, instantaneous attractiveness: "I daydreamed chiefly about beauty. . . . Daydreaming made my work easier." She dreamed of appearing naked in church for "God and everyone else to see."

Movies also filled in the gaps in her identity. They made her feel more alive and more conscious and better able to visualize and screen the world that otherwise excluded her. There was nothing she could not follow on the screen, and nothing that could diminish the intensity of her perceptions. She concentrated on movements "up there" "with the screen so big"—her phrasing dramatically recaptures what must have been the child's awestruck love of the magnification of human experience on film, which seems to have compensated for the diminution of her own experience outside of the movie house.

Occasionally incidents in her childhood seemed to presage her later envelopment in image building. The actress remembered, for example, the time of her return to the orphanage after having tried to run away. She feared punishment and instead was greeted by the compassionate superintendent, Mrs. Dewey, who took Norma Jeane in her arms, told her she was pretty, and powdered the child's face with a powder puff. No doubt the actress could not resist dramatizing this incident, for in another version she went on to describe how Mrs. Dewey had her look in the mirror and observe her face, soft and alabaster smooth like her mother's. "This was the first time in my life I felt loved—no one had ever noticed my face or hair or me before," Monroe told a publicity woman at 20th Century-Fox.

Norma Jeane was "buoyant for days" after this recognition scene, but when nothing resembling it was repeated, she began to doubt that it had actually taken place. Like so many of her other experiences, this one was fragmentary; it seemed to lead her nowhere. She felt incomplete, as orphans and adopted children often do. She really did not know what to expect from one moment to the next from people who did not have time for her. Since the gratification she did receive seemed equivocal, she apparently divided her personality in two. In her dreams, she was naked and unsullied, an immaculate figure. In reality, she submitted to degrading experiences—such as having to bathe in the water her foster family had used before her. She always came last, or so it seemed to her.

Gladys' unresponsiveness must have made Norma Jeane wonder if she made a difference to anyone. She needed to see herself reflected in her mother's eyes and mirrored in her mother's concerns. A child who cannot find herself in her mother's face suffers from the same alienation that prevents the mother from truly recognizing her own child. As a result, such a child, in Alice Miller's words, "would remain without a mirror, and for the rest of his life would be seeking this mirror in vain."

There have been cases of such children who become mirrors to themselves. R.D. Laing describes a child who actually used a mirror as a way of becoming "another person to himself who could look at him from the mirror." As Monroe turned toward mirrors for self-confirmation, as she mentions doing in *My Story* (her autobiography written by Ben Hecht), she may have experienced the duality that others have felt who fail to have their beings confirmed by their mothers or fathers, and so look for a means to make themselves seen as "real live persons." Certainly she suffered from the "persecutory features" that have been identified in persons who split themselves into two parts. They feel threatened with the disappearance of their own beings whenever others fail to endorse their presence.

Monroe's guardians provided contradictory definitions of her. What could she make of her various "homes"? The Bolenders were fundamentalists and teetotalers, the English couple were drinkers and allowed Norma Jeane to play with their liquor bottles, and Grace McKee, married to Erwin "Doc" Goddard when Norma Jeane returned to her in early 1938, ran a household considerably more easygoing than that of the strict Bolenders. Mutually exclusive environments were discordant. Norma Jeane could not confidently validate her feelings or believe that anyone trusted her. In *My Story*, Monroe says, "I knew people only told lies to children—lies about everything from soup to Santa Claus."

Of course, Norma Jeane was not entirely without resources or mentors. In fact, for nearly four years, beginning in 1938, she could count not only on her guardian Grace Goddard, but also on Grace's aunt, Ana Lower, a devout Christian Scientist. Until Ana Lower died in 1948, Norma Jeane and the starlet Marilyn Monroe tried to follow the teachings of a religion that emphasized the power of "right thoughts" in allaying pain and suffering. Illness and sin were illusions that could be overcome by the power of the mind. Christian Science must have functioned as a welcome mental hygiene in her early life and as a way of practicing self-reliance, as did her daydreams.

"I dreamed of myself walking proudly in beautiful clothes and being admired by everyone and overhearing words of praise," Monroe later recalled in *My Story*. The energy of what may have been an incipient erotic desire saved her from the severest feelings of self-loss, in which a person lacks not only the customary sense of "personal unity," but also, R. D. Laing suggests, a "sense of himself as the agent of his own actions . . . of being the agent of his own perceptions." At a very early age, Monroe seemingly invested her dream self with an attractiveness that at least partially transcended her public humiliation. Fantasies are often used to replenish a depleted identity. In acute cases, they become increasingly delusional, but as Monroe entered her adolescence, her craving for attention coincided with her growing physical beauty. Very quickly her fantasies were realized as she captivated her first male audiences.

2

Adolescence to Adulthood (1938–1945)

Suddenly everything opened up

By the age of eleven or twelve, Norma Jeane began wearing tight clothing that accentuated her rapidly developing figure. This sexual exposure
was exhilarating, and she seemed to revel in the attention of schoolboys,
workers, and other people on the street. Adulation made her feel a part
of things for the first time in her life. She could drop the oppressive,
inhibiting sense of belonging to nobody in exchange for an exuberant,
sensual contact with the elements of life itself, with the wind that
caressed her as she zoomed along on a bike borrowed from an admiring
group of boys. She felt, however, like "two people," the neglected
Norma Jeane and some new being who "belonged to the ocean and the
sky and the whole world." She grasped for the grandeur of life even as
she was riddled with anxiety about her rootlessness and failure to locate
herself in a specific world.

The mature Monroe reflected that her emerging sexuality "was a
kind of double-edged thing." It got her the attention she craved, but it
also resulted in "overly friendly" advances. Her guardians worried
about her high spirits, which could be so easily misinterpreted as hysteria. This shy girl had found a way to impress herself on others as soon as
she realized just how pleased they were with her presence. But what ties
would she make in a world suddenly so accessible? And how could
Norma Jeane handle these new companions when she had so little family, properly speaking, to guide her in her choices?

Grace Goddard seems to have been the first to suggest to Norma
Jeane, some time in the early spring of 1942, the idea of marrying James
Dougherty. Ana Lower apparently concurred with Grace's belief that
the twenty-one year old Dougherty would bring stability to this fifteen-
year-old girl's life. At first, Norma Jeane–still very uncertain about her
own place in the world– clung to Dougherty in grateful appreciation of
his genial effort to be, in his words, "her lover, husband, and father."

She would join with him in establishing the first home of her own. They were married on June 19, 1942, just three weeks after her sixteenth birthday.

In retrospect, at least, it is clear that Dougherty took on too much. After the United States entered the war, he was anxious to participate and deferred his decision to enlist only to placate a young wife terrified at the prospect of losing the sense of permanence that marriage initially promised. He was there, in part, to bolster her confidence, and she may have regarded his overseas duty in the Merchant Marine in early 1944 as an attack on the marriage itself. In her calmer moods, she did not resent his war service, but in her emotional periods she blamed him for wrecking their relationship—just as she faulted Gladys for abandoning her. His departure seems to have been a direct blow to her sense of self-worth, to her own reason for living, so that she had to find another way of surviving. The night before he was to ship out she became hysterical and pleaded with him "to make her pregnant," so that she would have a part of him if he did not return. She dreaded his leaving, refused to talk about it, and in desperation announced that she planned to call her father. This was evidently the first occasion on which she tried to contact him, and she may have been trying to certify her existence in still another way.

Norma Jeane had a terrible anxiety about being alone. There were too many gaps in her life, and like other women of her age and troubling background, she panicked. She was not depressed or sad; rather, she was out of control and absolutely at a loss when contemplating the absence of her husband's continued attentions. She was far from inconsolable, however, and quickly took up war work herself as a paint sprayer and parachute packer in an airplane factory. Of paramount importance was that she feel needed and recognized. As a diligent worker, she managed to cope with her husband's departure quite well. As a result, the marriage itself may have seemed less crucial to her well being and more like an interim identity, the first substantial role in which she had invested herself.

In her new role as aircraft employee, Norma Jeane had no trouble at all getting noticed. On June 26, 1945 David Conover came to the factory to photograph young women engaged in war work. He found Norma Jeane fascinating in her own right. For three days he marveled at how easily she performed for his camera. She was a quick study who sensed that a whole new world was opening up to her, and she began to make suggestions about how she should be positioned for shots at various factory locations.

With Conover's encouragement, a modeling and movie career suggested itself almost immediately and her commitment to Dougherty diminished considerably. She wrote him fewer letters, eventually quit her war job, and single-mindedly pursued her new goal. On his return to the States he tried to win her back, but he had very little interest in her dreams of stardom and could not identify with the success she had made of herself while he was away. Although they were not officially divorced until September 13, 1946, the marriage was surely over in Norma Jeane's mind by late 1945 when she was employed by Emmeline Snively's modeling agency.

In reflecting on her first marriage, Monroe bitterly regretted it as years that held her back. She was quite aggressive in dismissing the significance of her feelings for Dougherty, as though her real life only began with the moment of her photographed self's incarnation. She stressed that she had come to Hollywood after the breakup of her marriage out of more than a desire for fame and adulation; she was coming in a spirit of self-interrogation. She was going to live by herself, at nineteen, and she was going to "find out who I was." Dougherty would have kept her from even attempting this daring discovery of an identity.

In 1945 and 1946 she was reborn, mastering new images of herself the camera helped her to find, just as an infant manipulates images of itself duplicated in a mirror. Could a fully realized self emerge from her posing for the camera? With a lens focused on her, she was simultaneously learning to hold the world in her gaze. Perhaps the intense drama of her photographic sessions could make up for the insufficiency, the dullness, she had previously experienced.

Both Emmeline Snively and David Conover recall Norma Jeane's persistent scrutiny of photographic prints. She wanted to be able to recognize her mistakes and to make each shot as perfect as possible. She was a hard-working apprentice who was much more inquisitive than Snively's other models, for she wanted to know as much as possible about the powers of projection.

André de Dienes, who photographed Norma Jeane against various landscapes in early 1946, captures her ingenuous youthfulness and self-assurance. With her frizzy brown hair, uneven jawline, somewhat bulbous nose, and slightly protruding front teeth she is hardly ready to metamorphose into Marilyn Monroe. But she often gazes directly at the spectator and conveys the impression of a willing, malleable subject. Her sexual playfulness and the organic sensuousness of the scenes she is placed in are happily congruent. She is a pliable performer and utterly at ease whether she rests against a rustic fence railing or clings to the side of a mountain slope.

Norma Jeane's work habits were admirable. She was punctual and well prepared for each day's shooting session, and her resilience was extraordinary. Yet de Dienes observed that she was also curiously frail and that she would "curl up in the front of the car and fall asleep" when her assignment was finished. It is not surprising, of course, for a performer to let down after the excitement of a performance, but to de Dienes, Norma Jeane seemed out of focus when she did not have the camera's attention. His impressions echo what other photographers would later notice: "Her hours passed in a state of dreaminess that left her oblivious of the environment, and this began to irritate him."

De Dienes had illusions that this young woman would fall in love with him, but she seemed bent on demonstrating her independence and dated several young men who shared her ambition to be successful in Hollywood. Robert Slatzer, who first met Norma Jeane in the summer of 1946 at the studios of 20th Century-Fox, remembers her taking a deep interest in his poetry. In turn, he indicated that he might be able "to write a story about her." Occasionally they shared rented rooms during her early Hollywood years and, according to Slatzer, sporadically carried on a love affair. Apparently he never pressed his suit too ardently, and she found him a reliable sounding board. In his book, he seems to exaggerate the confidence she placed in him, but there is little doubt about the value of someone like Slatzer to her. With him she could be uninhibited about her love of poetry and even write some light verse for his amusement. Another male friend, Bill Burnside, remembers her liking for Shelley and Keats and how what she most wanted from him was his education. She built up a considerable library and a small circle of friends who could help her with reading she thought was essential to the development of herself as a person and a professional actress. Slatzer was only nineteen when he met her; she could appreciate a companion who understood her yearning to establish a big reputation and who was neither a rival nor an authority with whom she had to contend. She seemed to turn to him when the pressures of her career and personal life became more than she could handle.

Slatzer portrays himself as exceedingly tolerant of her wildly fluctuating moods and willing to respond immediately to her erratic personal overtures to him. If that was how he reacted to her, it is conceivable that she trusted him in ways that her other friends and professional associates would have found surprising. A far more aggressive lover like de Dienes could easily have seemed manipulative, and she would not submit to his plans, personal and professional, for her. His photographs — like all of the countless others she would pose for in this period — were not the definitive word on her; rather, they served as her threshold to a larger world.

3

Early Career (1945–1950)

It was the creative part that kept me going—trying to be an actress.

About a year after she began working as a professional photographer's model, Norma Jeane Dougherty signed her first movie contract as Marilyn Monroe with 20th Century-Fox on August 26, 1946. Modeling had been just a crucial step toward an acting career. She posed for department stores and industrial shows in a variety of clothing from sports outfits to negligees, diligently took lessons in makeup, grooming, and posing at Ms. Snively's school, and appeared on the covers of several magazines. But she had no clear idea of how to go about learning to become an actress. Of course she had to spend most of her time acquiring modeling skills, which to some extent would advance her toward acting, and she had to spend the rest of her time supporting herself through modeling jobs. Nevertheless, in the next three years—even after she was under studio contract and had taken courses in acting, dancing, and singing—she showed little promise as an actress.

She had virtually no acting experience when she was signed to her first contract at Fox, yet acting, she later insisted, "was this secret in me . . . something golden and beautiful . . . like the bright colors Norma Jean[e] used to see in her daydreams." It was not an art but a game about "worlds so bright they made your heart leap just to think of them." Acting was her compulsion: "a thing in me like a craziness that wouldn't let up." It would eventually become a transformative process capable of expanding the boundaries of her small and lonely being.

The year before she signed her first contract with Fox, Emmeline Snively told her, "You're very girl-next-doorish." Her face and figure were pleasing, sometimes provocative, but not yet compelling as perfect sexual shapes. She had to learn to smile with her upper lip drawn down in order to help minimize the length of her nose and to hide her gumline. The result of this adjustment was a wavering of her lips that is first glimpsed at the end of her second scene in *The Asphalt Jungle* and then emphasized in closeups of *Gentlemen Prefer Blondes*, where her undulating lip seems like a miniature of the movement of her whole seductive body. So that she could be adapted to a variety of modeling assignments, her hair had to be cut short, straightened, bleached honey blonde, and styled in a "sophisticated upsweep."

Such changes imposed a welcome redefinition of her person; now she had a specific role to play. Yet she had not chosen this identity and she resisted, momentarily, Hollywood's highlighting techniques. Emmeline Snively had to persuade her to consider both a screen name and the physical changes that would make her a negotiable prospect in the modeling agency's dealings with the studios. Thus a role was grafted onto her, and she had to fuse herself to it, which she did by joining Monroe, Gladys's maiden name, to Marilyn, the first name proposed for her at the studio by Ben Lyon, the executive in charge of new talent, who had been so deeply impressed with her youth and beauty that he immediately arranged for a screen test on July 17, just five weeks before she signed the contract he had promised her at their first meeting.

She was good visual material—this was the verdict on the screen test, which was silent and shot in color. She was directed to "walk across the set. Sit down. Light a cigarette. Put it out. Go upstage. Cross. Look out a window. Sit down. Come downstage and exit." She is supposed to have looked and acted like "one of those lush stars of the silent era." On screen she was palpable, kinetic—"all fire" one witness to the test exclaims.

Yet what to make of "Marilyn Monroe" seemed to puzzle both the actress and her studio. Publicity shots of the period 1946 to 1948 reveal nothing about her intense desire to act or about what kind of roles might best suit her. The arbitrariness of the shots is most striking. Monroe is there to make the poses, fulfill the assignments: in a makeup session, in a series of yogalike exercises, in skimpy bathing suits, in low-cut evening gowns, in a potato sack, in a babysitting sequence, in an acting lesson, in tights, in sultry poses, nightgowns and tee shirts, and playing baseball. This miscellany provides no apparent unity of image, no archetypal Monroe—although her vibrancy makes some of these ephemeral shots captivating.

After about six months of this modeling and some appearances as an extra, she was given an exceedingly small part in *Scudda Hoo! Scudda Hay!* Her role was not essential, and the closeups taken of her were eventually eliminated, so that her presence in the film was reduced to a long shot in which her face is indistinguishable. Rose Steinberg Wapner, a script assistant on several of Monroe's films, beginning with *Scudda Hoo! Scudda Hay!*, remembers a Monroe sweetly and innocently committed to dreams of stardom. "How do you become a star?" she asked Wapner as the two of them traveled by car to a movie set. At twenty-one, this starlet did not seem anything like a stunning, provocative female personality. Instead, she was like "many girls," Wapner remarks, who were eager to fit themselves into the proportions of stardom.

On August 25, 1947, after a year of very little film work, Monroe's contract was canceled. She continued to take acting lessons and to play a few stage roles. She did not create much of an impression in her theatrical debut at the Bliss-Hayden Miniature Theatre in Beverly Hills, where she appeared in *Glamour Preferred* from October 12 to November 2, but she was remembered for her subsequent willingness to play whatever role she was cast in. She had not yet made friends with the kind of people who could promote and guide her career, although she would start to do so in December of 1947 by signing a personal management contract with John Carroll and Lucille Ryman (husband and wife), who would be instrumental in securing her first featured role in *The Asphalt Jungle*.

Even as a model Monroe sometimes failed to demonstrate talent. John Engstead remembers her pose for a *Photoplay* photograph entitled "How a Star Is Born." Against a background of velvet draperies "the starlet would stand in an elaborate gown with her hands outstretched with an isn't it wonderful expression." A reticent Monroe arrived promptly for her assignment, "put up her arms, smiled, and that was that." Engstead was impressed with her pretty face, but he cannot account for what "transformed this sweet young thing into the superstar and sex symbol of a generation." Indeed, her "isn't it wonderful" photograph is lifeless; she looks like a mannequin, a stiff-limbed waxworks "star." Posing for this photograph was not so wonderful, her lack of a focused expression implies. There is an aimlessness about the whole composition; nothing about the frozen figure sustains attention.

Monroe's earlier photographs, especially those with Conover and de Dienes, were probably successful because a certain degree of improvisation was encouraged, and she was free to invent a repertoire of poses against settings in which she was extremely comfortable. In the series with Conover she was performing against the background of her working life in a factory. For de Dienes she had landscapes to which she could respond. What could she place herself against in the brief session with Engstead? Her arms are held up in this photograph, but they lack the force of a genuine uplifting gesture. Her mechanical posture may derive from the absence of continuity in the conditions of her employment.

It was at this point that Monroe's first powerful mentor began to shape for her a sense of what a whole career would look like. Sometime during the end of her first year at Fox she met Joseph M. Schenck, an executive producer, one of the founders of the studio and of the star system. Schenck took an early interest in Monroe for her "offbeat personality." She later described herself sitting around his fireplace listening to him talk wisely about "love and sex" as though he were a "great explorer." She was fascinated with his visage: "It was as much the face of a town as of a man. The whole history of Hollywood was in it." These were lean days for her, and both his food and dinner guests fed her ambitions. She believed Schenck would secure her status at the studio, and while she was not kept at Fox, he may have persuaded Harry Cohn, head of Columbia pictures, to sign her to a contract in March of 1948. She denied the gossip that she was "Joe Schenck's girl" and that she performed sexual favors for him in return for his support of her career. She was secretive about her sex life, but several of her friends believe she used sex as a way of saying thank you to men who had helped her.

In her first months at Columbia in the spring of 1948 Monroe struggled to find herself as an actress. Natasha Lytess, an acting coach, was instructed by her boss, Max Arnow, to see what could be done for Monroe. In Lytess's bitter and self-serving memoir she recalls that her pupil "was more than inhibited, more than cramped. She couldn't say a word freely." Single-handedly, Lytess would have readers believe, she shaped Monroe into the semblance of an actress. Lytess tried to make Monroe her protegee, even taking her into her home several years later during the making of *Clash by Night*. As a result, the actress became increasingly dependent on her coach for advice and insisted that Lytess accompany her on movie sets.

Under Lytess's supervision, Monroe would read scripts several times and underline or circle words to indicate the way in which they ought to be emphasized. She also marked scripts to indicate character traits or questions of interpretation that she wanted to discuss with Lytess. She developed a sense of deliberateness that simply would not allow her to be rushed. She was starting to treat her own body, her own strenuously acquired sensitivity, as instruments—a point she was to emphasize in her last recorded interview. Finally, with Lytess she could talk over the world of ideas without sounding pretentious. On movie sets male directors had been skeptical of her intellectual curiosity and ridiculed her reading of writers like Rilke and Tom Paine.

Of equal importance in the initial development of Monroe's talent were Fred Karger's efforts. Karger's ostensible role was that of musical coach, but in fact he became for her an exemplar of elegant style and clear performances. He was a handsome man with a compelling smile. His compact physique perfectly complemented his neat and efficient handling of a song. Nothing was wasted on this immaculate figure with whom Monroe quickly fell in love.

Although Karger responded warmly to Monroe by introducing her to his mother and sister and by frequently taking her out, he also had his reservations about her curious blend of immaturity and raw ambition. He was put off by her "embryonic" mind, which was also "inert" and barely conscious of the life around her. He hurt her, but she recognized the honesty of his remarks and valued his objective appraisals. It was at his urging, for example, that she submitted to the plastic surgery and dental work that removed the imperfections visible in the photographs by Conover and de Dienes. She progressed steadily under Karger's professional supervision and gradually withdrew from his equivocal courting of her.

Karger had shown Monroe that she could work according to a rigorous, concentrated schedule and produce a convincing performance. Natasha Lytess might be preparing her for her future as a serious artist, but Karger had gotten her ready in a very short period for her immediate assignment, second lead in *Ladies of the Chorus* (1949). This was her first sizable role, and she performed well. In his review of the film in *Motion Picture Herald*, Tibor Krekes noted that "one of the bright spots is Miss Monroe's singing. She is pretty and, with her pleasing voice and style, she shows promise." The movie—shot in eleven days—seems to have been designed to be forgotten, for the plot, the characters, and the songs are very bland and barely credible. The movie received very few reviews, and Monroe was not able to impress the studio with her performance. On the contrary, her Columbia contract was terminated after the first six months. It was hardly her fault, since her role had so little room for subtlety of characterization. She plays a chorus girl, Peggy, engaged to marry a wealthy young man (Rand Brooks). She is fearful that his family will reject her as soon as it learns of her lowly show business background. Her fears are happily dissolved when her fiancé's mother (Nana Bryant), convinced that Peggy loves her son, pretends in front of guests at an engagement party to have a secret show business background of her own in order to ease Peggy's entrance into high society.

For Monroe, this trite movie represented a tangible manifestation of her new life. She had finally been able to follow herself across a movie screen as she had followed so many stars in her childhood. That gloomy childhood—or at least her somber sense of her early years—was lightened by the glowing sign of her success. She had managed to have an impact on the world, at least briefly, in the enlarged brightness of her own image. No wonder she repeatedly drove past the theater featuring her film, for it was like watching the announcement of her new identity, an announcement even more exciting than the fifty-foot-tall skirt-flying likeness of herself, an advertisement for *The Seven Year Itch* later put onto the front of the State Theatre Building in New York City.

With no more than this token of success in hand, she was forced into other work after the expiration of her Columbia contract on September 8, 1948. In late August and early September she appeared in a production of *Stage Door* at the Bliss-Hayden Theatre, and she is reported to have worked briefly as a stripper at the Mayan Theatre in downtown Los Angeles. As an actress unattached to a studio contract, she was able to get only very small roles in *Love Happy* (1949) and *A Ticket to Tomahawk* (1950). The latter, in which she has one song and dance number with Dan Dailey and a few incidental appearances with three other dancehall girls, is almost as forgettable as *Ladies of the Chorus*. But the former, a Marx brothers production with a built-in audience, features her in an extremely brief but highly visible walk-on in a tight, low-cut, sequined gown.

Slinking into Groucho's office (he is playing a detective), she asks for his help. After asking "What can I do for you?" he saunters directly toward the camera and in an aside comments, "As if I didn't know." Then, in mock seriousness, he inquires, "What seems to be the problem?" She replies, "Well, men keep following me all the time!" The scene received extraordinary attention, which the film's producer, Lester Cowan, helped to generate by putting Monroe on a cross-country publicity tour. For the first time she had been really noticed in a film, and in spite of the brevity of the part, her entrance offered a foretelling of what was to become one crucial aspect of her screen persona: a curious blend of innocence and maturity. She has a puzzled, naïve quality, so she is the perfect target of Groucho's wisecrack, but her body and the way she uses it suggest that she knows the answer to her "problem." She rests her right hand on Groucho's upper chest and leans against him. Then her fingers move slowly up his shoulder in command of him, and her eyebrows are slightly arched as she sways past the camera with lowered lids. Surely a woman who can handle herself in such a deliberately provocative manner is conscious of the power of her sexuality. Her saucy hips playfully belie her sweet voice—that is part of the joking nature of her appeal.

Of course, there was no way to know if what Monroe could project for less than a minute could also be sustained for a whole film. She was still a figure, not even a face in films. With her anonymity still intact, and with a desperate need for some ready cash ($50) to make a car payment, she consented to pose for a nude calendar shot by Tom Kelley on May 27, 1949. Like her role in *Love Happy*, the two nude calendar poses, "Golden Dreams" and "A New Wrinkle," emphasize her body, not her face, as a decorative item. It was not the intention of either the movie or the calendar photographs to identify Marilyn Monroe as such. Indeed, it would be a few years before the discovery of her pose for the calendar. She would not be recognized immediately because she was modeled as a type of figure that was popular on such calendars at the time. Yet, as in the case of *Love Happy*, she brought an added dimension to the type; her pose stands out from other "girlie" pictures of that era.

Like her screen test, one of the calendar shots—in which she lies across a red velvet background—became an exercise in the creation of striking visual effects and a composition that has been called a work of "perfect symmetry." The overall picture is one of harmonious movement between the model and her background. Her long blonde hair cascades across the flowing diagonal folds of red velvet drapery. There is a sexual tension in the way she thrusts her right hand into her hair, a bit of coyness in her seeming to glance back at the viewer from her twisted pose, and an impression of subtle delicacy is conveyed by her fingers, which barely touch the velvet.

A vivid, self-directed personality is portrayed in this photograph. Note, for example, how the model has framed her face with her right arm, tilted her head upward and to her right, opened her red lips slightly—her upper front teeth are showing—and shifted her eyes to the right as well. Although such girlie pictures ordinarily depict passive women who open themselves up to lascivious inspection, Monroe's calendar shot seems a new wrinkle indeed, for the model is nothing if not active and in control of the sight lines in this pose.

Did Monroe intend precisely these effects? Was she conscious of compositional techniques? Her photographer, Tom Kelley, has stated (probably in hindsight) that he was "convinced that she had a genius for sensing what the camera saw as she posed." She worked for two hours without any specific coaching from Kelley. He recalls that "she was as graceful as an otter, turning sinuously with utter naturalness." The inhibitions Lytess had observed in the young actress "vanished as soon as her clothes were removed," Kelley remembers. Monroe later recalled that the "striking [of] joyous poses" while nude reminded her of childhood dreams and momentarily saddened her until "after a few poses" she realized how much she liked her body. As usual, the star was trying to tie up the loose ends of her life by transforming them into a coherent narrative of her self's slow emergence, yet it is also likely that her

Figure 2.   "A New Wrinkle," 1949
Nude calendar pose of Marilyn Monroe by Tom Kelley.
(®*Tom Kelley Studios; courtesy Movie Star News*)

absorption of the photographic medium was having a cumulative impact upon her, so that she could begin to gather together her experience and express it coherently.

Monroe's work on *Love Happy* and the nude calendar suggests that she was learning how to attract professional notice. She was also meeting people like John Carroll, a movie actor who bore some resemblance to Clark Gable, and Carroll's wife, Lucille Ryman, who was also active in the motion picture business. They were friends of Ben Lyon, the studio executive who offered Monroe her first contract. Carroll and Ryman were moved by Monroe's vulnerability and seeming lack of guidance. They decided to manage her, even though she had her own agent, Harry Lipton. For a short period she lived with the couple and may have had a brief affair with Carroll. In their company, she also met the powerful Hollywood agent, Johnny Hyde.

Shortly after the release of *Love Happy* in March 1950, Hyde, charmed by her scene with Groucho, decided to represent her. He was the first influential professional who expressed unreserved faith in her star quality. He did not take her apart in Karger's merciless fashion; he did not follow Lytess's dictation of how an actress should carry herself; and he did not emulate Schenck's reserved counsel. Instead, he seemed to reach inside of her as he would reach inside himself for an organic understanding. Monroe noted that after her success in *The Asphalt Jungle*, he was beaming and acting "as if he had made good on the screen, not me." Certainly she made good as his client, *his* discovery, but he was also happy for her, Monroe insisted. He was a deeply kind man without any selfishness in his treatment of her because, according to Monroe, "he not only knew me, he knew Norma Jean[e] too. He knew all the pain and all the desperate things in me. His primary contribution was to get her to see herself without always relying on the evaluations of others, to have faith in her own genius. Paradoxically, she could only sense her autonomy by imagining how great his need was for her. They became lovers, but she did not feel in love with him, and she refused several offers of marriage from the ailing agent, even though it would have given her financial security.

On the advice of Lucille Ryman, Hyde convinced John Huston to test Monroe for the part of Angela in *The Asphalt Jungle* (1950). The actress secluded herself with Natasha Lytess in order to explore every facet of Angela's personality and to understand her character's relationship to the film as a whole. At the audition she felt sick and had to remind herself of her years of study in preparation for her "first chance at a real acting part with a great director." She doubted that she would be any good, but Huston was kind and patient and allowed her to do her lines lying on the floor as a simulation of Angela's lounging on a couch. As soon as the scene was finished, she asked to do it again. Huston said that was not necessary—he had already decided to give her the part—but he allowed her to do so anyway.

Huston was sensitive to her requirements; she was to praise him for that. It was typical of her to ask for a retake of the scene, and her need for retakes would grow as her roles in films expanded. She kept pushing herself long after her directors and fellow actors were satisfied. The retakes had to do with her sense of perfectionism, which was linked with her dread of incompleteness, of a role that was unfinished. She had thought of herself as having been born a second time through her Hollywood career. That second birth had to be better; each role had to be in some way an advance over the previous one—an impossible demand in Hollywood.

Huston had a sense of a production in its entirety that most directors, as far as Monroe was concerned, did not have. To her, other directors seemed more concerned with photographing the scenery than the actors. Superb shots and set-ups, framing techniques and editing, were their major interests. They wanted to please the "Front Office," whereas Huston worked for his actors and seemed, indeed, a part of their acting. Even though her role was small, he made her feel that she was an important performer.

She shared with her fellow actors many of the complaints they had against directors. Huston was unusual because he showed her that everything an actor feels—including a bad case of nerves—contributes to the energy of a scene. She needed to know the whole script, not just her lines, he insisted. For "acting was also reacting—listening to other actors, losing herself." Each piece of advice had its incremental effect, until she could see how all of it was integrated into a coherent approach to the art of film. He had objectified a process of creation for her that had been previously narrowed to her nervous preoccupation with herself, or to the constricted concerns of less talented professionals.

Monroe found the role of Angela in *The Asphalt Jungle* deeply satisfying. Although she had only a few lines and two scenes, her character had an indispensable function in both the plot and the themes of the film. As in the famous calendar shot, the first shot of Angela shows her sleeping in "the twisted posture" which emphasizes her voluptuous body and her attention to that body, "one hand entangled in her hair." She is in a position of extreme passivity and is startled by the staring face of the attorney, Emmerich (Louis Calhern), who has been her lover, but who now manifests what is to her a "puzzling mixture of desire and contempt." In her sybaritic waiting upon him, she represents a signifi-

Figure 3. Marilyn Monroe in *The Asphalt Jungle*, 1950
From the MGM Release *The Asphalt Jungle* ® 1950
Loew's Incorporated; ren. 1977 Metro-Goldwyn-Mayer Inc.
(*Courtesy The Museum of Modern Art/Film Stills Archive*)

cant aspect of the corrupt lifestyle he has grown to deplore but from which he cannot seem to release himself. She is one of his collectibles, an extravagant example of what he calls his "absurd" style of life.

Angela will lie for him and give an alibi to cover his involvement in a jewel robbery only as long as she is under his direction, but when he fails to supply her with her cues she is uncertain, meek, scared, and finally devastated by the harsh police interrogation. When Emmerich bids her to tell the truth, she quickly offers the last bit of evidence that will convict her lover. She has her moment of anguish when she says, "I . . . I tried. . . . I'm sorry, Uncle Lon." He has expected her to acquiesce to whoever controls the situation, and so he replies, "You did pretty well—considering." Considering what? Considering that she did lie for him, that she was loyal to him for at least a few moments under intense police pressure? She did pretty well considering the kind of amoral, conniving creature she is? Such questions would seem appropriate given that she immediately asks him if she will still be able to go on the trip he has promised her. She knows he will be going to jail, but she thinks only of herself. His answer "(shaking his head) 'Some sweet kid'" ironically exposes just how self-preoccupied she is in pursuit of her happiness. She lowers her eyes and moves away to dictate her state-ment to the police. Is she disappointed, or is she aware that she has asked an inappropriate question? She is easily cowed by circumstances and willing to shift with the prevailing momentum of the scene.

The role of Angela deserved the keen concentration Monroe gave to it because it was meant to suggest one of the four choices made by women in an asphalt jungle dominated by hard, brutal, and greedy men. Emmerich's wife (Dorothy Tree) seeks refuge in invalidism. She hopes that she will be able to ensure her husband's affection and keep him in the home. Emmerich simply installs Angela in another "home." Doll Conovan (Jean Hagen), in love with stickup man Dix Handley (Sterling Hayden), tries to keep her man by observing strict loyalty to masculine codes of toughness, which means that she refrains from overt displays of affection and from openly confessing her need for Handley lest he react by regarding her as an obligation. He softens under her tactful care, and she discovers why he has adopted such a mean exterior. Maria Ciavelli (Teresa Celli) is the faithful housewife and mother who knows nothing about her husband's job—he is expert at cracking safes—and is bewildered by his sudden death in the jewel robbery, since she has been so cut off from the realities of his life. As the most beautiful of these women, Angela has room in which to maneuver and to manipu-late men, but she is also undermined by her own youthful stupidity, which makes it difficult for others to take her seriously. As a very young woman, she has not yet learned how far her scheming can take her. She does not size up situations well, and as a result she can appear to be ridiculous, as in her response to the policeman who knocks on her locked door: "Haven't you bothered me enough you big banana head?"

In such a part Monroe had to portray an unusual variety of emotions. If her character's psychology were shallow, her character's behavior was devious enough to allow room for a full play of gestures and facial expressions. If she were acting a type, the kept woman, she nevertheless was interpreting lines and script directions that gave her the opportunity to fashion a whole person. Angela had to be passive, seductive, innocent, solicitous, puzzled, vulgar, scared, angry, stupid, nearly hysterical, anguished, and calculating in just two brief scenes. There was plenty of room for mistakes, for missing the transitions from one emotion to another, but Monroe was flawless in her fulfillment of the script's demands.

In *The Asphalt Jungle* Monroe gave her first thoroughgoing performance, and it must have seemed that the future held endless possibilities. Hadn't she shown an impressive authority as an actress, an especially important matter for one who struggled so grimly to be creative? Joseph Mankiewicz was impressed with her work, and with Johnny Hyde's encouragement he cast her as Miss Caswell in *All About Eve*, a film she welcomed as another chance to work with a fine director. It was an exceedingly small role, but again it presented her with the opportunity to make a vivid impression in a film sure to receive wide distribution and publicity.

The role of Miss Caswell solidified Monroe's "dumb blonde" stereotyping. The variation on the type, in this case, is Miss Caswell's absence of innocence. She is hard, ambitious, and corrupt—in spite of her youthful beauty. She is less dependent on men for her cues than Angela is, although she is just as ignorant. When she fails to get a part in a stage production, she asks whether they have auditions for television. Rather than cultivating her own talent, she entertains important producers whom she hopes will help her acting career. Her understanding of success is couched in crass materialism. Seeing a fur coat she admires, she says, "Now there's something a girl could make sacrifices for." Although the character is vulgar, Monroe plays her in a fairly restrained manner; that is, there is no awkward gesturing, no obvious attempt to render Miss Caswell's lack of subtlety in visual terms. Yet Monroe has Caswell—in her first appearance in the film—always on the verge of smirking, suggesting the wanton attitude just behind her soft, beautifully displayed figure. In other words, Monroe employs a sensitive tactfulness in portraying a tactless character. The point of such restraint is to prepare for the right dramatic moment when Miss Caswell's predatory sexuality can emerge in its most appropriate form. Monroe saves Caswell's exaggerated use of sexual innuendo for a brief scene with a producer, in which she drops her eyelids, smiles provocatively—her lips almost pucker—and delivers a heavily suggestive thank you by lowering her voice.

Monroe's three brief appearances in this film amounted to something less than what she was given to work with in *The Asphalt Jungle*, and the range of emotions in Miss Caswell is extremely narrow when compared with that of her previous role. So it is difficult to say what a shrewd professional observer might have been able to make of her performance in November 1950 when *All About Eve* was released. Given the obviousness of her character, she was wise to take Natasha Lytess's advice to understate the character's mannerisms. Her coach exhorted her *"not to act,"* so as not to destroy the credibility of Caswell's simple insights into people. As Fred Guiles suggests, one of the best lines in the script is Caswell's perceptive description of a producer (Gregory Ratoff) she is encouraged to cultivate: "Why do they always look like unhappy rabbits?" It is very easy to laugh at this blonde, and it would have been easy for Monroe to turn the character into a kind of cartoon; instead, she endowed Caswell with a complete personality, and in doing so she contributed to our understanding of Eve, the main character of the film.

Eve (Anne Baxter) is the sophisticated, truly successful version of Miss Caswell. Eve wants to become a star in the theater, and she does so by ingratiating herself into the lives of the most important theater people. She is adept at dissembling, at making herself indispensable to others. She is always careful to prepare for her exploitation of others and for the sexual advances she hopes will help to secure her success. She is able to fool nearly everyone and she achieves her career goals, for she has assumed the role of acolyte to the famous actress Margo Channing (Bette Davis). At the beginning of the film she tells Channing that acting has made up her life, and Margo misses the irony of the statement. Not only does Eve mean she has become obsessed with the stage and with following its stars, she also means that she is acting—making herself into a kind of character who will trample the lives of those who help her. Everything Eve does is an act; she is nothing as a person, everything as an actress. She plays the role of Margo's secretary so she can grasp the role of the star, which she does by insinuating herself into the role of Margo's understudy and then seeing to it that Margo misses one of her performances. It is essential that Miss Caswell also audition for the understudy role to show that only Eve's shrewd kind of "acting" can

prevail. Miss Caswell lacks Eve's insight into the necessity for ubiqui-
tous acting.

In many ways this film about the actor's personality had great relevance for Monroe's life and career. Many people in Hollywood already
equated her with Angela and Miss Caswell. She was given credit for
skillfully playing parts according to her type, and not for imaginatively
exploring a type according to her talent. As in *The Asphalt Jungle*, she
was featured as a blonde siren who could not possibly perform any of
the other female roles in the film.

It would seem to be an elementary observation that an actor who
performs a part well need not be just like the part she or he plays, and
yet particularly in the case of film the person and the role often get
confused not only in the eyes of the audience but in the eyes of film
professionals. Celeste Holm, one of the stars of *All About Eve*, recalls that
she "saw nothing special about [Monroe's] Betty Boop quality. I thought
she was quite sweet and terribly dumb, and my natural reaction was
'whose girl is that?' "

Various aspects of Angela and Caswell seemed similar to aspects of
Monroe's life. Both characters were under the protection of older men,
just as Monroe had been protected by Schenck and Hyde. Monroe, like
Miss Caswell, was viewed by some as a schemer. Nunnally Johnson, for
example, saw her as one of the "eager young hustlers" of Hollywood.
She was "Johnny Hyde's girl" and not worth talking about outside his
presence. Natasha Lytess, speaking in rancor after Monroe had rejected
her, claims in her memoirs that her pupil found Hyde an "expedient"
tool in her rise to stardom. Monroe acknowledged this questioning of
her motivations when she complained that no matter how truthfully she
spoke or how honestly she behaved most men and women "believed I
was trying to fool them."

Two reporters for *Life* and *Look*, Stanley Flink and Rupert Allan,
witnessed other sides of Monroe that reflected a young woman making
the transition from obscurity to stardom, a transition that inevitably
provoked conflicting responses in the subject and in her observers.
Flink's memories of late 1949 or early 1950, when he first met Monroe,
center on how she seemed to be caught "in the swirl" of Hollywood
glamour and publicity. She was not absolutely sure she wanted to be an
actress, but the possibilities of such a career dazzled her and seemed
better than anything else she could imagine. She was quite willing to
take direction; indeed, Flink remembers a highly nervous young woman
who seemed quite dependent on her directors whenever he visited her
movie sets. It was her peculiar combination of innocence and ambition

that charmed Flink much more than her appearance, which he found "pleasant but not startlingly pretty."

Rupert Allan, on the other hand, was immediately impressed with the actress's stunning beauty and dedication to her craft, to her physical fitness program, and to every aspect of her professional career. He had to work hard to prevent *Look* from turning his article on her into the typical celebrity piece. Instead, he wanted to impress readers with her intelligence and wit. He had no doubts about the great career she was about to begin, and he looked forward to the fulfillment of the youthful promise he detected in early 1950. In a few years he would go to work for her as a press representative, and they would remain close friends for the rest of her life.

Allan provides the best evidence of a complex performer who was learning how to inhabit many roles, including her assumption of injured innocence, behind which—Lytess claims—was hidden a hardened shrewdness and guile: "It was always like that. When you disagreed with her she was like a little flower in the grass, a poor thing whom no one loved. At the smallest suggestion she might be wrong, she could make *you* feel guilty." There is a clear-eyed sharpness in her characterization of Caswell that is strikingly different from the soft, droopy-eyed vagueness of some of her later roles. The tableau shot from *All About Eve* that is often reproduced shows Caswell's vivid focus on Eve as Eve aggressively focuses on the critic Addison DeWitt. This is a tough, competitive period for Monroe, as she implies in her description in *My Story* of Hollywood parties to which she would go for self-advertising. Such behavior clearly labeled her a young woman on the make. She was much more than that, however, if one considers Lytess's intriguing description of Monroe's behavior: "Whenever she explained something her right hand darted forward, weaving to the left and right like a serpent. It was a gesture of evasiveness and survival through expediency." Certainly Lytess's favorite epithet, "a veiled woman," evokes a Monroe far more secretive, canny, and devious than Angela or Miss Caswell could ever hope to be.

Films fused Monroe to her personae and standardized responses to her. In the theater, it might have been somewhat different for her, since there is a distance between the actor and the audience, and it is the actor who can increase or decrease that distance. The actor can accentuate or diminish certain features and gestures according to the demands of the role. In film, the camera moves in and away from and around the person of the actor, so that a personality is created that somehow survives and transcends individual roles, and audiences gather to see how different roles reflect the same film personality. This is basically a tautological process, in the sense that films perform as mirrors which throw back to audiences images of stars that have already been reflected by other films, mirrors. On stage there is no screen; even a stage star does not have to contend with replications deposited, so to speak, onto strips of celluloid. It is easier for the stage actor to outlive earlier roles, since it is merely the memories of past performances with which he or she must contend. Memories are also mirrors, of course, but memories fade and change; the celluloid strips, on the other hand, continually refresh reflection.

In the images of her face, her figure, her voice, it was easy for Monroe to confirm the impressions of those directors who typed her as dumb blonde. In other words, they were able to fill in their visions of what a dumb blonde was like by elaborating on those aspects of her that resembled the type. They missed the whole person—or perhaps it is more accurate to say that they were not looking for one.

Although so much attention has been drawn to the resemblances between Monroe and the parts she played, the irony is that no one has seen that she experienced the kind of psychological pattern that would prepare her to play Eve's role. Like Eve Harrington, Marilyn Monroe desperately wanted to be a star; she was willing to sacrifice most of her personal life to attain her goal. She had relatively few friendships outside of those people who were in a position to support her career. She moved in with people who helped her and became intimately involved in their lives, just as Eve moved in with Margo Channing and began to run her life. Monroe appeared to be "kind and soft and helpless. Almost everybody on meeting her wanted to help her. Marilyn's helplessness was her greatest strength," asserts Sidney Skolsky, her Hollywood columnist confidant. Similarly, Eve appears to be a naive and tender young girl who appeals to the hard-boiled, cynical theater crowd.

Monroe may also have been like Eve in her ability to deceive herself, so that she would not have to admit that she had occasionally deceived others. This was Lytess's opinion expressed in her memoirs: "She cannot face herself, she keeps her back to herself." Certainly Monroe was like Eve in her fanatical belief that only through acting could she be a success, be somebody deserving of respect. After noting several instances of Monroe's thoughtless cruelty to her, Lytess reports telling her, "You knew how ill I was and you never called. . . . I want to love you, but you make it difficult." Monroe replied: "You don't have to love me, Natasha, as long as you will work with me." This brutal refusal to deal with her coach's feelings of betrayal reveals just how far Monroe's monomania may have taken her toward Eve's ambitions. She may also have found it necessary to separate harshly her personal and professional feelings regarding Lytess because of the latter's all-consuming interest in her life. Lytess never seems even to have considered that Monroe had to protect herself from a mentor who tried to supervise every aspect of her life. There is no way of knowing, at any rate, how Monroe evaluated the sincerity of the role she played in relation to Lytess.

All About Eve makes this point when its characters accuse one another of playing scenes rather than expressing sincere emotions. To complicate matters further, there is the possibility that actors will believe in the characters they create, just as some famous figures including Monroe have been suspected of believing their own publicity. Fiction that is strongly conceived, in other words, can replace fact—or as Mailer puts it, "the most mysterious property of a factoid [a fiction that masquerades or functions as a fact] is that it is believed by the people who put together the factoid printed next to it."

Perhaps her work on *All About Eve* made Monroe especially conscious of Addison DeWitt's notion that actors are not like "normal human beings," for they are particularly susceptible to realizing their own fictions and to showing off their emotions. She may well have thought of herself as part of a separate category of human beings, for Skolsky points out that Monroe often quoted her own version of DeWitt's remarks: "Once in a while somebody writes an article saying that actors and actresses are just like other people. We're not. It's because we're not that we're actors and actresses." DeWitt's view of the actor's abnormality leads him to conclude that all "theatrical folk" are "the original displaced personalities." Certainly Monroe's own version of her life stressed her displacement, her alienation from the conventions of ordinary life. Acting was a form of compensation for her many deprivations, and the warm response of an audience—which Monroe experienced for the first time in a movie theater showing *The Asphalt Jungle*—replenished her identity. It is easy to imagine Monroe's fervent delivery of Eve's description of her commitment to acting:

> I've listened, from backstage, to people applaud. It's like—like waves of love coming over the footlights and wrapping you up. Imagine . . . to know, every night, that different hundreds of people love you. . . . they smile, their eyes shine—you've pleased them, they want you, you belong. Just that alone is worth anything. . . .

Monroe consulted Sidney Skolsky, just as Eve consulted DeWitt. Monroe even used to leave messages for him signed "Miss Caswell." With Skolsky as perhaps the crucial manager of much of her very early publicity, she was able to model herself into a strikingly sympathetic and attractive personality who could compel the adoration of audiences in just the way Eve describes. In retrospect, at least, Skolsky insists on the deliberateness of Monroe's self-creation. She "knew how to sell herself" and had an immediate, intuitive grasp of "the value of publicity." She refined stories about herself that proved colorful, carefully embellishing them to provoke "even more publicity." Skolsky never could figure "how much of the story of her bleak childhood" was factual, although he was certain she was "not quite the poor waif she later claimed to have been." She kept increasing the number of her foster homes "because she knew it was a good selling point." She was doubtful about her identity, but not about how she should picture her biography. It should play like a good movie. Similarly, she was remarkably astute about her movies and knew far better than the studio executives what a successful Marilyn Monroe movie ought to contain, Skolsky concludes.

Without a definitive sense of herself, Monroe was free to engage in endless mutations of her biography. Whether she was calculating or relatively unconscious about her fictionalizing or cynically performing what was expected of her is difficult to determine. Surely at one time or another she engaged in all of these different behavioral possibilities and perhaps mixed them together in ways that cannot be distinguished. It may have become difficult for her as for others to know when she was just being herself.

It is impossible to describe confidently the state at which Monroe had arrived in the evolution of herself and her career in 1950. Norma Jeane, Angela, Miss Caswell, and Marilyn Monroe are some of the changing phases of her identity. But she—what name is appropriate for her at this point?—cannot be associated too closely with any of these phases. She is not as young as the Angela she plays so well. Unlike Miss Caswell, she passes her audition and is praised for her talent. Marilyn Monroe, the star and the mythic figure, has not yet emerged, and Norma Jeane never really had the opportunity to develop as an adult.

Clearly, Monroe was tentative about herself and elusive to others. Joseph Mankiewicz remembers her as a solitary actress carrying around an edition of Rilke's *Letters to a Young Poet*. She was unsure of herself, and in the social gatherings of his cast after the filming of *All About Eve* she was pleased at their invitation to join them, "but somehow she never understood or accepted our unspoken assumption that she was one of us. She remained alone. She was not a loner. She was just plain *alone*."

Monroe put her whole trust in only one person: Johnny Hyde. Although she had lost her first contract with Fox, he was able—on the strength of her performances in *The Asphalt Jungle* and *All About Eve*, plus very small roles in *The Fireball* and *Right Cross*—to get her another Fox screen test with the actor Richard Conte in early December. On December 10, she signed a seven-year agreement with the studio. In the minds of Joseph Mankiewicz and others, Hyde was responsible for whatever self-esteem and professional confidence Monroe could muster.

Troubled by a weak heart for years, Hyde finally succumbed to his ailment on December 20, just ten days after ensuring his client's professional future. Monroe went to pieces and, according to Lytess, tried to kill herself with a pill overdose. Joseph Mankiewicz is still convinced that she never fully recovered from Hyde's death and, in fact, "gave up on herself." Hyde's son remembers her at his father's funeral, overcome with grief, and throwing herself on the coffin. She shook everyone with her screaming over and over again of Hyde's name. Monroe grieved for him as if for herself.

Grief did not prevent her from doing her work, although on the set of her next film, *As Young as You Feel*, she would weep and go "off to a corner sometimes to be by herself," her director, Harmon Jones, explained. Just two weeks after Hyde's death, she was visited on the set by Elia Kazan, her friend and perhaps her lover, who was attracted to "her wit and her lack of pretension." He wanted to introduce to her his friend, Arthur Miller, who had brought to Hollywood an original screenplay he hoped would be produced. Later that same week, Miller and Monroe met at a party given by Charles Feldman, an important Hollywood agent, producer, and confidant of the Kennedys. Monroe and Miller easily became involved in an intense conversation about their lives and literature. Although there were relatively few contacts between them until she moved to New York City nearly six years later, it is clear that she began almost immediately to console herself with the idea of someday joining with this celebrated playwright in establishing the whole career and identity that Johnny Hyde had promised for her.

4

Becoming a Star (1950–1952)

And I want to say that the people—if I am a star—they made me a star—no studio, no person, but the people did.

On January 1, 1951, Marilyn Monroe made her first appearance on the cover of *Life* magazine. Throughout the next two years her popularity grew steadily, yet she was given parts that were usually brief and undistinguished versions of what her studio biography called "the blowtorch blonde." Stories about her in such magazines as *Life, Look, Collier's, The American Weekly, Photoplay,* and *Modern Screen* noted her serious pursuit of acting, but the career Hyde had carefully charted seemed about to lose its direction because of her studio's lack of imagination. To Robert Cahn in *Collier's,* Monroe appeared to be "the standard Hollywood blonde" with a "vague smile that seems to include everybody." *Life* wondered if she could really achieve "the universal sex appeal of Jean Harlow."

Monroe was not taken seriously, perhaps because her photographs and films appeared to be self-contained; that is, they did not put the question—who am I?—that Monroe herself was always addressing. Instead of showing her as the half-finished, fragmented personality she *said* she was, the photographs often portrayed her in a partially aroused state which stimulated the viewer imaginatively to elaborate on her erotic provocations. A typical publicity pose displays her with half-closed eyes and half-open mouth, for neither seeing nor speaking—her potential intellectual attributes and capacities—are meant to form part of her appeal. Parts of her body—the darkened lips, the long black eyelashes, the smoothly shaped and elongated eyebrows—are heavily outlined, and other parts—her neck and torso—are ringed with jewelry and clothing that accentuate the roundedness and fullness of her figure. The luminous makeup, the lustrous jewelry, the self-encompassing use of her hands, and the bent-forward attitude of her head and upper body

Figure 4. Marilyn Monroe, 1953
Publicity pose by Frank Powolny.
(*Courtesy The Academy of Motion Picture Arts and Sciences*)

fashion a fully equipped and seductive self-image that contradicts the cryptic off-camera self Monroe was trying to fathom and to define.

Photographs and films projected a dazzling array of Marilyns, an enormously passionate display of a person who wanted to believe that she was a remarkable individual, who wanted to see and hear how she sounded and looked to others. But her replications were, in a sense, all pretense; she was producing shadows of selves and not living out her life in her own way—unless she was willing to have "her own way" dictated by the studio. Like many creative persons, she wanted to reinvent herself, to give birth to herself in her own image.

If Kennedy Fraser is right that "women get accustomed to chopped-up images—eyes, nose, and mouth in a powder compact; the back of the head in the hand mirror; the feet and ankles in the sloping glass at the shoe store," then imagine how Monroe became accustomed to polishing parts of her reflected image, so that she was deflected from the deeper sense of self she claimed to be seeking. It was not enough for her to recognize herself in her mirrored image, she said—although this is literally one of the few forms of self-recognition she was allowed in most of the films she worked on from 1950 to 1952.

In *The Fireball* and *Right Cross* (released in August and October 1950 respectively), she plays sexy blondes in roles that gave her no opportunity to develop complete characterizations. Her sexy blonde secretary role in *Hometown Story* (May 1951) is no better, and it is not until her performance in *As Young as You Feel* (June 1951) that she makes a specific impression on the critics. She is a secretary to a corporate executive (Albert Dekker), and as usual her sexual appeal is emphasized: the camera holds on her wiggling walk down a hallway; she takes shorthand in a low-cut dress; and she is prominently featured as a kind of decoration in her boss's office. She's given just a little more to work with in this role, and she is on screen long enough to suggest an alert attentiveness that is quite atypical of the giddy blondes of some of her later films. Her lines are almost all brief, monosyllabic replies to her boss, yet there is a scene in which she is pictured as very deliberately attending to herself—looking into two mirrors, smoothing her face and dress, arranging her hair, and sticking out her tongue—thus offering the first direct view of the self-involved figure who emerges in later films. "It is my business to be sexy, that's the way I define myself," Monroe seems to be saying.

Love Nest immediately followed *As Young as You Feel* in October 1951, and it makes clever use of Monroe's developing screen persona as a woman with such formidable sexual appeal to men that she belongs in a category of her own. Monroe plays an ex-WAC, Roberta Stevens, the friend of Jim Scott (William Lundigan), a veteran recently returned home to his wife, Connie (June Haver), who has just purchased a building in New York City as a means of supplementing their income. With her first appearance, Monroe's character is set up as the kind of provocative female that other women suspect. Connie eyes Roberta suspiciously, even though Roberta behaves quite properly and dresses formally in a business suit and veil. When Jim comes out to meet his old friend—he has offered to rent her a room—he is somewhat ruffled by his wife's insinuations and perhaps overwhelmed by the impact Roberta has already made before she even enters his home. He trips over himself as he follows her up the steps. Monroe plays Roberta as a confident, outgoing model, who is mildly amused by Jim's friend, Ed (Jack Paar), who makes enthusiastic passes at her. She laughs at him tolerantly, just as "the Girl" Monroe plays in *The Seven Year Itch* good-naturedly accepts her male companion's sexual gambits. In both cases, Monroe's characters imply a certain degree of sexual knowledge that is never revealed. The quick shots or scenes in which Monroe appears during the rest of *Love Nest* excite curiosity about her and convey the sense that there is a personality that never gets fully expressed on the screen. There are brief glimpses of her in a bathing suit and of her taking off her nylons. There is also a short sequence of her undressing to reveal a silky slip and lacy bra, of her wrapped in a towel getting into the shower, of her coming out of the shower in a bathrobe, smiling seductively at Jim.

June Haver's recollections of working on *Love Nest* provide a fascinating insight into how Monroe regarded herself in the first stages of her stardom. More importantly, Haver touches on the sources of Monroe's universal appeal: her vulnerability, her quick and confident response to an appreciative audience, and her way of eliciting an elemental reaction in others who enjoyed just watching her effortless movements. Monroe was a shy and nervous actress, and she seemed very young and pretty to Haver. She had an "electric something," especially noticeable in a scene "where she was supposed to be sunning in the back yard of the apartment house we all lived in." The entire crew seemed stunned by her appearance in a bathing suit and stared silently as she walked across the set. Work stopped. Haver had never seen a film crew act so impressed, and she marveled at their attention to Monroe, since they were used to seeing actresses in "brief costumes" in musicals and beach scenes. There might be some playful flirtation with actresses, but never this kind of complete devotion. Haver could tell that Monroe loved their reaction, and "in her shy way, she smiled."

Having an audience gave Monroe confidence and made it easier for her to say dialogue that was always difficult to get out—just "on the first word or two," Haver observes. Then Monroe relaxed, warmed up, and "suddenly seemed to be another person," as if she had gone through "a complete metamorphosis; she became completely uninhibited in her movements, the way she sat in that chair—so gracefully, naturally graceful—and seductive at the same time. Suddenly, she seemed to shine like the sun," Haver concludes. This tender reminiscence is similar to what other women felt on the set of *Love Nest,* and it suggests that Monroe could charm both sexes, in spite of all that has been written about her appeal to men. In such moments she attained the goal for which she and Natasha Lytess had striven: "freedom of self."

Movie sets were difficult places for Monroe to practice self-expression, for making movies is often a dull, repetitive, and frustrating business. Scenes are shot over and over again, with checks for lighting, makeup, sound, changes in script, various camera adjustments, and so on. An actress wonders exactly when the crew will really be prepared, when she should give all of her effort to a scene. Film making is guided by rhythms of mechanization and industry, not by rhythms of actors. Since movies are very rarely shot in the sequence of their final edited versions, there are few opportunities to build toward the climaxes that are rehearsed into stage plays.

In spite of these obstacles, Monroe continued to give energetic, humorous, and fully committed performances in forgettable films. For example, in *Let's Make It Legal* (October 1951), her physical appeal—"she is a 'beautiful blonde' who trades on her looks to get what she wants"— is gratuitously used at the beginning, middle, and end of the movie. In 1951 and 1952 she compelled the attention of audiences by honestly playing every bit part as if it really mattered, which it probably did to her, since making movies had become the objective of her life. Such an extraordinary expenditure of creative energy on insignificant roles may very well have damaged her, in the sense that she became less and less able to cope with the fragmentations of herself that film making fostered.

What was left of Marilyn Monroe once her screen selves were discounted? Very little. She felt "terribly dumb" about many of the things people discussed: painting, music, books, history, geography, sports, and politics. She decided to go to school and enrolled in extension courses at the University of California, Los Angeles. She studied Renaissance art and literature, Freud and other psychologists, and though she did not have the time to pursue a degree, she learned enough to see just how superficial her studio upbringing had been.

Through her friend, Jack Palance, Monroe made contact in the fall of 1951 with Michael Chekhov who, along with Lee Strasberg, should be regarded as the major influence on her mature acting style. Palance had suffered from his own inadequacies as an actor and from a cadaverous appearance, and so Monroe, worried over her own professional weaknesses and physical typing, seems to have been prepared to listen carefully to his confident recommendation of Chekhov's acting class.

Monroe revered her acting teacher, a descendant of the playwright Anton Chekhov. She called him Russia's "best actor" and a "brilliant man." He was "selfless and saint-like and witty, too," and a heroic figure to be compared with her beloved Abraham Lincoln. In several Hollywood movies he established himself as a premier character actor, and then he had retired to write, to garden, and to teach. From him she "learned more than acting. I learned psychology, history and the good manners of art—taste."

Working with Chekhov gave her a sense of tradition; she felt like a carefully chosen and honored disciple. His virtuosity, particularly his ability to play a range of roles, naturally appealed to an actress whose work had been so depressingly limited. Doing a scene with him "was more exciting" than acting on movie sets, for it became for the first time an art that belonged to the actor, not to the director or producer.

Chekhov had an extremely powerful idea of the actor as a disciplined interpreter of life rather than as an imitator. He encouraged the same blending of intellectual and esthetic interests Monroe had been trying to achieve on her own. His book asks the actor to imagine himself into the psychology of persons from other periods of history and from different nations, and of persons around him toward whom he feels unsympathetic. Chekhov adopts both an esthetic and a moral stance toward acting when he speaks of making the body "sensitive, noble, and flexible."

As Monroe continued to chafe against an inflexible studio system, she was laboring at a set of exercises designed by Chekhov to produce "sensations of *freedom* and *increased* life." She learned a very concrete way to "open" and "close" the self: after a preliminary series of "wide, broad but simple movements, using a maximum of space," so that the whole body was involved and utilized, there followed an enactment of what might be called Chekhov's organic enrichment of the actor's sensations:

> *Open* yourself completely, spreading wide your arms hands, your legs far apart. Remain in this expanded position for a few seconds. Imagine that you are becoming larger and larger. Come back to the original position. Repeat the same movement several times. Keep in mind the aim of the exercise, saying to yourself, "I am going to awaken the sleeping muscles of my body; I am going to revivify and use them."
> Now *close* yourself by crossing your arms upon your chest, putting your hands on

your shoulders. Kneel on one or both knees, bending your head low. Imagine that you are becoming smaller and smaller, curling up, contracting as though you wanted to disappear bodily within yourself, and that the space around you is shrinking. Another set of your muscles will be awakened by this contracting movement.

As part of the same exercise, the actor is to resume a standing position and then employ various thrusting, stretching, throwing, lifting, holding, dragging, pushing, and tossing movements—all of which are aimed at getting the actor to know his or her body and its capabilities. Command of the space in which the actor works is a way of exerting control over environment. Very gradually—as her film roles from *Don't Bother to Knock* to *The Misfits* demonstrate—Monroe would find ways to inhabit more fully the frames of her films and to go beyond her early intuitions about the right position in the frame.

In Chekhov's view, the actor is a sculptor, a shaper and molder of movement and space, and there are concrete exercises that demonstrate how the actor can create himself or herself as a "movable form." The fingers and hands are trained separately to combat vagueness and shapelessness. There can be nothing amorphous, aimless, or accidental about the actor's movements. Similarly, his sense of hearing has to be sharpened through deliberate exercise, so that in every sense of the word the actor becomes a finely tuned instrument.

Much of what Chekhov covers in his book on interpreting a role Monroe would have already learned from Lytess, but perhaps his emphasis on the autonomy of the actor was new to her. Chekhov has actors work on imagery associated with their characters, and with "images of fantasy" in order to develop imaginative flexibility. He explores in considerable depth the process of perfecting a character's dominant psychological gesture, and he combines his initial physical exercises with certain psychological themes the exercises explore. He then progresses to the principles underlying the composition of a good performance and the structures of plays. At every step, his aim is to broaden the actor's sense of responsibility and insight.

Chekhov stresses the organic relationship between life and art. His view is that the same laws of composition govern the universe, "the life of earth and man," and all of the arts. As a corroboration of his insight, he recommended that Monroe study Mabel Elsworth Todd's *The Thinking Body*, which became, Monroe later told her friend Ralph Roberts, her bible. She would take years to absorb *The Thinking Body*, and she never claimed to understand all of its technical information, but she practiced many of its exercises and was influenced by Todd's way of situating the body within the continuum of human psychology and physiology.

Of the five films in which Monroe appeared after beginning her work with Chekhov, only *Don't Bother to Knock* (July 1952) called for anything like the full deployment of his method, for that film supplied her with the starring role of a mentally disturbed young woman in which she had to sustain a whole character. She had earned the role by giving a strong supporting performance as a young cannery worker in *Clash by Night* (May 1952) and a flashy rendition of a beauty queen in *We're Not Married* (July 1952). A moviegoer in the summer of 1952, alerted to Monroe's growing popularity and her sudden emergence in a variety of roles, might have grasped some notion of her potential as a fine film actress, although as usual it was not her screen performances but her publicity in this year that brought her notoriety. The revelation in February about her posing for the nude calendar, the discovery in May that she had misled the public about her orphanhood and her mother, the controversy in September over the plunging neckline of a dress she wore to pose with servicewomen, and her growing intimacy with Joe DiMaggio—all confirmed her status as a national celebrity.

The publicity solidified her appeal even as it revealed the contradictions in her character, for she was somehow able to exploit her sexuality in the most deliberate, self-conscious way and yet appear to be an innocent, a naif, a child surprised at all of the commotion she has caused. Economic exigency forced the struggling starlet to pose for a nude calendar. Was it so wrong, she joked, when all she had on was the radio? No, she was not exactly an orphan, she told Hedda Hopper, but her mother had been mentally ill and institutionalized, and reporters had assumed that Gladys was dead. She was hurt over the army's attempt to censor one of her photographs with American servicewomen because her dress was too revealing. According to Monroe, the photographer was at fault, since he had shot her from above and not straight on as he was supposed to do. In every case, what could have been adverse publicity was turned into a touching account of how Monroe had been misunderstood or mishandled, and it seemed that almost every story contained her plea for understanding. Yet the plea never become tiresome, or simply maudlin, because she was always brightly facing the future and planning her programs of self-improvement. As Mailer suggests, she broke through some kind of publicity barrier in this year, so that everything she did was made to seem interesting. The various views of Marilyn Monroe in 1952 and 1953 in popular circulation and fan magazines, in *Time*, *Newsweek*, and the daily newspapers, were nearly all unfailingly generous. Most of the movie reviews of her were approving or tolerant, and beginning with *Clash by Night* a few reviewers began to credit her with acting skill.

Figure 5. Marilyn Monroe in *Clash by Night*, 1952
(*Courtesy of RKO General Pictures; Wisconsin Center for
Film and Theater Research*)

Unfortunately, her films were not carefully assessed, and most viewers did not see her versatility. In *Clash by Night* she is forceful as a working class woman, Peggy, who does not feel the urgent need to defer to men, to seduce them, or to complete her life by marriage. She is not a liberated woman by today's standards, but she plays her part with a vigor that is directly attributable to her independent stance, to her awareness of male domination, and not just to natural vivacity. She is a convincing worker as she plunges her hands into an assortment of fish, a tense determined expression on her mouth. The film still of this scene (which does not appear in the film's final cut) is a study in the concentration of human labor uncharacteristic of most of Monroe's other roles. Yet there is nothing about her aggressiveness that diminishes her sexual attractiveness. Indeed, a study of the different postures she assumes in this movie suggests an upright, bold personality who can be sensitive and affectionate with women as well as men.

In *We're Not Married* Monroe has a role that is much closer to the conventions established by *Let's Make It Legal*, where she is paraded in bathing suits and other costumery of sex. In *We're Not Married* she is a beauty contest winner who is referred to as "that cute little girl." It ought to be easy to condescend to Monroe as the simple-minded housewife whose ambitions hinge on her looks, yet she plays the role with a verve and lack of pretension that make it difficult to dismiss her as simply giddy. There is none of the sultry posing of her publicity shots in her performance; there is even a down-to-earth determination and ambition to be the best, even when that means inconveniencing her husband (David Wayne) by shifting the burdens of housekeeping and child raising to him. All the same, the film is a rather typical example of the unreal movieland environment that enveloped Monroe, for the housewife dimension of the beauty she plays is never presented. Furthermore, it is impossible to locate her character in a specific locale, even though she is explicitly identified as coming from Mississippi. Of course, none of the characters in the film speaks in regional dialect, yet Monroe suffered more than most actors and actresses from the distortions of movie making typified by this homogenization of language because her roles so often centered on her figure, her presence, as if what she said, or what she was as a whole person, could not possibly be as interesting or as impressive as her body.

In *Don't Bother to Knock* Monroe had trouble playing Nell Forbes, a young woman whose personality is disintegrating, mostly because the role was poorly written. Unlike the vigorous working class character in *Clash by Night*, Nell is a retiring, waifish introvert. She has a dreamy, unfocused look about her eyes and a listless, passive expression about her lips that make her seem blank, out of touch with others. Her primary means of expression is her hands; she grips her fingers together at about waist level as if she is holding herself together. At the beginning of the film the gripping gesture seems normal and casual, or at most a nervous habit occasioned by her meeting the Joneses, for whom she will babysit. But later in the film—when her suicidal tendencies become evident, when the camera tilts down to her scarred wrists—it becomes clear that all along she has been trying to get a grip on herself. It is through her hands that Monroe develops what Chekhov calls the "psychological" or "archetypal gesture" that conveys the essence of a personality, and that "serves as an original model for all possible gestures of the same kind." Monroe plays Nell as an unobtrusive person who is on the edge of insanity, but as Manny Farber points out, Monroe "lulls you into always believing the girl is more normal than she is."

As soon as Nell is alone, she gazes into the mirror and puts on Mrs. Jones's perfume, jewelry, and attractive evening dress. She admires herself in the mirror and suddenly begins to create a whole scene out of her glorious transformation. She behaves—as *Mischief*, the Charlotte Armstrong story on which the film was based, suggests—like "some movie star." There is something "perfectly fresh" about the way Nell works her metamorphosis; she does it in the wondering manner of a child, and her apprehensive clutching of her hands gives way to much more forthright hand motions as she deliberately composes herself in the mirror and loses her inhibitions.

She really comes alive when Jed Towers (Richard Widmark), who is staying in a hotel room directly across from her, spots her through the open blind of her room dancing with herself. After some hesitation she invites him over, and in response to his admiring glances she says, "You like the way I look." It is the first time that the familiar Monroe appears with her undulating lips and provocatively lowered voice. She gazes in the mirror as she tells Towers the story of *his* life, for she has confused him with her lover (a flyer like Towers) who had died in the war. She kisses Towers passionately in her desperate attempt to make him her former lover, and with her dreamy eyes and lowered lids, she briefly recites the sad details of her abused childhood. Monroe takes her character through several successive changes of mood and makes her transitions from lethargy to seductiveness to sadness to desperation very compelling.

Nell is so self-absorbed, so intent on incorporating Towers into her fantasy life—the only world over which she has control—that she turns murderously on the child she is babysitting, almost pushing her out of a window (Towers stops her) because the youngster interrupts the dream

Figure 6. Marilyn Monroe in *Don't Bother to Knock*, 1952
® 1952; ren. 1977 Twentieth Century-Fox Film Corporation. All Rights Reserved.
(*Courtesy Wisconsin Center for Film and Theater Research*)

Becoming a Star 51

of personal fulfillment Nell has tried to consummate. Similarly, she strikes her uncle (Elisha Cook, Jr.)—the elevator operator who has gotten her the babysitting job and who apprehensively checks in on her—because he violates the make-believe atmosphere of her hotel room. When Nell is finally subdued after having brought herself again to the point of suicide, she subsides into the self-effacing mood that characterized her at the beginning of the film, except that now she seems to have been momentarily shocked into recognizing her debilitating tendency to merge her fantasies with reality.

Manny Farber calls Nell "a small-town Alice in the Wonderland of the 'Franklin Hotel,'" an apt phrase, for it captures the way she is mesmerized by the fantasies of her own adventures in front of a mirror. Towers can be anything she likes so long as she looks at him in the mirror. He is nothing to her as a three-dimensional figure, but he is everything to her as a screen on which she can project the images of her dreams. At first she pretends the hotel room is hers; she makes up a story about why she is there; she even projects the glamorous personality she has created for herself into the future when she talks to him about a trip to South America, but her perceptions of the present and the future tend to be ungrounded, disconnected, and fragmented just like the flat, distorted surface impressions of a mirror, which supply only the illusion of depth.

Nell is a frustrating character to read because there is no sure way to connect with her; she is not lucid enough to invite explorations of her personality. A few more details about her past would clarify what her personality disorder stems from, but such details would not explain her person. While Roy Baker's direction and Monroe's acting are good, Daniel Taradash's screenplay deflects attention from Nell by having Towers conveniently rescue her from another suicide attempt and gently enforce for her the distinction between her illusion and reality. Such an ending does more to show how Towers the wise guy has learned to be compassionate than it does to show how Nell will cope—or fail to cope—with her inveterate need to transform her cryptic life into the dream of a whole self.

To Hedda Rosten, Monroe declared that Don't Bother to Knock was one of her favorite films. She believed that in it she had given one of her strongest performances. Of Monroe's acting in this part, Anne Bancroft, who played a character reacting to Nell's breakdown, observes: "It was so real, I responded; I really reacted to her. She moved me so that tears came into my eyes. Believe me, such moments happened rarely, if ever again, in the early things I was doing out there." Richard Widmark was less impressed with her talent, but he conceded her powerful screen impact.

In many ways, *Don't Bother to Knock* became a test case for her, a show of strength in which she had to prove she could create a major dramatic character. "Seen in retrospect," David Robinson remarks, her performance "is far from being her least impressive," and it raises pertinent questions about her reactions to a role that appeared to correspond painfully to her own biography. Certainly she must have felt close to Nell's waiflike attitude, her dreamy mirror gazing, her desire to be glamorous and to dominate her environment by means of that glamour, and her generally fragmented sense of the world and human relationships. Monroe's own diffidence and remoteness, the impression she created that she was not "all there," had been observed by Nunnally Johnson on the set of *We're Not Married*.

Most of Monroe's other films of this period merely skimmed her own character and broke it into sexual segments. With no narrative links between her segments, she just appeared and radiated, as if the integument of her person covered everything it was essential to know about her. Thus she was used in *O'Henry's Full House* and *Monkey Business* (released in August and September of 1952 respectively) as a showpiece. In the former, she is seen briefly as a streetwalker who is surprised when a gentlemen (Charles Laughton) in the street treats her with respect. "He called me a lady!" she exclaims in wonder, almost in disbelief, as if to indicate what a poor opinion she has of herself. There is perhaps just a hint of plaintiveness in her reaction that can be read autobiographically, since Monroe was always seeking respect and yet was startled to receive it. But the film's intention is to display rather than probe her personality, so it is impossible to say exactly what the person-to-role relationship is in this instance.

In *Monkey Business*, on the other hand, the person is completely subordinated to the role. Monroe plays Miss Laurel, a comically stupid secretary, whose special skill is swinging her hips and behind. She never really seems to understand what is going on around her, but because of her buxom figure (accentuated by a bra that thrusts her breasts forward and upward) her competence does not matter. As her boss Oxley (Charles Coburn) says, "anyone can type." She is allowed an earnest line in which she offers to type for her employer, but he explains that his letter is important, and clearly Miss Laurel belongs to the unimportant side of business. She comes to the office early, she says, because Oxley has been complaining about her "punctuation." She is asked to check all the Ford dealers in town and find Dr. Fulton (Cary Grant), the inventor of a youth serum who has gone off on a joy ride after taking his own serum. She asks, "Which should I do first?" Throughout the film she is photographed and treated in terms of her sexual parts. She begins this splitting up of herself by ostentatiously raising her dress part way up her thigh and offering one of her nylon-clad legs for Dr. Fulton's close inspection, since he has invented a new kind of acetate stocking. The scene is positioned so that Dr. Fulton is sitting on a couch and Miss Laurel is standing above him. Naturally he has to look up her leg as she smiles encouragingly down at him. Later there is a scene with Fulton in a car lot in which there is a cut-away shot to a pair of legs—and Fulton naturally says, "Hello Miss Laurel," which is followed by a shot of her face (still missing her torso).

The effect of this shooting style is to dismember Monroe, and to concentrate on her gorgeous face, on her slim legs, on her rounded behind, or on her full breasts. When Oxley catches Fulton gazing at Miss Laurel's leg, Fulton replies that he has been looking at her "acetates." This vulgar way of punning on her anatomy is continued in the form of other innuendoes. When Fulton jumps in alongside Miss Laurel in his sports car, she asks, "Is your motor running?" He replies, "Is yours?" During the sports car sequence, in which Fulton recklessly maneuvers his way through innumerable near-accidents, Miss Laurel laughs unconsciously and actually seems to enjoy the danger. She acts like an adolescent—she's taken no youth serum—and is flattered by Fulton's attraction to her. In spite of her obvious interest in him, she never attempts anything like a mature seduction. Indeed, she is the only character in the film who is doomed to be perpetually adolescent, and as such she is the proper target of those adults who momentarily abandon their sense of decorum after swallowing the serum. So Fulton's wife, Edwina (Ginger Rogers), shoots Miss Laurel twice in the behind with a slingshot. Again, this scene is arranged to give maximum exposure to Monroe's body, for Miss Laurel has to twist her torso twice to slap Oxley's face and then Fulton's, for she thinks the two men on each side of her have pinched her. Later Oxley, intoxicated with youth serum, chases her and shoots seltzer water at her behind.

Monkey Business was the first film since *Love Happy* to make deliberate sport of Monroe's figure. *The Asphalt Jungle* and *All About Eve* treat her with some humor, but *Monkey Business* stands alone in its exploitation of every opportunity to amuse itself at her expense. As in the case of *Love Nest*, *Monkey Business* spreads what is actually a very small role over several brief sequences, so that the character Monroe plays heightens interest in the film as a whole. In *Love Nest*, however, Monroe's character has an adult attractiveness; in *Monkey Business* she is portrayed with a cuteness that is on the same level with that of the monkeys featured in the film.

Monkey Business was a substantial success, and it suggested that Monroe would be good in comedies; she had a sprightly, daffy, perfectly timed insouciance—the breezy sports car sequence shows that much. And she was already a star, not so much because of the movies she had made as because of the images she was able to impress on the public's consciousness. As a representation of sexual provender, she had arrived.

In *My Story* (written two years after *Monkey Business* by Ben Hecht, one of the screenwriters of the film), Monroe recalls that success arrived in a rush and surprised studio executives but not her, since she had carefully noted how much publicity her bit parts generated. In her last recorded interview, she acknowledged how strenuously and shrewdly she had worked for public acclaim, yet she wondered if she could carry the load of adulation, if perhaps she had tricked herself into believing she could be greater than she actually was.

5

Fame (1952–1954)

*Fame to me certainly is only a temporary and a partial happiness—
even for a waif and I was brought up a waif. But fame is not really
for a daily diet, that's not what fulfills you. It warms you a bit but
the warming is temporary. It's like caviar, you know—it's good to
have caviar but not when you have it every meal and every day.*

Sometime in the spring of 1951 Joe DiMaggio saw a newspaper photograph of Marilyn Monroe posing with a baseball player. It excited him to
think that this young actress, with a baseball bat in her hands and a
baseball player at her side giving instructions, took an avid interest in
the sport that had made him an American hero. He dreamed of meeting
Marilyn Monroe, with whom, he presumed, he had something in common.

In March or April of 1952 DiMaggio managed to arrange a meeting
with her through a mutual friend, David March. She was pleasantly
surprised by his neat appearance, quiet demeanor, and calm self-
confidence, since she had been expecting a "loud, sporty fellow." Perhaps because of her own fastidious attention to every detail of her
appearance, she could not help commenting on how carefully he put
himself together for the evening: "There's a blue polka dot exactly in the
middle of your tie knot. . . . Did it take you long to fix it like that?" He
merely shook his head and gave no immediate indication of his response
to her. His silence was his way of being himself, Monroe learned, and
his eyes tended to reflect the true state of his alertness. She found him
an exciting man because he was so different from Hollywood's brash,
self-serving confidence men. DiMaggio, it appeared, wanted nothing
from her but herself. If he was first attracted to the sight of her in a
photograph, it later became clear that he had almost no interest at all in
her career, in watching her movies, in discussing her roles. That she was
a beautiful person—not simply a coveted image or an approximation of a

desirable woman—is what counted with him. It must also have counted heavily with Monroe, since others had seldom been able to comprehend the nexus between her self and her roles.

DiMaggio was a powerful and protective figure, and she would rely on him for his strength for the rest of her life. Their romance was a strain, however, since he had so little respect for her career or her intellectual interests—an attitude she found useful only when her frustrations with Hollywood caused her to consider retirement. According to Robert Slatzer, Monroe continued to see Slatzer and to exchange books of poetry. Their affair was briefly alluded to in late August 1952 in a Dorothy Kilgallen column, and Slatzer himself in the same newspaper wrote about sharing with Monroe an interest in the works of Edgar Allan Poe, Edward Fitzgerald, and Kahlil Gibran.

Giving herself completely to DiMaggio apparently frightened Monroe, and Slatzer was her buffer. Marriage troubled her, yet she was also anxious about being alone. Clearly, Slatzer was not an imposing enough figure to satisfy her need for a famous consort—at one time she and Shelley Winters composed a list of eligible prominent men. On the other hand, he made very few demands, and she could be sure of his loyalty. She may have been disturbed enough about her growing commitment to DiMaggio to offer herself, very briefly, to Slatzer in a marriage made in Mexico on October 4, 1952. A few days later, according to Slatzer, she had second thoughts and their union was dissolved.

It was like Monroe to waver between alternatives in this way. Slatzer was aware of her instability and perhaps realized from the start his inability to keep her. For her part, the brief marriage may have been her way of acting out the very role she feared to play in reality. Marrying Slatzer was a safe dress rehearsal for the far more potent performance that would be expected of her in becoming DiMaggio's wife. Whatever her motivations in pursuing Slatzer, Monroe's behavior reflects a divided and confused mind bordering on an hysteria that left her susceptible to engaging in conflicting and contradictory actions.

Yet associating with DiMaggio also instilled confidence in her and a growing sense of her public prominence. Even as her relationship with him promised to pull her clear of the film role/person framework, her first major film, Niagara (February 1953), made her face, her figure, her voice, and the way she employed them, the subject of the screen.

There is, for example, the celebrated tracking shot that focuses on her rear end and her swaying gait as she moves away from the camera. Other films will develop other aspects of her screen presence, to be sure, but Niagara initiates the many "Marilyns" to come, a point Andy Warhol has grasped brilliantly in his many portraits of "Marilyns," all of which

Figure 7. Marilyn Monroe in Publicity Pose for *Niagara*, 1953
® 1953; ren. 1980 Twentieth Century-Fox Film
Corporation. All Rights Reserved.
(*Courtesy The Museum of Modern Art/Film Stills Archive*)

derive from the image of her singing "Kiss" in *Niagara*. She has to be understood, Warhol implies, in the plural. The basis of her appeal is her ability to be reproduced; the public wants to see that walk over and over again, and film—unlike any other medium—is equipped to replicate that sequence indefinitely.

Unfortunately for Monroe, the lurid color in which she is framed resembles that used in the boxed-in strips of comic books. Like the parodic sexual siren of cartoons—say, Betty Boop—Monroe's character, Rose Loomis, is the target of quips and innuendoes. When the nice, neat, and clean young honeymooning husband (Casey Adams) kiddingly asks his bride (Jean Peters) why she doesn't wear tight-fitting dresses like the ones Rose wears, the bride responds that a woman has to "start laying plans" for such a dress when she's about ten years old. Such remarks define how far Monroe's character has strayed from the conventions most women follow in presenting themselves and how deliberately she is consigned to her own peculiar realm of being.

Monroe is isolated in her singing of "Kiss" dreamily, moodily, and so suggestively that the crowd of young people who have been dancing recede from her in hushed wonder. As in her most suggestive publicity photographs, she seems to be caressing herself, to have retreated into the deepest recesses of her private fantasy life. She holds her passions so far away from both men and women in this film that when a young man asks her to dance, she warns him, "better not." In this scene she seems warmed by her own sensuousness as she sings to the record she has asked a young man to play for her, and as she embellishes the song the camera tightens on her ecstatic countenance. In closeup, in revery, her face clearly is meant to arrest attention and to fashion Monroe as a fantasy.

The film's hackneyed plot matters very little, except insofar as it furthers the implications of "Kiss." Rose Loomis's depressed husband (Joseph Cotten) is tortured by his awareness that he cannot satisfy his sensual wife and that she must be looking for other men who can gratify her. He interrupts her singing of "Kiss" and breaks the record, foreshadowing the fulfillment of his barely suppressed urge to destroy her, when he learns that she has plotted with her lover to take his life. She is bound to die, evidently, because her sexual energies go beyond the bounds of what people can tolerate or the screen can show.

Niagara gave Monroe her only opportunity to portray an evil woman solely concerned with herself and willing to commit any crime to accomplish her own ends. Near the beginning of the film her anxious husband stands over her bed softly calling her name as she pretends to sleep. There is yearning in his voice; he is halfheartedly seeking her sexual favors, although the censorship of the time and his diffidence forbid the making of an explicit request. What he wants from her is clarified later when Rose says of him to her lover: "there's always a way to get around George." George's momentary relaxation and humor in a bedroom scene shortly afterward prove her point. This venal employment of sex deeply disturbed some members of Monroe's audience, and she never attempted anything like the role of Rose Loomis again.

Publicity for *Niagara* demanded that its female star engage in crude exploitation of her sexuality, and Monroe obliged by appearing at public gatherings in skin-tight costumes from her movie wardrobe. DiMaggio refused to accompany her on such occasions and bitterly protested the show she was making of herself. Hollywood columnists played up her exhibitionism, and soon newspapers and fan magazines were receiving letters criticizing her vulgar behavior. Monroe created such a sensation at a Photoplay Awards dinner that Joan Crawford publicly condemned her for conduct unbecoming an actress and a lady.

Besides adopting her familiar guise of injured innocence, Monroe wrote a public letter to Dorothy Kilgallen, shortly after the release of *Niagara*, that drew a distinction between the actress and the women she played. In *The Asphalt Jungle*, she noted, "I played a vacuous, rich man's darling attempting to carry herself in a sophisticated manner in keeping with her plush surroundings. I saw her as walking with a rather self-conscious slither and played it accordingly." Her succinct summing up of her characters—"in *All About Eve*, I was an untalanted [*sic*] show girl walking with deliberate exactness"—emphasizes the intelligence and clarity of her professional work, especially in her attention to the small physical details that indicate a character's mental state. She was articulating what Chekhov taught her. As for *Niagara*:

> the girl I played in that was an amoral type whose plot to kill her husband was attempted with no apparent cost to her conscience. She had been picked out of a beer parlour, she entirely lacked the social graces and she was overdressed, over madeup, and completely wanton. The uninhibited deportment in the motel room and the walk seemed normal facets of such a character's portrayal. I honestly believe such a girl would behave in that manner.

Monroe believed her acting ability entitled her to try more challenging roles—Gretchen in *Faust*, for example. She had impressed Chekhov with her Cordelia in acting class, and she had pleaded with her unsympathetic studio to test her for serious roles. Her employers were content with her popularity as evidenced in box office receipts, in fan mail, and in two awards she received in March of 1953: "Best Young Box Office

Personality" (*Redbook* magazine) and "Fastest Rising Star of 1952" (*Photoplay*).

In the spring of 1953, with her concern over craft mounting, she enrolled in mime classes at Lotte Goslar's Turnabout Theater, a small repertory house in Hollywood, where Monroe had been impressed by a production of one of Anton Chekhov's plays. She wanted to work alone with Goslar, but the teacher convinced her she would benefit most by interacting with an exciting class of ten other pupils studying dance mime, movement, and acting. Although she was reserved at first, she eventually grew comfortable with the group, and Goslar was struck by her serious and modest appearance and by her exceptional talent. This talent manifested itself in an ambitious project that called for each student to develop a character from infancy to old age. In every phase—childhood, youth, maturity—the actor had to be convincing as the same person. The whole class was moved by Monroe's mastery of this difficult exercise in creating the full range of human behavior.

In these moments of intense creativity, Monroe asserted total control over her own person and filled in the gaps in her own development. Goslar's exercises complemented Chekhov's and the ideas of Mabel Elsworth Todd, whose book Chekhov recommended as essential to the completion of an actor's training. *The Thinking Body* emphasizes that all of human life is involved in a struggle for balance and that human beings can consciously promote and control the forces that motivate sensations and physical activity. Monroe had dramatized her life precisely as a struggle to achieve harmony.

Hadn't the actress's own experience, at least since adolescence, confirmed Todd's initial pronouncement? "Living, the whole body carries its meaning and tells its own story, standing, sitting, walking, awake or asleep. It pulls all the life up into the face of the philosopher, and sends it all down the legs of the dancer." Here was a holistic view of human activity Monroe could identify with and practice, a teaching that could turn her toward a therapeutic inspection of herself and away from Hollywood's mechanical magnification and distortion of what were supposed to be her better parts.

Like Chekhov's approach, Todd's is integrative: "Mechanically, physiologically and psychologically, the human body is compelled to struggle for a state of equilibrium." Through a better understanding of the body's structures and functions, Todd concludes, man could better preserve his unity and cope with the world. Monroe needed to believe that the greatest sources of her strength came from within, that she projected her power through a camera and onto the screen rather than the reverse, in which the camera produced and then stripped away some personal unreplenishable essence. Todd taught that the proper treatment of the body stimulated and rekindled its energies. Thus Monroe's constant study of *The Thinking Body* may have been one of the primary ways of fighting the fear that films not only enhanced her self-image, but had also robbed her of a more fundamental existence.

Todd develops a series of exercises (with appropriate illustrations) designed to demonstrate the body's intrinsic balance and the way that balance can be consciously managed. Rather than simply describing what she means, however, Todd has the reader participate in thinking about the body, so that her prose often resembles the language of acting manuals. For example, after a passage on the spine, in which she carefully describes how human weight is balanced by the pelvis, thigh joints, and femora, she shifts to a concrete, imagistic passage that puts this knowledge about how weight is economically distributed into practice:

> Think *down* the back and *up* the front. Let the spine drag. Picture it extended like the dinosaur's tail, but keep the front wall of the body up. The spine travels the whole length of the back, while the whole front of the body is suspended from the spine and head, directly and indirectly, through connecting bone, muscle and soft tissues. Thinking "up the front" of the body without lifting any of its bony parts will establish proper traction in the connecting muscles to keep the ends of all bones in the front of the body-wall at proper levels for a balance of weight at their spinal attachments. Thus tensile members at the front balance compression members at the back.

Monroe confessed that she found Todd difficult reading, but she was grateful to know what to look for, and Todd's thinking up and down the body neatly paralleled Chekhov's exercises on the opening and closing of the self. Both teachers required Monroe to *act*, to discover for herself her own unity. Several years later, when Ralph Roberts met Monroe and became her friend, he found they shared an enthusiasm for Todd's book, from which the actress had adapted her own set of physical exercises.

Acting is a matter of finding a concrete, functional way of interpreting character, of developing the right psychological gesture, Chekhov counsels, and Todd says much the same thing about "learning consciously to employ the *motivating picture* to create the conditions for appropriate movement responses." One has to know "three things: exact location, direction and desire to move. When conditions are right, movement takes place."

Monroe's other life—the romance with DiMaggio and movie making—worked against her dedication to art. In 1953 and 1954, she had to contend with exhaustion, frequent colds, and headaches that probably resulted from her feverish schedule. She completed three major films — *Niagara, Gentlemen Prefer Blondes,* and *How To Marry a Millionaire* — in less than two years and began work on a fourth, *River of No Return.* In the preceding period, 1952–53, she was rushed into five films. It is hard to see when she had any time for DiMaggio, and he resented taking second place in her life. Like Rose Loomis's husband, he hated his woman's exhibitionism. The contact points of Monroe's character — on and off screen — ignited the same charged reactions, so that the rudiments of her personality seemed to blend into a single celluloid life.

In *Gentlemen Prefer Blondes* (June 1953), Howard Hawks and his screenwriter, Charles Lederer, grasped the evolution of Monroe's style: she was becoming self-referential. She was playing characters like Rose Loomis who had no past, needed no past; they just had to *be.* Hawks and his crew helped Monroe to transform herself into a self-generating phenomenon, a perpetuum mobile of desire. The allure of the movie is the way it stands apart from, divisible from reality. *Blondes* begins with Lorelei (Monroe) and Dorothy (Jane Russell) singing "We're Just Two Little Girls from Little Rock," although no attempt is made to make them look or sound like two little girls from Little Rock. On the contrary, we get the distinct impression that Monroe and Russell are entertainers playing roles and setting scenes; we are not to take them seriously. They are on stage, backstage, or off stage; almost everything they do is defined by the stage setting. As soon as they begin singing or dancing, their world becomes a stage, a series of scenes. When Lorelei sings to her fiancé in the ship's cabin, when Dorothy sings for the U.S. Olympic team around a swimming pool, and when both women sing "When Love Goes Wrong Nothin' Goes Right" in a French café, crowds gather as audiences and private emotions are transformed into public performances.

Dorothy, however, is allowed to slip out of her role as performer, so that she can function as a person who often advises Lorelei against acting. At the very end of the film, Dorothy's differentiation from Lorelei is apparent. At their double wedding ceremony she says, "Remember, it's all right now to say yes." Her comment implies that Lorelei may not be clear about the limits of her role, that she might just go on playing it because the role is not a means to an end (marriage) but just a means, a way of being (a women *in pursuit* of a rich husband) in which she has fully invested herself.

More is under consideration in such a scene than Lorelei's dumbness. She is distinguished by her ability to hold on to a role, to retain nothing of herself for other times, other settings. What Lorelei is as a person is forever elusive. Sometimes she seems just plain dumb, as when she does not know the difference between a tiara and a necklace. But then she confounds her future father-in-law (Taylor Holmes) by getting the better of him in argument by frankly admitting that she can be smart when she wants to, "but most men don't like it." Just how much does Lorelei know about her dumbness? On occasion she is dumb with Dorothy. Has her role overtaken her? Somewhere apart from her role Monroe is having fun with her audience; she is parodying her own glamour-girl style. But where exactly is that parody located? Billy Wilder will exploit this ambiguous aspect of Monroe as put-on in *The Seven Year Itch*.

Throughout *Gentlemen Prefer Blondes* Lorelei polishes her role, not her person. Dorothy, on the other hand, asks "is there anyone here for love?" She chafes against the restraints of role playing; she wants to be herself and to be loved as herself, although she enjoys impersonating Lorelei in one scene and sees nothing wrong in scheming and staging scenes for her own protection. She can dissemble, but her identity is intact, mature, even motherly in the way she guides Lorelei, whose babyish voice implies an identity that is undeveloped, despite her shrewd understanding of how to play her role.

The justly famous "Diamonds Are a Girl's Best Friend" musical number elevates and consecrates the glamorous child-woman myth that envelops Lorelei-Monroe throughout the film. She appears in a fetching satin dress and glossy makeup reminiscent of her most lurid publicity photographs, but there is an elegance in her long gloves and in the men in tuxedos who attend her. At the same time, the gentle way these men carry her through the number, and the conspicuous way her dress trails what almost look like a chick's tail feathers when she hops, indicate an infantile, unconscious nature (first glimpsed in *Love Happy*) that belies her cynical song about how women lose their charms (looks), but rocks (diamonds) don't lose their shape. As in her nude calendar, the heavy use of red throughout most of this number is obviously intended to evoke the heat of passion, and the glare of diamonds is the brilliant reward for the shrewd application of that passion. In this complex mix of contradictory implications—all myths have this affinity for blending conflicting impressions (in this case cute naïveté and adult seductiveness)—the reds recede and a single beam—Truffaut calls it "a kind of dim church light"—isolates her with her arms straight above her head and her fingers outspread as she smiles and luxuriates in her self-love and in the adoration of her gentlemen, who are on their knees with faces and arms uplifted. Notice how she places her hands on her chest and shakes her breasts and how many of her gestures are self-referential even as she plays to a worshipful audience. If *Niagara* first defines the visual angles

Figure 8. Marilyn Monroe in *Gentlemen Prefer Blondes*, 1953
® 1953; ren. 1981 Twentieth Century-Fox Film Corporation. All Rights Reserved.
(Courtesy Wisconsin Center for Film and Theater Research)

of her appeal, then *Gentlemen Prefer Blondes* explores audience reaction to that appeal, so that the sound track includes a long admiring chorus of "ooh-ooh" timed to coincide with her exaggeratedly slow side-to-side hip movements.

While "Diamonds Are a Girl's Best Friend" burlesques Monroe as sex symbol, the number's extravagance is more than humorous, for it heightens her symbolic status. Such a lavish production goes well beyond anything required to embellish Lorelei's personality. The setting, the costumes, the jewelry, the makeup, and Monroe herself are designed to be thoroughly dazzling. Every move she makes sparkles and glitters; her voice and the accompanying music are amplified and modulated to project both the raucous response of unrepressed sexuality and her soft, mellow, caressing tones. "Diamonds" is a scene that in every possible way has been arranged for Monroe, so that by the end of the number she has moved in every direction and filled in every corner of the movie frame. As a result, the frame is transformed into her vehicle of self-incorporation.

After *Gentlemen Prefer Blondes*, every film would be more or less written to play off against the person/symbol Marilyn Monroe. Nunnally Johnson wrote the part of Pola in *How to Marry a Millionaire* (November 1953) with Monroe in mind. He wanted to treat comically and compassionately what he saw as her insensitivity—her way of cutting off the world—and her self-absorption. He created a myopic Pola who refuses to wear her glasses because she fears that she will not be able to attract the millionaire husband she is seeking. The contradictions of Pola's plight are amusing, for how can she find her rich consort without seeing him?

Johnson seems to have identified a crucial aspect of Monroe's personality. She was certainly self-involved, especially during the making of this film. Lauren Bacall recalls that Monroe "just had to concentrate on herself and the people who were there only for her." At the same time, she had to reach out; she would persistently try to overcome her self-preoccupation because it made her vulnerable, shutting her off from others and causing misunderstanding, as it did with Johnson, who thought she was stupid. So as she did with Jane Russell, Monroe inquired about Bacall's children, her home life, her happiness. Monroe "seemed envious of that aspect of my life—wistful—hoping to have it herself one day," Bacall observes. In one of the most acute capsulizations of Monroe's character, Bacall concludes that she was "afraid to trust—uncomfortable. She made no effort for others and yet she was nice. I think she did trust me and like me as well as she could anyone whose life must have seemed to her so secure, so *solved*."

Like Pola without her glasses, Monroe could not perceive people as they were; they had to be within her myopic range. She had to feel that others were *with* her; if one were not a sympathetic soul she sensed an enemy. Jean Negulesco, her director on *Millionaire*, noted that "it is difficult to come close to her. She becomes vague. She puts up a curtain between herself and people." In his autobiography he recalls the sudden appearance of the hooded expression that disturbed Natasha Lytess: "With a soft-spoken voice, helpless as a sharp knife, her eyes at half mast like a cobra watching its prey, she was a cruel child tearing off butterfly wings—gay, mean, proud, and inscrutable."

Negulesco was willing to cultivate her, to explain carefully the necessity of wearing glasses—she was afraid she would be made too unattractive—by mixing personal and professional relations in the course of having several dinners with her. He made a point of his interest in her as a person, and like Karger, Lytess, and Chekhov, he discussed art and literature to establish a rapport with her. He even painted her portrait and pointed out various techniques. She was intrigued by his discussion of postimpressionist artists and asked "sensible" questions about them. She was slow to absorb his direction and hated to adjust to script changes, yet her stamina over very long work hours and her total concentration impressed him. Several years later he remembers how "she had such a right sense of knowing the character she was playing—the way to enter a scene, to hold singular attention as the scene developed, the way to end a scene—so that no other actor existed around her."

There were times, however, when it seemed virtually impossible to mediate between her self-absorption and the corporate film world of cast and crew. During one trying afternoon on the set of *Millionaire*, Monroe kept "blowing one take after another, fluffing her lines, or forgetting them." Everyone was tired and tense in the late afternoon, and Johnson—sensing growing resentment and feeling sorry for Monroe—prepared to console her as she compulsively consulted a mirror to adjust her makeup. He told her she was doing well. There was nothing to worry about. She looked up from the mirror and seemed puzzled, for, according to Johnson, it was clear that she let him and Negulesco "do the worrying." All she cared about was her own part.

A publicity still from *Millionaire* elaborates on Monroe's posing for herself. The mirror shot has her in a typical position, with her right arm parallel to her face and her forearm bent backward as if to suggest, once again, a self-caress. The four-part mirror reflects four different angles of the same pose, with each angle gradually turning her face from distant profile to a three-quarter open view. The photograph encloses Monroe

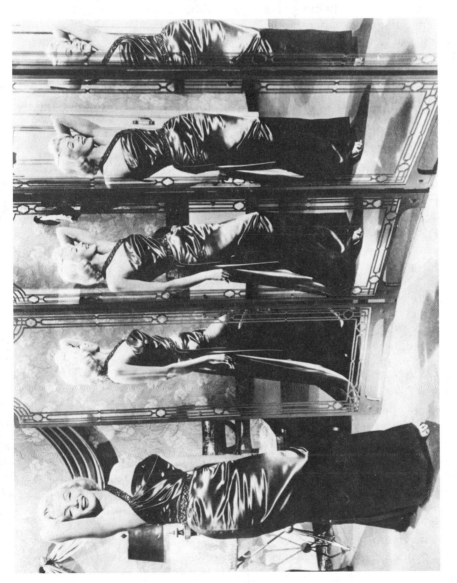

Figure 9. Marilyn Monroe in *How to Marry a Millionaire*, 1953
® 1953; ren. 1981 Twentieth Century-Fox Film Corporation. All Rights Reserved.
(*Courtesy The Museum of Modern Art/Film Stills Archive*)

within the panels of her own appeal; her images revolve around her person, or is it the person—who is smiling dreamily—revolving around the images? With the aid of a mirror, one pose begets four different images; this is precisely the sort of self-amplification that Monroe seems to be enjoying in the photograph.

In the film, however, the scene in which this mirror appears is quite brief, and Pola only uses the mirror to check that everything is in the right place. *Millionaire* does not explore Monroe's interesting polarities of self-commitment and self-to-world involvement. Pola is too naïve, too limited in experience, and cannot approach Monroe's complexity. Or, put another way, Monroe's psychological myopia is played for laughs by giving Pola a physical disability and various sight gags. Pola runs into walls and takes the wrong airplane, and Monroe is very skillful and funny in performing the physical business of her role. It was characteristic of her to call on Chekhov to help her with the timing of her comic scenes.

Because Pola moves blindly through the world she cannot see herself, a point that is vividly made in her encounter with Freddie Denmark (David Wayne) who wears glasses. He is sitting next to her on a plane and observes her reading a book upside down. "Why don't you wear glasses?" he asks. At first she denies her need for them, then hesitantly admits to her blindness as Denmark freely confesses his own reluctance to wear glasses until the day he said hello to three different men to whom he owed money. Denmark is extremely forthright and obviously comfortable wearing glasses. He encourages Pola to wear hers and confides that he thinks that with or without glasses she is "quite a strudel." Monroe plays Pola's reactions perfectly. Waves of panic move across Pola's face as she tentatively puts her glasses on. Denmark's response is immediate, positive, and decisive. He tells her the glasses give her a "certain difference or distinction," and Pola glows with a happy idea of importance she has never felt before. She is directed to a sense of self-worth, just as Monroe sometimes depended on the sensitive guidance of others for a belief in her own strength. But while Pola's salvation is accidental, Monroe sought and perceived ways of building a better self. Pola is passive; Monroe, who could retard her progress through inertia and timidity, was nevertheless dynamic and inventive in working out her own career.

Appearances, however, suggested otherwise, for there was a strong man in Monroe's life who provided the male protection her screen personae often seem to need. DiMaggio was also decisive, and she would call on him for help during the filming of *River of No Return* (April 1954) when she tore a ligament. She had been feebly struggling under Otto

Preminger's abrupt direction, and DiMaggio arrived with a doctor to shore up both her mental and physical defenses, which were crumbling rapidly. Or were they? According to Shelley Winters, Monroe may have staged her accident to scare Preminger and her studio and to create sympathy for herself. After her accident Preminger became amenable and DiMaggio ardent. She and DiMaggio had a lovers' quarrel before the start of the film, but sometime during its making they decided to marry.

In *River of No Return* Monroe plays a dancehall girl, a "whore with a heart of gold," as Joan Mellen puts it. It is a poorly conceived movie, as Monroe knew, but that does not excuse her stilted, mannered speech, which is completely out of character, and which Preminger blamed on Natasha Lytess's emphasis on enunciation. Monroe is persuasive in her dancehall songs (Lotte Goslar helped her with them) and even compelling in her singing to a young boy (Tommy Rettig); here she appears utterly at ease, charming, tenderly maternal, and at one with the Western setting and her role. But her character, Kay, is passive. She has been misguided by the disreputable men in her life, collaborating in their shady dealings. With her poor background she has had few opportunities to be as good as she should be, although she does evolve emotionally and with some feistiness when she makes Matt Calder (Robert Mitchum) abandon his "preconceived notions" about her dancehall career and acknowledge that she is capable of change. She seems less than the "real woman" Molly Haskell professes to see, however, and at the end of the film Calder literally carries her off to become his wife and the mother of his young boy. All she needed, the film implies, was one good, clean, hardy, honest man to set her straight.

On January 14, 1954, shortly after the completion of *River of No Return*, she did indeed marry a good, clean, hardy, trustworthy hero, Joe DiMaggio, the Yankee Clipper. The marriage was a sensational event. The couple found themselves on the covers of magazines, in the headlines of newspapers, and at the top of gossip columns all over the world. Monroe's studio had suspended her for her refusal to do *Pink Tights*, but it had to revoke the suspension and send congratulations to the honeymooning couple in Japan. "Joltin' Joe" was her slugger, Monroe told the press. Their marriage was another chapter in the American Dream. Two of the beloved national pastimes, sports and movies, had been conjoined—"the merger of two worlds," *Life* (January 25) called it.

En route to Japan an army officer invited Monroe to entertain the troops in Korea, and without DiMaggio's enthusiastic approval, she headed off to respond in person to the headlines that elevated her in the public consciousness to a level she had never imagined possible. She

Figure 10. Marilyn Monroe and Joe DiMaggio, ca. 1954
(*Courtesy Movie Star News*)

had to improvise an act quickly, since she had not come to Japan with performing in mind, but she had no great problem with this change of plans. She took a few songs from her films and choreographed a personal triumph. Altogether she entertained approximately 100,000 troops in ten performances. Pictures of her singing and dancing in subzero temperatures were published all over the world. By all accounts she put on a remarkably poised and witty act—quite a feat for an actress who was not used to live audiences.

She returned to DiMaggio in Japan with a slight case of pneumonia, but the cheering she had evoked warmed her immeasurably, even if this kind of fame could not fulfill her permanently. In *My Story*, she recalls that backstage before her first performance in Korea she could hear "music playing and a roar of voices trying to drown it out." An excited officer told her that she would have to "go on ahead of schedule. . . . I don't think we can hold them any longer. They're throwing rocks on the stage." The repeated roar of her name demonstrated that her identity had an echo and an impact. She told Sidney Skolsky,

> I felt I belonged. . . . For the first time in my life I had the feeling that the people seeing me were accepting me and liking me. This is what I've always wanted, I guess. That's why, without realizing the full meaning of what I was saying, I told Joe that for the first time I felt like a movie star.

In Korea, Monroe was able to fuse herself with her filmic and photographic image, to be exactly what her audience had supposed her to be. In Korea, she became one with the imprint of her fame.

6

Half-Life (April–November 1954)

Who is she—who does she think she is, Marilyn Monroe?

In the spring of 1954, just after their honeymoon trip to Japan, Monroe and DiMaggio began quarreling. They were in San Francisco, his home town, where he apparently took up a "semi-bachelor" routine while she waited impatiently to resume her career in June on *There's No Business Like Show Business*. Although he grudgingly moved to Hollywood, he was not on the movie set to give Monroe support, as he had been for part of *River of No Return*. She, in turn, devoted little time to home life and conferred continually with Natasha Lytess, whom DiMaggio detested. Indeed, it is during this film that Monroe began to encircle herself with the hangers-on who would cater to her on subsequent movie sets. DiMaggio, no doubt, felt excluded from this group of syco-phants, and some of Monroe's coworkers came to deplore her menag-erie of helpers, preferring to believe that she would have been better off relying on her own strengths rather than using others to shore up her weaknesses.

In *Show Business*, Monroe plays Vicky, a hat-check girl who aspires to be an actress. Like Monroe's, Vicky's lowly beginnings provoke people—like Tim Donahue (Donald O'Connor), who will become her boyfriend in the film—to scoff at her pretensions. She is pictured in front of a mirror, posing for herself, rocking her head, and her lack of inflec-tion, her way of pronouncing every word with equal emphasis, as in her line, "This gentleman was just leaving," make her a wooden, uninspired copy of Monroe's earlier film characters. It is as if one of the well-worn pages of Monroe's studio biography were simply inserted into the film. Her first musical number, "After You Get What You Want You Don't Want It," is an embarrassingly bad imitation of "Diamonds Are a Girl's Best Friend." Although she sings the number well, so that the song's wry sensibility is sophisticatedly poised in her warm, delicate phrasing,

Figure 11. Marilyn Monroe in *There's No Business Like Show Business*, 1954
® 1954; ren. 1982 Twentieth Century-Fox Film
Corporation. All Rights Reserved.
(*Courtesy The Museum of Modern Art/Film Stills Archive*)

she is forced to throw herself at the various couples seated at nightclub tables while she eyes men and turns her body at various angles to make her legs or her breasts more prominent. She also uses a familiar gesture from "Diamonds," placing her hands on her chest and shaking her breasts, but the scene as a whole fails to sustain the rapport between her person and her audience that the earlier film establishes.

There is something very static and remote about this scene, in spite of the fact that Monroe is maneuvered into filling the movie frame in ways similar to those employed in *Gentlemen Prefer Blondes*. In a still often reproduced from this scene she is captured with her arms extended upward and with her hands bent at the wrists and turned toward each other over her head, so that once again she frames herself in her own appeal, emphasizing her smiling, open-mouthed self-intoxication. Unlike her avatar, Lorelei Lee, Vicky is slightly freakish, a bizarrely angled bird with too much plumage, too much frippery that turns her into a prop, a thing on which to attach items of sexual provocation. Note the studio's description of the costume Monroe wears in this still: a "high necked, long-sleeved, slit-long-skirted evening gown of white illusion net over flesh crepe, with white-beaded lace appliques embroidered in strategic places." Monroe's Vicky is essentially a character to gawk at, and much the same can be said of her in the other big production number, "Heat Wave," where her repertory of gestures is severely limited and the camera often concentrates on her crotch and other body parts.

The film never attempts to integrate the vulgarian of these musical scenes with the poor naive Vicky who is seen in short episodes with her boyfriend Tim. Somehow, more or less like Monroe, Vicky has become a rising star after having been on her own since she was fifteen. This cheap use of Monroe's by then already well known biography does nothing to enhance the characterization of Vicky, but it does demonstrate how Monroe was forced into dull formulaic work. It is difficult to appreciate her presence in this terrible film; her role is negligible, and she must have felt marginal, overshadowed by such musical comedy stars as Ethel Merman and Dan Dailey.

Monroe was ill throughout the making of *Show Business*, suffering from ailments variously reported as anemia, a low-grade virus, and just sheer physical exhaustion. Rose Steinberg Wapner remembers Monroe on the set going over and over again the same scene until Wapner could see physical weakness in her eyes. It is the only film in which she observed this kind of weariness in Monroe and a dissipation of creative energy. Reports of Monroe's excessive drinking, addiction to sleeping pills and amphetamines, and her need to consult a psychiatrist first surfaced during the making of this film. Not all of these reports are verifiable, yet it is apparent that she was under more stress than in any previous picture or period of her life. Her dress designer, Billy Travilla, remembers her crying and expressing fears about losing her mind. "My brains are leaving me. I think I'm going crazy," she told him.

DiMaggio was extremely jealous and, according to some of Monroe's friends, physically abusive. He suspected she was having an affair with her voice coach, Hal Schaefer, who has recently admitted as much. As with Slatzer, she was deeply grateful for Schaefer's guidance and for his professionalism. Like Fred Karger, Schaefer did not allow his feelings for her to interfere with the cultivation of her talent, and the intimacy between Schaefer and Monroe did not develop until several months after their film work ceased. Their affair, in fact, was an ordeal for him and contributed to a suicide attempt he barely survived.

Monroe's faltering marriage made work difficult, as Susan Strasberg observed on a visit: "Marilyn was perspiring heavily and kept falling out of step. Joe DiMaggio was on the set that day, so she was under additional tension. She slipped in the middle of a complicated step and fell soundly on her backside. Taking a break she came over to us, still embarrassed from her fall." On the set of *Show Business* Monroe seemed to flounder. "She didn't appear to have any guidelines," Wapner remarks. In retrospect, it seems as though a phase of the actress's career was nearly over, and she would have to find some way to avoid these base imitations of herself.

Monroe had already begun to consider alternatives to Hollywood. In September of 1953 she had met the photographer Milton Greene who began to encourage her to join him in the formation of her own film production company. And she had probably heard from Elia Kazan and others about Actors Studio in New York, so that when she finally met Paula Strasberg—the wife of the studio's eminent head—she declared on the set of *Show Business*: "I've heard so much about your husband, I think he's wonderful. . . . I've always dreamed of studying acting with Mr. Strasberg." In sum, she had already made tentative contacts that make her move to the East less abrupt and less arbitrary than it appeared to the press who reported on it in her day. When Monroe went to New York on September 9, 1954, to do location shooting for *The Seven Year Itch*, she resumed meeting with Greene and began confiding in him and his wife about her career and her troubles with her husband. She was also keeping in touch with Arthur Miller by telephone, writing a few letters to him, and occasionally visiting Brooklyn, where he lived. She particularly enjoyed the heterogeneous life of urban streets and spoke to reporters about retiring to Brooklyn. Apparently, Monroe was meditating on a break with Hollywood long before she actually took up permanent residence in New York.

The Seven Year Itch may have represented a kind of culmination for her that made a break easier to contemplate, for the film epitomizes the screen persona that had first been fully manifested in *Gentlemen Prefer Blondes*. Her character in *Itch*, The Girl, is given no name until near the end of the film, when her would-be lover, Richard Sherman (Tom Ewell), says in swaggering fashion to another male that maybe The Girl is Marilyn Monroe. In a recent showing of the movie, an Ann Arbor, Michigan, audience exploded with laughter at this in-joke, just as audiences must have roared their approval in 1955. In *Itch* Monroe plays at being herself; that is, she parodies the screen persona she has become. Many of The Girl's lines are similar to Lorelei Lee's. For instance, Lorelei could easily have said The Girl's line about knowing how to identify a piece of classical music, "there is no vocal." When The Girl does her commercial for "Dazzle-dent" toothpaste, she couches her words and her figure in the simpering attitudes of Monroe's early publicity photographs.

Better than any movie up to this point, *Itch* exemplifies Monroe's range of appeal. In *Gentlemen Prefer Blondes*, she is paired at various times with a precocious young boy with a mature voice, a wimpy young man with an adolescent outlook, and an old man with some sexual vigor left in him. In *Show Business* she is charmed by an ordinary-looking song-and-dance man. In *Itch*, she fills in the middle ground of her democratic attractiveness by becoming the object of the middle-aged, middle-class male's sexual fantasies.

Monroe arrives as The Girl everyone can enjoy. She is no longer someone else's mistress (*The Asphalt Jungle*, *All About Eve*), someone else's secretary (*As Young as You Feel*, *Monkey Business*), or someone else's wife or girlfriend (*We're Not Married*, *Niagara*, *Show Business*). Indeed, The Girl has no boyfriends or bosses, and she does not see herself in competition with other women. She is readily available even for the most passive male: Sherman, like the moviegoer, only has to dream about her in order for her to appear. She remains accessible even after Sherman blunders badly in his seduction of her; she is, in short, the perfect plaything, a *living* doll, as one of the characters in the film keeps insisting. "You're just elegant," The Girl tells Sherman at a strategic moment when he is feeling particularly inept and unattractive, and she earnestly hopes that his wife will value him more highly. She constantly strokes his middle-aged ego. She tells him he has powerful thumbs as he "pops" the champagne cork, which is clearly a not so covert allusion to his wanting to pop her, a girl who is as effervescent as the champagne she loves to dip her potato chips in. Similarly, his twitching thumb is a barely disguised token of what is no doubt—the audience is invited to imagine—his other pulsating member, the strong sexual drive he tries to suppress in loyalty to his seven-year marriage. The Girl delivers puns on phallic penetration without a flicker of self-consciousness, and she is oblivious to Sherman's "grown-up" leer about her "interesting point of view." She seems infinitely innocent and willing to follow every turn of Sherman's erratic stop-and-go romancing.

The celebrated skirt-blowing scene is, of course, the finest instance of a Monroe character's ability to suggest simultaneously both childlike pleasure and sexual delight. Photographs of Monroe straddling a subway grating with her dress forced high above her thighs by the rush of air coming from below appeared in magazines and newspapers around the world. It seemed that she was caught in a spontaneous moment of joy and relief on a hot city summer night, and that moment was suspended above ground and defined from nearly every conceivable angle. She was shot in profile, straight on, with her head tilted backward, forward, or turned three-quarters of the way toward the camera. In one pose she is holding her dress, so that it fans out in front of her, revealing her panties, and fans out behind her, as she twists her neck in ecstasy. In another pose her whole body surges forward with one of her fingers seemingly shooting in the direction of the camera that is shooting her. The self-reflexiveness of such shots does not carry over into the filmed scene. On the contrary, the film version seems subdued and understated after one has become accustomed to the plethora of poses available in the photographs. In the film, the forced air lifts her dress rather sedately above her knees, although in a second shot the camera fastens on and moves along the surface of the subway grating as if tracking the gust of air shooting up from a speeding train, and simulating the rush of feeling exemplified in The Girl's lifted spirits and skirt.

Monroe is something else besides an object of male fantasy, or an airy symbol of a nature goddess almost able to raise herself in her magical skirt above the grimy subway grating to fly as high as her soaring orgasm of delight. She also plays The Girl as a woman who is herself; that is to say, there is a matter-of-factness about her, a down-to-earth directness reminiscent of Clara Bow that is disconcerting for Sherman. She is kind to him, but she makes clear that his air conditioner, in this hot city summer, is one of his main attractions. She is less impressed by his efforts to be suave than she is by his more genuine modesty and self-effacement. What he excites most in her is compassion and sincere respect for his homely strengths. She makes it clear that she rebuffs good-looking, conceited young men who try to overwhelm her with

Figure 12.   Marilyn Monroe in *The Seven Year Itch*, 1955
® 1955; ren. 1983 Charles K. Feldman Group Productions.
Twentieth Century-Fox Film Corporation. All
Rights Reserved.
(*Courtesy The Museum of Modern Art/Film Stills Archive*)

their high opinions of themselves. Although one could interpret her preference for Sherman as another one of his middle-aged projections, there is a solidity to The Girl, a sureness that surprises him and makes it unlikely that she is just *his* fantasy. In fact, her lack of embarrassment about her motives, and her charming way of conveying them to him, make her seem—at least in this respect—not at all dumb, but rather far more mature than Sherman. Take, for example, the scene in which she discovers that by simply pulling up a few nails she can open a trap door that leads immediately to a set of stairs that descend from her apartment into his. As she reaches the landing, she pauses with a hammer poised delicately in one hand and a toothbrush in the other and sweetly announces, "You know what? We can do this all summer." The camera holds on her wide-eyed child's face, and she subtly shifts to a narrow-eyed, adult concentration conveying an unmistakable sexual innuendo—to which audiences respond with both laughter and the verbal asides that one expects in connection with double entendre. Such minutely perceptible modulations in the way Monroe plays The Girl, and the camera's facility for fastening on her long enough to suggest that more is there than the initial impression of naïveté has the audience, rather than the actors, doing double takes. In other words, Monroe's character is as infinitely suggestive as she is innocent.

As usual, the publicity surrounding a Monroe film virtually obliterated any consideration of her talent. Instead, primarily because of the skirt blowing scene, she was treated as having shown more of herself than ever before. The filming of this celebrated scene at 2:30 A.M. on September 10, 1954, in New York City attracted a crowd variously estimated to have been between one thousand and four thousand people, who watched Monroe's skirt fly up fifteen times as the scene was rehearsed. DiMaggio had arrived two days earlier and could be seen drawing the attention of some fans and the press. Amid shouts of "higher" and "hurrah" as the wind-blowing machine puffed her skirt overhead, DiMaggio retreated in silent anger.

At about 4:00 A.M. Monroe returned to her hotel room and DiMaggio arrived somewhat later. Evidently they quarreled over her night's work, for "some shouting and scuffling was overheard by other hotel residents nearby, followed by hysterical weeping." The next day DiMaggio departed for California, and Monroe remained heavily sedated. In less than a month, on October 4, her attorney would announce the end of her marriage, and she would proceed to finish *Itch* without the breakdowns, tardiness, and falterings that now were customary on her sets. She became adamant in her decision to dissolve the marriage and

Figure 13. Marilyn Monroe in *The Seven Year Itch*, 1955
® 1955; ren. 1983 Charles K. Feldman Group Productions.
Twentieth Century-Fox Film Corporation. All Rights Reserved.
(*Courtesy Movie Star News*)

seemed just as determined to demonstrate her commitment to her career.

Monroe also seemed intent on exploiting every opportunity for publicity. Sidney Skolsky, who was present during the preparations for Monroe's appearance before the press to announce her divorce, recalls how Jerry Geisler, her attorney, acted like a movie director, explaining the mood he wanted, and how Skolsky was to offer his support while the attorney held her tightly in his grip. The newsreel footage of the announcement certainly suggests a rather staged, melodramatic scene, so that Monroe's sorrow is made public in the way Geisler planned. She walks out of the house, faces the microphones, begins to speak, falters, and wells up with tears. As her attorney supports her, she slowly shakes her head from side to side as if to signal that she cannot trust herself to say anything.

Why did Monroe have to face the press and cameras in this carefully framed way? Because she learned to view her life in terms of camera set-ups. Her real distress over the breakup with DiMaggio had to be used as another scene in her star script. Another eyewitness account of Monroe's preparations for the press has her "numb from emotional fatigue. New floods of tears ruined her mascara every few minutes so Marilyn was obliged to spend much of her time in front of a mirror in her second-floor bedroom." She was *obliged* to put a face on her emotions, to repair her image in the mirror repeatedly, because that was the only way she knew how to put herself together.

Monroe was living with the consequences of having become a performing self, the kind of self for which, Shelley Winters remarks, reality has to be heightened by turning one's private life inside out:

> Sometimes I'll be weeping and I'll look in the mirror and I say, "Why do I twist up my face?" I'm right in the middle of agony and I'm sort of remembering how I got to this feeling of agony. . . . I'm not sure that this is good, in fact, I think it's bad, but maybe you can't help it if you're an actor.

The actor's only instrument is herself, and she has to be on view for every occasion and know how to project her life into her roles. As a result, much of her experience is filtered and stored up for public exposure. Actors are conducting constant raids on their own lives. For Monroe, the accretions of photographs, films, and mirror images tended to prevent her being entirely direct with herself. Working with her life had come to resemble working with the paste-up she had done for *Show Business*, in which she recorded the "Heat Wave" song twenty-five times for one of her singing coaches, Ken Darby, who took "the twenty-five pieces of tape home with him and cut them up and put them together so that she had the proper phrasing in each part of the song" and could then recreate it in the studio.

Given Monroe's superb command of Hollywood publicity, it came as a shock a few months later when she announced that she was leaving 20th Century-Fox and moving to New York. Almost immediately, however, her move was suspected to be a publicity ploy, and few people seemed to appreciate that she had become saturated with her own stardom to such an extent that she felt stymied. Although she would indulge in various kinds of publicity maneuver for the rest of her career, never again would her life be quite as public as it has been during *The Seven Year Itch* and her divorce from DiMaggio. In her last years she was—in a way that anticipated the Beatles—in revolt against herself, or against the popular personality she had created. Like the Beatles, she had served a long apprenticeship in which she had worked much harder than others reaching for the same kind of recognition. Like John Lennon, she voiced the "infantile longing behind every star's obsession. 'Why didn't anybody notice me?' " She shared the Beatles' talent for turning everything into an event, a spectacle, and she succeeded—as they did—because on and off stage and screen she was good theater, a good ad-libber, a wit, a vivacious creator of comic cross-talk that foreshadowed the Beatles' press conferences. She regarded her appearances before the press as little comedy shows that she deftly directed. She acted out her personality in films just as the Beatles created their personalities through their music and movies. She became increasingly skilled and sophisticated in her film work just as they became more musically ambitious and adept. Finally, like them, she mythologized herself, drawing on her past and future as, in essence, her only subject, even while withdrawing from the public and focusing more on her art than on public acclaim.

7

Search for Self: The Method
(November 1954–May 1956)

Goethe said, "Talent is developed in privacy," you know? And it's really true. There is a need for aloneness which I don't think most people realize for an actor. It's almost having certain kinds of secrets for yourself that you'll let the whole world in on only for a moment, when you're acting.

Monroe had been consulting with Milton Greene for over a year about her own production company. His idea included the possibility of buying screen properties in which she could extend her capacity as an actress. If she could manage her career through her choice of sympathetic directors and producers, then she was prepared to entertain Greene's enthusiastic belief that she could play the roles she coveted. By the end of 1954, Marilyn Monroe Productions had been formed, with Monroe as president and Greene as vice president. She had become convinced that her contract with Fox could be shown in court to have no legal standing, or at least that the formation of her own company would pressure Fox executives into giving her better roles and more control over the film-making process.

Greene's reputation had been made as a superb photographer, not a producer. In his early thirties, he was very young, many people thought, to be taking on Fox, to be supporting Monroe during what turned out to be a year-long battle with her studio, and to be masterminding the making of movies he promised would be far more sophisticated than her earlier Hollywood products. Some of Monroe's friends distrusted his motives and suspected him of exploiting her. She was cautioned to pick someone with more experience, with more Hollywood savvy. Undoubtedly Greene appealed to her precisely because he was not part of the Hollywood establishment. Moreover, she was hardly naïve about her association with the ambitious Greenes, and she was careful about what she confided to Milton's wife Amy, who seemed particularly keen to ingratiate herself with influential people.

Greene had been introduced to Monroe by their mutual friend, Rupert Allan, and he had come to Monroe, on Allan's advice, with his portfolio in hand. Greene was brash and youthful looking – "he appeared to be about eighteen years old in those days," Allan recalls. "You're just a boy," Monroe exclaimed. "You're just a girl," Greene immediately replied. Could Greene somehow take Monroe just for what she was and work with her identity from scratch? It is hard to say which of them was more excited by that prospect, since they were nearly equal in age and hopeful that their best years, their finest accomplishments, were ahead of them.

Greene was more than just a charming talker, a young man with a quick wit remarkably like Monroe's own quips, or a wit cleverly adaptable to her own spontaneous humor. His photographs of her captured that rare luminescence she could have in person, a brilliance even greater ("if you can imagine that," Lee Strasberg told Fred Guiles) than what appeared on the screen. Norman Mailer has captured some of the impressive range Greene was able to get in his photographs; they convey "a mist of glamour, tenderness, amusement, sex, and subtle sorrow."

Of Women and Their Elegance is the finest record so far of Greene's photographs of Monroe, and it reveals a great deal not only about his relationship with her but also about the kind of performer she was becoming as she realized her freedom from the restraints of earlier poses and positions. One black and white sequence, for example, demonstrates the evolution of a far more intriguing personality than was found in her earlier photographs. Monroe seems much older; in part, at least, the sense of age arises from the austerity of the setting. In the cover shot her figure from the bustline downward is encased in a dark garment that is virtually indistinguishable from the black background. Her blonde hair, which is usually luxuriantly displayed, is barely seen and seems almost wispy at the sides and shrouded by black at the top of her head. Her long, dark eyelashes enhance the mysteriousness of her hooded expression. She is almost smiling but her lips are not parted. Her right eye is slightly open, and the left appears to be closed. The familiar teasing pose – half revealing, half concealing the sex symbol – is shaded here, suggesting ambiguity and perhaps a divided self, which is the insistent theme of Mailer's narrative in *Of Women and Their Elegance*. This particular photograph is suggestive of a sexuality about which more needs to be known, but that sexuality seems rooted not simply in the body but in what could be the sadness of the woman's eyes and smile—if she is indeed smiling. This woman's complex thoughts, her conflicting emotions, are not apparent in her earlier photographs. For the first time, perhaps, Monroe's sexuality and wry wit are seriously linked but remain almost somberly elusive. She is a figure of shadow and light, a delicately poised dark impenetrable body, more nearly a part of the photographic medium than she had ever been before and at the same time defined more provocatively as a person than any photographer had been able to show thus far.

Like many of Monroe's other photographers, Greene points out that Monroe was hardly a passive subject for the camera. She almost never initiated the idea for a pose, but once he began to suggest things to her, she would respond immediately by adding her own distinctive touches. No photograph could work, Greene emphasizes, without her full cooperation and understanding. What is fascinating about their collaboration is that she appears to have adopted different attitudes toward the camera—at times, she plays up to it; occasionally, she seems aloof and keeps her distance. Then there are poses in which her awareness of being photographed seems problematic altogether, so that it is not certain whether she is entirely caught up with herself or seeming to be so in front of the prying lens. Or is it the photographer's selection of camera angles and focus that determines the diversity of feelings encoded in the photographs? Even if Greene was at the controls, so to speak, he had to navigate by Monroe's moods and to track an intricate and evanescent personality with the mechanisms at his disposal.

However Greene's photographs are read, they offer indisputable evidence of maturation. Certainly they parallel Monroe's sense of having been liberated from Hollywood. By the end of 1954, she was in New York City and had already contacted Arthur Miller. In the next several months they drew closer and closer together. From December 1954 to February 1955 she stayed in relative isolation with Milton and Amy Greene in Weston, Connecticut, before coming to New York to romance with Miller, to investigate working with Lee Strasberg at the Actors Studio, and thus to begin her life and career anew. Soon she would be firmly in the tow of Greene, Strasberg, and Miller—the triumvirate—as she had been previously with Lytess, Karger, and Hyde. Although she retained some of her Hollywood connections—staying in close touch with the Karger family, for example—her professional relationships, particularly with Lytess, were broken. She allowed nearly a year to pass before having Lytess officially notified by telegram that she would no longer serve as an acting coach.

Milton Greene's influence on Monroe was at its greatest during her nearly three-month stay in his home. His wife Amy warmly welcomed Monroe and included her in all household activities. The actress avidly read Amy's books and was particularly taken with biographies of Napoleon and his wife Josephine. She was attracted to powerful mistresses of historical figures like Lord Nelson and to artists like Isadora Duncan. Of particular interest to her were women who invented themselves, so to speak, and imposed their personalities upon an age. Monroe, Amy Greene recalls, had a powerful need to hear stories, encapsulizations of lives, perhaps because she was trying to get a grip on her own. She kept a diary full of her observations on conversations, on magazine articles, and on other items that caught her interest. As the Greenes describe this period, a remarkable sense of the actress's restlessness and drive emerges. They could hear her staying up very late at night—sometimes reading, sometimes playing the radio—but nearly always sleep would come only after her regular dosage of Seconal.

To Amy Greene, Monroe confided the hurts she felt as a woman. She confessed to having had a child while still a teenager. Later with her maid Lena Pepitone, she would again mention the child and her guilt feelings over allowing her guardian to take it away for adoption. The actress in her may have been dramatizing events that never actually occurred—like the numerous abortions she alluded to in the presence of Greene and other female friends—but the episodes of severe distress occasioned by her periods were undeniably real and made Monroe weep over an internal ache no analgesic could assuage. Her Los Angeles physician, Dr. Lee Siegel, has noted that she suffered from endometriosis, "a condition in which womb-lining tissue forms in places other than the womb, such as the ovaries or Fallopian tubes." As a result, she was often in agony and felt the pain acutely in her reproductive organs, a pain that increased due to the progressive nature of her ailment.

The actress, as her psychiatrist Ralph Greenson learned four years later during the making of *Let's Make Love,* dealt with her cycles of pain and insomnia by resorting to a wide variety of drugs: Demerol (a "narcotic analgesic similar to morphine"), Phenobarbital HMC and Amytal (barbiturates), and sodium pentathol ("a depressant of the nervous system, primarily used in anesthesia"). She impressed Greenson with her knowledge of drugs, but she also scared him because she would mix several kinds together and was adept at getting prescriptions from several different doctors. Some of these drugs—especially Demerol—she took by injection, and Greenson put a stop to that dangerous practice.

Although there is no doubt about the debilitating consequences of her drug taking, previous accounts give the impression that she was immobilized and totally dependent on stimulants and sedatives, including alcohol. Yet this is misleading, as Greenson implied in his reluctance to term her an addict. She did not experience withdrawal symptoms when she abstained from medication. Although drugs sometimes impaired her ability to perform, they also became a crutch and gave her the lift some performers find in cocaine today. In other words, she was caught up in intense moments of creativity while battling equally intense moments of fear and pain. While she rationalized her drug use, it is also clear that doctors, including her psychiatrists, could not identify the source of her pain or alleviate the anxiety that prevented her from sleeping, so that she turned to these quick-fix remedies in order to cope with the relentless pressures that were a part of her position as one of the premier performers of her time.

The Greenes were a calming influence. Milton was irrepressibly upbeat about her battle with Fox to have some creative control over her career, and Amy conducted herself with an authority the actress admired. Monroe took to heart some of Amy's advice on how to dress in a less flamboyant manner and on how to handle herself in a more understated fashion. She was learning to husband her talent after years of profligacy in Hollywood. If she was becoming more circumspect about herself, she also knew that Milton Greene had to be a showman and needed to keep his business partner in the public eye, so she consented to riding a pink elephant in Madison Square Garden in March of 1955 as part of a charity event. On the whole, however, Monroe became part of his rather elegant style, as is easily grasped by observing how his photographs of her closely match those of other models in *Of Women and Their Elegance*. These photographs give evidence that for all her troubles, she had attained a fair amount of mastery over herself.

In the Edward R. Murrow *Person-to-Person* interview done on April 8, 1955, in the Greenes' home, Monroe appears exceedingly modest, as if she is indeed under the tutelage of this couple. Many of Murrow's questions are directed to Milton and Amy, and there is an air of condescension in his queries about whether Monroe is a good house guest. It is almost as if they are discussing a child, and Monroe's tiny voice and diffidence certainly suggest something like a child's embarrassment in front of a camera. When asked about her new production company, she speaks of wanting to make good pictures and agrees with Murrow's leading question that she got tired of playing the same roles all the time and wanted to try something different. She offers a very brief capsule history of her career, mentioning her work with Huston, Chekhov, Lytess, and Wilder, and she attempts to make a significant comment on the importance of a director who "is with you . . . really with you every moment." There is more behind her faltering comments than she conveys, but she appears vacuous and at one point shrugs her shoulders as though she is belittling what she has just said. She sounds like a little girl when she describes what joy it was to ride on the elephant in Madison Square Garden. All the while, Amy appears to be feeding Monroe cues, and as Amy strokes the dog that is lying beside them, Monroe does the same.

Monroe's confidence in the Greenes seems to have weakened after the Murrow interview. It was one thing to learn a more subtle way of presenting herself in the privacy of their home. It was quite another to have her tentativeness exposed on television, which was more than she—or probably anyone—could bear with equanimity. Monroe made no overt effort to break with the Greenes, but her suspicions were aroused, especially since she found it difficult to cope with the ambitions of others and could not accept that inevitably their motivations would be mixed. She wanted to believe, on all counts, in their selflessness, or, in a short time, she would not believe in them at all.

Perhaps the Greenes were to her something like temporary help in her quest to revamp her career. She could never give herself to them as wholeheartedly as she did to her acting teacher, Lee Strasberg. At a dinner party in March, about a month before her interview with Murrow, Monroe met Cheryl Crawford, a Broadway producer and one of the cofounders of Actors Studio, the principal agency of Lee Strasberg's formidable influence on American acting. Apparently Monroe was quite candid about her ambition to act larger, more complex roles, and Crawford responded by recommending a visit to Strasberg, who would size up her talent. It is quite likely that Monroe had been angling for an appointment with this acting master, but at the same time she probably dreaded his legendary reputation for incisively evaluating the actor's method, for she had Elia Kazan accompany her on her first meeting with Strasberg.

That initial encounter was nothing less than a comprehensive examination of her reactions to very personal, embarrassing questions designed to gauge her sensitivity, to ascertain how easily, quickly, and imaginatively she could react to what Strasberg termed "the stimulus." Her extraordinary responsiveness surprised him, since he would have expected such acuteness to have been killed by her Hollywood milieu. Instead, it had "remained fresh and alive . . . without really having been hurt." If anything, the sum of her experience had made her more sensitive than she had ever been before. As he described his impressions of Monroe to Guiles nearly five years after Monroe's death, Strasberg's voice still carried something of a sense of wonder and a note of incredulity that must have arisen during his first discovery of the miracle of her sensitivity. In his direct, even blunt treatment of her, and in his unshakable faith in her talent, Strasberg may very well have reminded her of Michael Chekhov, a man, Strasberg observed to Guiles, who intrigued Monroe.

The change from Chekhov's to Strasberg's teaching was not disruptive for Monroe. After all, both men had developed with the Stanislavsky approach to acting, and Strasberg professed nothing but respect for Chekhov, emphasizing Chekhov's contributions to her discovery of herself as an actress. Thus Monroe came to Strasberg not to learn a whole new way of acting—although newspaper accounts would make it seem so—but to work on, as Strasberg told Guiles, her conscious control of herself as an actress, on her discipline and concentration. Although Strasberg doubted that she read much of Stanislavsky and suggested it was enough for her to absorb his principles in acting classes, it seems more in character for her to have read part of Stanislavsky seriously, to have attempted him—just as she tackled but could not totally master Todd—and then turn to Strasberg for further inspiration. Like Chekhov, he was a scholar of the theater, and he responded to her out of his deep immersion in theatrical history, comparing her favorably to the finest stage performers, like Jeanne Eagels in *Rain*, who haunted his imagination.

Strasberg took Monroe out of what must have seemed like the vacuum of her search for self and method, out of those necessary but now more-than-sufficient three months of quiet study at the Greenes. He urged a fundamental recovery of her roots as a person and a basic reassessment of her techniques as an actress, so that the sources of her creativity could be revealed and channeled into finer performances. He saw that she was already an accomplished actress—especially in *The Seven Year Itch*—but he also saw her uncertainties. Even though audiences had been satisfied with her performances thus far, the actress acknowledged the futility of not knowing how to achieve her best work. For both personal and professional reasons Monroe worked privately with Strasberg. He explained to Guiles that "it was too difficult for her to subject herself to public scrutiny. Work at the Studio is done before members who then take what you've done apart." Edward Easty, a fellow student at the Studio, found Monroe's reluctance to act in public unusual, but Strasberg stressed that she was terrified of a live performance because all of her professional work had been done in film. Moreover, she was braving an intimidating situation that many actors and actresses—even those who had gone through the trials of opening on Broadway—would not countenance. James Dean, for example, walked out of a Studio class that he felt was sterilizing him with severe criticism.

Stella Adler, one of Strasberg's Group Theater associates, attacked him for having stripped actors of their personalities by encouraging what is commonly known as the Method: an intense concern with how the actor's private life informs his or her acting roles.

Monroe's use of the Method remains controversial, and opinions of her directors, casts, and crews on the sets of her final films, from *Bus Stop* to *The Misfits*, remain deeply divided about its usefulness. Even Strasberg's supporters do not deny that the Method makes actors vulnerable because it demands so much concentration on self. Ellen Burstyn points out that the increased sensitivity produced by the Method might threaten the equilibrium of the self, might make life more painful. But actors require that excruciating sensitivity, she believes, and have to be willing to risk themselves for their art—an art that by its very nature, Helen Hayes suggests, makes actors "volatile" and "overly emotional because we are so aware of our own pain and doubts and fears in life, just as we are aware of those of everyone around us. And when you are in on those inner secrets of people's hearts and souls, you can't just become as wonderfully detached and cool-headed as a surgeon or a legal mind."

Some of Monroe's friends opposed her use of the Method because they believed it fractured her ego by having her recall traumatic past experiences. Arthur Miller, always wary of the Strasbergs, has contended that the Method imprisons actors in their subjectivity and turns the social life of theater too far inward, so that the reciprocal relationship between characters and their audience is ruined. In film, on the other hand, the Method is more acceptable, he concedes, because it is adaptable to the camera's proximity to private emotions.

Miller may be thinking of film's singular ability to suggest inner feelings by focusing so precisely on an actor's features and gestures. Monroe claimed that before her film career began her feelings were not reckoned; they simply vanished unrecorded and unheeded by others. It is easy to conceive of how she would find the Method attractive, for it made acting excruciatingly intimate, close to the actor's person, thereby fusing—or at least bridging—the break between private and performing selves. Strasberg, then, was responding to both sides of Monroe, and she found it necessary to center her career hopes on his efforts to unite her disjointed identity. As Strasberg put it to Maurice Zolotow, "what was going on inside was not what was going on outside, and that always means there may be something there to work with." Strasberg would serve, in many ways, as the integrating force in her life and would earn the gratitude and respect of many of her professional associates. John Springer, who would work as Monroe's East Coast publicist for the last three years of her life, had ample opportunity to witness the positive difference Strasberg made in his client's life. Indeed, listening to Springer describe Monroe's deep involvement with Strasberg and the Actors Studio is to realize how close she came, under Strasberg's guidance, to making acting and her life all of a piece. With Michael Chekhov's death in September of 1955, Strasberg became the sole focus of Monroe's highest aspirations as an actress.

On first hearing of her work with Strasberg, Billy Wilder suggested that it would spoil Monroe's natural instincts; she would become self-conscious and lose her audience. He was subscribing to a rather common belief that she was a "natural" and ignoring much of her deliberate preparation for earlier films. His view of her was as an essentially passive actor, that is, Strasberg was doing something *to* her; strenuous acting exercises would burden her with extraneous techniques. Yet for all of Wilder's difficulties with her on their later film, *Some Like It Hot,* he had to admit that, if anything, her acting had improved. As John Huston put it to Fred Guiles, she acted from "the inside out," allowing the camera to record emotions as they rose to the surface of her whole visible self. Like many other accomplished screen actors, she learned to let the camera trigger her feelings and target her attention. Both Strasberg and Josh Logan, her director on *Bus Stop,* suggested as much.

Strasberg realized that the Method was the actor's means of collaborating with the camera's pinpointing of action, and his insistence that every gesture, every movement, have its motivation made clear his affiliation with psychoanalysis. He used terms like "sublimation," by which he meant the actor's ability to free his or her own experience, to make it available for contact with the character he or she is playing. With Monroe, Strasberg found it necessary, as he had with other actors, to recommend that she see a psychiatrist, so that the deeply emotional re-creations of her past in acting exercises would receive appropriate clinical treatment. If it was dangerous to evoke her childhood traumas, there is no evidence to suggest that Strasberg burdened her unduly with recollections of the past or that he emphasized them inordinately. On the contrary, his practice was to use no more of such past experience than was absolutely necessary for the part. He had little patience with self-indulgence and could abruptly dismiss a student by saying "Don't enjoy your ability to weep." Robert Hethmon observed Strasberg handle personal emotions "with great delicacy and tact, and with great watchfulness"—as can be seen in this tape-recorded example of his instructions on the use of "affective memory":

> [Y]ou try to see the people that you saw. You try to hear the things that you heard. You try to touch now the things you touched then. You try to remember through your senses what your mouth tasted and what you wore and the feeling of that garment against your body. The emotion you try not to remember at all.

He sharply cut off any attempt to withdraw from the actuality, the objectivity of the actor's performance: "Really look at us. Don't just make believe. Really see us. Make clear to yourself that you're real and we're real. . . ." There had to be an engagement between actor and audience, not a retreat into fantasy.

Instead of causing further distress by recalling what was sometimes a painful past, Strasberg found in his own practice that "the work [at the Studio] helped the [psycho]analysis, and the [psycho]analysis helped the work." Certain "very sharp or strong things" aroused in Monroe's acting could be further explored in therapy. Or certain things that were "blocked" in her psychoanalytical sessions were revived and clarified in the concrete acting exercises designed to stimulate sensory memories. Thus psychoanalysis and the Method were mutually beneficial.

Strasberg's Method promised Monroe a renewed sense of authenticity. Of her struggle with her Hollywood career, he observed: "Sometimes when an actor is in her position the successful playing of the same kind of thing causes you to feel that you are getting away with something. A feeling of guilt develops." Throughout his talks at the Studio, Strasberg stressed the actor's frustration with the repetition of what Hethmon calls "essentially the same element of himself that brought him initial success." Like many other actors, Monroe regarded the Actors Studio as a sanctuary and a laboratory where she was free to experiment with herself, to confront openly the questions many typecast actors ask: "Can I do it again?" "Can I do anything else?" "Can I work with a different director?" "Can I play a different type?" "Do I really have talent?" On the set of *Show Business* Monroe had been terribly embarrassed meeting Susan Strasberg and her mother Paula because she had performed clumsily; at the Actors Studio she could hear Lee Strasberg say something like, "This is a place where you can fall flat on your face," because actors deliberately came there to admit and to solve their problems. The Studio offered the only kind of institutional support, and the only kind of artistic continuity, available to Monroe and most American actors who had nothing like the English repertory system, where actors are more or less constantly employed in a variety of roles. In describing how it was for even the most successful actors, Strasberg reveals why it was possible for Monroe to feel such acute distress in spite of having performed well:

[T]he actual conditions of work are for the actor extremely poor. The actor works, let's say, on a movie. It takes him months. He works in a disjointed way that hardly permits his imagination to be aroused. Then he loafs around because he's glad to loaf around after getting up all those months at six o'clock in the morning and finishing at six at night. He gets pretty tired. Then he does another picture somewhere else.

The disruptive routine of picture making is exactly what Monroe had forsaken in an effort to rouse her deepest creative instincts. It was a courageous move to give up Hollywood at the height of her stardom, and Strasberg responded to her risk taking by very carefully timing her transition into acting at the Studio. After about three months of private study in his home, Monroe was confident enough to enter one of his classes with about thirty students that met twice a week. This did not make her an Actors Studio member, for that privilege was earned only through a rigorous series of auditions. She was also admitted to the public Studio classes as an observer, as were other interested parties like Gloria Steinem, who met her briefly. Monroe was quiet, rarely asked a question, and occasionally took notes. According to one observer, she exhibited "an avid interest in every scene performed by her fellow actors and in every word of criticism and instruction offered by Strasberg." She had difficulty understanding his classes—perhaps because of terminology like "justification" and "substitution"—and one of her fellow students helped to "translate" the teacher's words. She behaved like a neophyte, as did other actors and actresses with significant reputations who felt humbled by the experience of probing so profoundly the fundamentals of acting. This group activity encouraged a sense of equality, and Strasberg never felt that Monroe's modesty was affected. Indeed, for the first time in her career, she probably felt that she was genuinely part of a group just as dedicated as she was to a search for the appropriate acting method.

Strasberg called upon all actors to engage in what Stanislavsky called "living the part." This meant both observing and internalizing not just human emotions and actions, but also animal behavior and the function and placement of objects. As she had been with Todd and Chekhov, Monroe was called on in Strasberg's classes to identify with principles of structure and composition, while at the same time *feeling* her way into the shapes and positions of things and into the gestures and rhythms of creatures other than herself. For example, she had to improvise her version of a kitten. She prepared by borrowing one, studying him intensely for two weeks, and presenting herself to the class as "a playful, lazy, stretching, scratching, purring kitten."

This classic Stanislavsky exercise, with its call for acute, penetrating observation of life in all of its specificity, contributed to her ease of movement on stage even as it sharpened her concentration and control. It is not as if she had not moved well before, of course; rather, she recognized that even greater ease of movement was the product of an intimate contact with nature—another cardinal goal of Stanislavsky's approach that made her achievement seem, once again, organic, an aspect of existence itself and not an external copy of it.

One can readily imagine Monroe identifying with the kitten's feline grace, but more significantly, to *be a kitten* involves shedding adult inhibitions to recover a primordial spontaneity free from stereotyping, from the Hollywood manufacturing of Marilyn Monroe. Not Hollywood alone but society as a whole imposes rigid codes of behavior, and theater, similarly, contributes its cliches, Stanislavsky noted. To enact life, to embody a character with originality, he counseled that "an actor, like an infant, must learn everything from the beginning, to look, to walk, to talk, and so on." We do these things badly in ordinary life and our faults show on stage, he concluded. To behave as a cat is to loosen up immediately, to become aware of how we have learned to contract our muscles in conformity to social habits and public decorum, so that we stiffen on the stage unless we learn how to release physical tenseness. Monroe too may have felt as if she were learning everything from the beginning, not just in the sense that she was a new Strasberg pupil having to go through the entire regimen of his Method, but also in the sense that life was revealing itself to her in its origins as layers of conventional behavior were stripped away. Fresh characterizations are obtained only through exacting training of the body and the self. She was instructed to sing a popular song without moving her body, "so that she used the inner nervousness subjectively instead of leaking it out through random, unconscious bodily tics and jerks." Again Strasberg was following Stanislavsky's emphasis on "the necessity for 'gestureless' moments of immobility on the part of the actor, to concentrate on his *feelings* all the attention of the spectator." Various exercises were used to induce relaxation and to stimulate spontaneous expression.

In a normal fashion, Monroe progressed from acting exercises to the performance of scenes in class. She first chose to prepare a scene with a fellow student, Phil Roth, from Clifford Odets's *Golden Boy*, a drama about a young man, Joe Bonaparte, who abandons the development of his "real self," of a career in music, for the monied success of the prize ring. Harold Clurman, Odets's good friend and Group Theater colleague, calls the play a story of the artist who becomes a "thing" and notes that "Hollywood and what it represents provided the play with its inner theme, its true subject matter." Monroe had acted in *Clash by*

Night, written for the screen by Odets, and they were friends. Odets's own struggles with his integrity as a writer in Hollywood would obviously have interested her as a kind of subtext, and she would have seen quickly how the play defined not only the writer's dilemma but her own. Odets, like his character Bonaparte, had once been a Golden Boy enticed by fame and fortune to Hollywood, where he put off achieving the promised great work of his theatrical career. Monroe, in every way a Golden Girl, had now to wonder if she would ever get the opportunity to fulfill her artistic ambitions after putting them in abeyance during her rise to stardom.

Monroe's character, Lorna Moon, has "a certain quiet glitter . . . and if she is sometimes hard, it is more from necessity than choice. Her eyes often hold a soft, sad glance." She feels like a "tramp" because she is always the mistress, never the wife; she is looking for legitimacy and for someone to authorize her worth, just as Monroe felt outcast, demeaned, and hoped to marry the highly principled Arthur Miller, who could confirm her probity. Lorna is very much like Monroe in finding it difficult to hope for her heart's desire, yet hoping for it nonetheless.

Through Lorna, Monroe was able to make contact with the incisive, somewhat hard-edged, working-class side of her personality, the side that Richard Meryman found in his *Life* interview with her, and that Stanley Flink calls "street smarts." Flink remembers that she was especially good at sizing up people and gauging their motivations, as Lorna does on several occasions. Monroe-Lorna is also reminiscent of Peg, the supporting character Monroe played in *Clash by Night.* Peg expresses an uninhibited, robust physicality and firmness of speech and gesture. "When I want you to kiss me, I'll let you know," she curtly tells her boyfriend, Joe (Keith Andes). She sticks out her tongue at him and will not be bossed. Unlike Monroe the glamour girl, Peg does not slur her words suggestively; instead, she is very direct with all the characters in the film. She punches Joe, who jealously tries to deflect her interest in another man (Robert Ryan), and this raw energy reflects the off screen Monroe who delighted in telling Stanley Flink how she would perform the physical business of her roles. Peg does not hesitate to order Joe to get her sweater or to bring coffee for visiting friends. She is ebullient, and she can be roughly affectionate, as Monroe could be when jumping off the scaffolding of a movie set into the visiting Flink's arms.

Lorna Moon is a harder, more cynical version of Peg, "a conniver of the first order" who is "overwhelmed by a feeling of genuine love for the first time in her life" for the fight manager, Tom Moody, who will turn Bonaparte away from music decisively. Edward Easty was particularly taken with Monroe's "ease of movement" as Lorna: "Gone were the strained efforts of artificial behavior and cliches. . . . She held nothing back." After the scene, Strasberg "could not resist turning full way around in his front row seat, facing the entire assemblage and asking or rather demanding, 'Well, was the scene excellent or not?' To this the answer was resoundingly unanimous in the affirmative," Easty concludes.

Monroe's triumph had come in difficult circumstances, for many students at the studio distrusted Strasberg's championing of Monroe and believed themselves far superior to this Hollywood "import." This was the audience that Monroe had to satisfy, a part of which suspected that their teacher had been corrupted by recent favorable publicity and was abandoning his principles. According to Easty, this audience sat in stunned, silent appreciation of her truthful rendering of Lorna Moon. Monroe had moved slowly in her preparations for this scene, and he suggests "we might have had quite a long wait before seeing what she could really have done professionally. The sad part is that we all thought she had time." His use of "we" after carefully noting the previous division of opinion on her talent is suggestive of the community of feeling she was able to arouse and share, a solidarity of sentiment so different from the acrimony on her movie sets.

In December of 1955, after nearly ten months of study, Strasberg judged Monroe ready to do a scene from Eugene O'Neill's *Anna Christie* for Actors Studio members. As early as the fall of that year it had been decided that she would rehearse a scene with Strasberg's son, John, from Tennessee Williams's *A Streetcar Named Desire* for her private class as a way of practicing for her public debut, which finally occurred in early February 1956. The characters she chose to portray while at the Studio must have clearly stimulated her own profound feelings of orphanhood, exploitation, and alienation: Anna Christie, in search of her father and feeling abused by life, prostituted; Lorna Moon, "a lost baby," whose mother was a suicide and whose father was an alcoholic; Blanche Dubois, caught up in dreams of a romanticized self and terrorized by fears of fading beauty. These women reminded her of the attenuated hopes of youth, of how difficult it was to achieve a mature identity. Approaching the age of thirty, Monroe knew that she had to move on to the next stage of her career, to take full possession of these roles.

She chose scene 5 of *Streetcar*, in which Blanche tries to seduce the young man collecting for *The Evening Star*. The scene demands that the actress convey the character in all her loneliness, coquetry, sensuality, romanticism, and resignation. Blanche dreams of a better, idealized world while acknowledging the sordid one that is partly of her own making. In playing this role Monroe confronted her own propensity for aggrandizing reality: "Young man! Young, young man! Has anyone ever told you that you look like a young Prince out of the Arabian Nights?" Blanche asks in a desperate attempt to hold on to this youth as her own. Strasberg believed that Monroe rendered Blanche with a "strangely poetic quality." For him, there was not only sensitivity but a grandeur in her evocation of Blanche's sadness and suffering. Monroe had brought beauty to the part, he concluded. Evidently she understood that like herself, Blanche Dubois, properly played, is a tragic, not a pathetic character.

The opening scene from *Anna Christie*, which Monroe had used for an exercise with Natasha Lytess, was much longer and more ambitious than what she had attempted in *A Streetcar Named Desire*. In Strasberg's words, Anna is supposed to be "nervous . . . sick, she comes back [to her father], she doesn't know what's going to happen." The dialogue at the beginning of the play was not of much help to the actress conveying Anna's feelings, Strasberg observed, for at the moment of her entrance "you almost don't know who the girl is," and she is not ready to speak directly about her feelings. Monroe's success in adapting her "tremulousness" to suit Anna's febrile character was extraordinary. Strasberg emphasized how surprised the audience was that she could use her sensitivity so precisely.

The precision had been developed in Monroe's serious study of the whole play. With Arthur Miller's aid, she went over the text for a couple of hours, exploring Anna's identity, her way of thinking, her view of life. Did Anna want to die? Monroe's query derived from her perceptions of an exhausted, played-out character, and she wanted to know exactly what accounted for Anna's fatigue, since her actions, not her words, would have to convey first her listlessness, then her growing anxiety about meeting and coping with her father. Monroe's questions cut two ways: toward the character and toward herself, since, like Anna, she set out on at least one quest to find her father and had on more than one occasion intimated to friends her desires for death. Like Monroe, Anna is quick to resent people she thinks are laughing at her, and she feels she has been put upon, deprived of her integrity, and exploited by her foster family. Anna implies that she had been sexually violated at sixteen by a cousin on the farm.

If Monroe was reaching into the innards of her own life to play this part, she was also employing questions to get at what Strasberg called the "subtext," that portion of the character's thinking that is indicated but not fully expressed in words. Even the character's life before he entered a scene should be considered as a way of getting at Stanislavsky's notion of "the imaginative fiction of another person." The playwright leaves certain aspects of the character unexpressed, and it is the actor's responsibility to go beyond the "scraps and bits" out of a life to create a whole person, a complete role with "comparatively unbroken lines," Stanislavsky points out. What was the unbroken line of Anna's emotional life? This is what Monroe wanted to know, so that she could establish the continuity of her performance and make Anna's life her own.

Strasberg was unequivocal in his praise for Monroe's handling of Anna Christie, and he was struck with her presence, "the unusual quality which she was able to maintain . . . to keep and somehow to create and also to transmit more on the stage even than on the screen." Was he responding to her aura, to the uniqueness of her original self? Strasberg speculated that the "self-consciousness of the screen," the fact that everything has to be framed, blocked some of the brilliance he saw in the immediacy and exceptional control of her live performance. Evidently her concentration was perfect, and even those in the audience who were not particularly taken with her brilliance admitted that she did not blow a line and that she had at least been competent, although one male studio member vigorously rejected the idea that she was "capable of playing Anna Christie." Kim Stanley, on the other hand, remembers her initial skepticism and how Monroe's performance "was just wonderful. She *was* wonderful. We were taught never to clap at the Actors Studio— it was like we were in church—and it was the first time I'd ever heard applause there. Some of us went to her privately and apologized."

Strasberg acknowledged to Fred Guiles that doing the scene had been very difficult for Monroe, and he was not certain that she could "follow through" with a complete performance, but he persisted in his belief that she was making her way toward a stage career. Cheryl Crawford rated Monroe's acting "quite extraordinary—full of color," but she could not credit Monroe with a place in the theater: "she was paralyzed with fear. It was too rough. She'd have a spasm every time she'd go on." Maureen Stapleton, Monroe's partner in the scene, tried to relieve the tension by suggesting they put a copy of the play on the table in front of them. "Lots of people do it," she reassured her earnest colleague. But Monroe treated the scene as though it were opening night on Broadway and refused to regard her performance as informally as Stapleton suggested. Rehearsals were repeatedly interrupted because Monroe forgot her lines, yet her actual performance of it was flawless, and "that exceedingly wispy voice of hers seemed to carry all right, for all her worrying about it," Stapleton recalls. Afterwards she accompanied Monroe to a bar on Tenth Avenue, and "celebrated having cheated death one more time." Performing well for this high-strung actress was tantamount to surviving as both a person and a professional.

Monroe herself is said to have been distraught immediately after her Anna Christie scene: "I was terrible," she sobbed. Friends tried to console her in terms of Strasberg's superlatives, but she remained unconvinced and insisted that "the only thing that was great was Maureen." Her anguish could not have been unexpected, for she had so much at stake, and it was part of her nature—as Milton Greene and Rupert Allan have stressed—never to be content with her work. Susan Strasberg, on the other hand, attributes to Monroe a ploy performers often use: criticize yourself before others get the opportunity, and you may be able to elicit sympathy and to create a protective coating for yourself. Certainly Monroe had used such a strategy in her Hollywood career. About a week after she did the scene, Fred Stewart, an actor who knew Strasberg well, complimented Monroe on her Anna Christie by emphasizing the actress's strength, her way of making "the character herself." Monroe was still very unsure about her success because she had no way to measure it; doing a scene in front of a live audience was new to her, she told Stewart. She was happy to receive his support and gradually began to believe in the power of her stage performance—so much so that she was "exhilarated" and tremendously grateful for the opportunity Strasberg had given her. Even years later Ralph Roberts, John Springer, and other friends vividly recall how significantly her work with Strasberg had loomed in plans for her future.

Monroe had completed assignments on three difficult roles and was acting with renewed conviction as she made plans for *Bus Stop*, her first film since leaving Hollywood in late 1954. In late December of 1955, prolonged negotiations with 20th Century-Fox culminated in a new seven-year contract, in which it was stipulated that she and the studio would draw up a list of directors acceptable to her and also that she would be allowed to do outside productions. She would have to appear in only four Fox films, for which her corporation would be paid $100,000 a film, to be split evenly between herself and Milton Greene. After having spent a rather quiet year on her own, she left New York on February 26, 1956 for Hollywood, raising intense curiosity among the press. To one reporter she seemed somehow different, and she replied almost shyly that her suit was new but otherwise she was the same person. It was a typical lighthearted, self-effacing comment that belied the new confidence and control she would soon display in her portrayal of Cherie.

Monroe's progress from Strasberg's classes to the set of *Bus Stop* is comparable to the advance in sophistication from *An Actor Prepares* to

Building a Character, Stanislavsky's classic texts on acting. In the first two chapters of the latter work, one is able to observe closely the actor moving beyond his exercises in *An Actor Prepares* to mastery of a whole role in a complete performance. Indeed, Monroe's creation of her character, Cherie, reads almost like a textbook case, an idealized version of the collaboration between script writer, director, and actor that the great film theorist Pudovkin called for but regretted not realizing in his own work. After completing his direction of *Bus Stop*, Josh Logan said that Monroe "conceived the basic approach to Cherie." The director, of course, helped her "get it on film," but it was "her feeling about the whole story" that stimulated Logan and the screenwriter, George Axelrod, who would incorporate the actress's interpretation of her role into his rewriting of certain scenes. Only very rarely have actors had the opportunity to influence a film so directly, and Logan's supreme trust in Monroe, built on his belief that she was "one of the great talents of all time," has been occasionally matched by other directors but never surpassed.

Logan was not predisposed to praise Monroe. When she was first mentioned for the part of Cherie, he recalls exclaiming "Marilyn Monroe can't bring off *Bus Stop*!" He acknowledged that she was a popular success, but he was certain she could not act. He was astounded by Strasberg's belief in her greatness, even though he found her teacher "a bit smug and pedantic." It was the first time he had "heard Marilyn praised by anyone in the theatre." Logan decided to risk working with her.

He dropped his prejudice against her during their first meeting. She talked persuasively about *Bus Stop*'s story. She had carefully observed Kim Stanley's portrayal of Cherie on the New York stage and demonstrated how easily she could catch her character's Southern accent. Then Logan had one of those perceptions that seemingly join the realms of film and reality: "of course she was the perfect girl to play the part. Kim Stanley had had to readjust her looks, her height, her weight, and everything else to appear as this girl, but Marilyn *was* Cherie, presto in the flesh." Monroe had her character's childlike enthusiasm and dreaminess, but she was much more lucid and perceptive than her counterpart—as Logan indicates: "she struck me as being a much brighter person than I had ever imagined" whose "accurate reactions to each well-made point" filled the director with a wonderful sense of promise about the whole production of *Bus Stop*.

It is likely that Monroe was following Stanislavsky's injunction about "living the part," and sought to show Logan her mastery quickly, for as they worked together, Logan recalls, "she wanted to know all about my studying with him in Moscow. She wanted to know all about the way actors lived and acted there. How Stanislavsky talked to them and they talked to him—intimate details." She used Freudian terminology somewhat clumsily and self-consciously, but Logan was certain that Strasberg "had opened a locked part of her head, given her confidence in herself, in her brainpower, in her ability to think out and create a character."

Lee Strasberg had provided Monroe with "an outline, a kind of map" to consult en route to her role, his daughter Susan Strasberg explains. Susan's mother Paula was the "great technician" who helped Monroe explore "the streets, the towns, the rivers," the fine details of a role. Like Natasha Lytess, Paula Strasberg was in an uncomfortable position for a coach every time Monroe insisted that she be present on the movie set. Paula would be suspected of usurping the director's responsibility for guiding the actress during her performance. Few directors, not even the sympathetic Josh Logan, cared to witness the way Paula and Monroe worked on scenes together—such as the "Old Black Magic" sequence that called for the subtlest execution of a bad performance. Overdoing the song would coarsen Monroe's character; underplaying it would diminish the character's vitality. How to interpret the number's every note engrossed the actress and her coach and irritated others, who were intolerant of Paula's claim on Monroe's time. Even Logan, the most generous of Monroe's directors, does not recognize the style Paula helped to develop, a style her daughter identified immediately because of her years of work with her mother.

Why did Monroe, who had such good instincts in her reading of a role, need a coach at all? She often spoke poetically, in similes and metaphors that someone had to help her unravel and interpret. Hers was not a logical way, Lee Strasberg explained to Fred Guiles. Rather, she would make comparisons: "isn't this like or so on," and she would be completely right about a part but still in need of locating the precise terms that writers and directors commonly deal in. She could seem very "kooky" to a professional who did not have the patience to follow her: "What do you mean the character should be burning as if she's sitting on a stove?" is Strasberg's example of a frustrated response to her figurative language. "She would become clearer as she went on," he remembers, and "she would always see the character; she would always see what the real event was, not just what the people were saying." She was so good at evaluating scripts that Paula Strasberg planned but never carried out her intention to publish Monroe's marginal notations after the actress's death. Monroe attacked her part with a dynamism that invigorates Logan's prose as he recalls her taking charge. When the costume designer delivered a set of clothes that were "too grand, too movie star—not pitiful, comic, and humorous enough for Cherie," Monroe laughingly told Logan that they were going to "shred it up, pull out part of the fringe, poke holes in the fishnet stockings, then have 'em darned with big, sprawling darns. Oh, it's gonna be so sorry and pitiful and it'll make you cry." She then proceeded to rummage through the costume department to find "the oldest, the most worn, the saddest" bits of clothing that would still somehow express the spirit of a character whose reach would exceed her grasp. Similarly, Milton Greene eschewed using Monroe's usual "honey-colored" makeup in favor of a "light opalescent color, very thin and white." It was a daring experiment that the actress and her coworkers enthusiastically accepted as appropriate "for a little nightclub singer who always went to bed at five or six in the morning after drinks, and woke up way past noon to a breakfast of black coffee and aspirin—a girl who never really saw the sun," Logan remarks.

Although her studio bosses vehemently protested the risks Monroe and her collaborators were taking with the film, Logan insisted on artistic control, and Monroe had her way—with Logan's consent—on most of the major decisions in the production. As a result, she exuberantly put herself into the making of the whole film, even suggesting ways of staging certain scenes and of setting up cameras. In only two instances did she exhibit the temperament that bedeviled her earlier, less sensitive directors: when Logan found her still looking at herself in her dressing room mirror hours after she was due on the set, and when she lost her composure with her costar, Don Murray, and raked him across the face with her sequined costume, scratching the corner of his eye. Murray dismissed her aggression as that of a "childlike personality." She operated from "a very self-centered viewpoint. She wasn't deliberately mean." Both incidents are indicative of the self-absorption she was still attempting to overcome.

That self-absorption was only one side of her personality, however, and it cannot account for her development as an actress. For she also had a special talent, perhaps an unusual need, for taking people on their own terms. Rupert Allan remembers the way she would "work a party," making sure that she met as many people as possible, sitting down with them and really taking an interest in their lives, while remaining accessible herself. Logan observes that "she was always . . . the most fun to talk to, to listen to—warm, witty," and enthusiastic. If this outgoing, empathetic quality was natural to her, it was also encouraged by her training in the Method, a part of Stanislavsky's legacy—first adumbrated for her by Michael Chekhov—that urged actors to take in "everything," to "adopt a broad point of view . . . to interpret the life of human souls from all over the world." Strasberg speculated that the painfulness of her own past and her wounded sensitivity created an "avidness for life," a "reaching out that she had when she would listen to you. . . . her eyes were all wide, and I don't think she was just acting. . . . she really took in whatever it was that she was interested in." Similarly, Rupert Allan recollects her relish for *The New York Times*, the excited interest she would exhibit in speaking of world affairs and one specific instance of her calling him to make a shrewd comparison between front-page stories in *The New York Times* and *Los Angeles Times*. Monroe's correspondence about politics with Lester Markel, then Sunday editor of *The New York Times*, corroborates Allan's memories of her keen engagement with current events.

In "dressing" her character, to use Stanislavsky's term, Monroe was employing everything she knew about self and society and turning away from her own reflected image in previous films, in which she had been encouraged to act from the outside in, taking care to have her look like the part before she felt the part in her. As a result, both her self and her roles were somewhat specious. Now she proceeded from the opposite direction by delving within herself to authenticate both her person and her character, Cherie.

Since Monroe could not think of Cherie as simply a role given to her, she had to come up with a Cherie of her own. Like the actor in *Building a Character*, she found there is no quick route to rapport with a role; the actor begins in uncertainty not only about his character but about himself: "I was not I, in the sense of my usual consciousness of myself. Or, to be more precise, I was not alone but with someone whom I sought in myself and could not find." It is as if the actor abnegates the self, holds it in suspension to create room for the role to emerge: "I existed, I went on with my usual life, yet something inhibited me from giving myself up to it fully; something was disturbing my usual existence. I seemed divided in two." The actor becomes aware of a "secret subconscious life," a second life after confronting the fundamental "question of whom I was to play." Looking into the mirror does not aid the actor in discovering his or her identity, because the actor has not yet found the source of it within himself or herself. The actor begins to feel in character as he or she alters his or her conventional theatrical makeup and costume and selects the props for a character he or she still cannot properly name; nevertheless, the actor seems compelled to apply the self to a characterization that is slowly rising from inside until, glancing once again in the mirror, the actor does not recognize himself or herself. He or she has, in fact, used the self as an instrument to transform the self. Every step taken in the creation of a character is the actor's own, yet the result is that the actor is not entirely himself or herself. The actor has created something new, original, fresh—much as Monroe, according to Strasberg, "took in" the feelings of others and had an extraordinary acting ability "to see something in a fresh way that was completely her own and to draw attention to it with a kind of directness" and precision "which couldn't be said or seen for that matter in any other way."

Now Monroe had a role that was not just bits and pieces of film but a role that had grown organically and that might survive, in large part, its edited version. This was certainly not the first time she had come to a movie set with her character well worked out, but it was the first instance of her total immersion in a character, speaking in that character's accents even when filming had stopped, as other Method actors like James Dean had done.

Monroe still found the actual process of filming discontinuous and profoundly disturbing. Sometimes she would hold onto a crew member's arm and pace around the edges of the sound stage. Occasionally she would retreat in total isolation from cast and crew. She would interrupt scenes and request time to think off to the side of the action. Logan remembers her "feverish concentration," and how in her effort to perform well she would "stop and wrinkle her face as though in pain before she could continue." Interruptions of filming would throw off her concentration, and it would take several minutes before she could resume her character's mood.

Logan decided to keep his cameras going in order to overcome her halting performances. Instead of crying cut after each take, he simply put her into the position appropriate for the beginning of the scene, or handed her the first prop in the scene, or had the script supervisor give her the first line, so that she and the camera kept moving. Logan had come to perceive that "the moment the camera started turning, Marilyn 'turned on' with it." This unusual and expensive way of film making yielded several interesting takes of scenes, with none of them "dull or routine," and he therefore had "a chance to piece bits and pieces of brilliance together until the final scene shone." Although Monroe's acting was mediated by film technology and the director's art, Logan was, in effect, inducing a live performance from Monroe by partially eliminating the stop-and-go element of film making for her. He suspected she was "inherently" a stage performer, and he treated her as one by also recording her "Old Black Magic" number live to get the spontaneity that would be lacking if she sang the song "to a playback" and then again for the camera by lip-syncing. "She could never memorize exactly the way she had sung it, breathed it, performed it, and still make it sound spontaneous," Logan concluded.

Film conventions disconcerted the actress, Maurice Zolotow reports, because "she had to keep fixed positions, marked out on the set." A "spontaneous reflex of emotion" might move her out of the designated position, so that the carefully set up camera framing would be destroyed. On the other hand, she delighted in the one-to-one relationship it was possible to have with cameras. Logan remembers the day she "was dancing around like a child in anticipation of having a big head closeup as Garbo had had." All the features of her face would be enlarged, for the lens could concentrate on "every vein, every tiny bit of facial fuzz, the watery depths of her eyes, the detail of her skin, her nostrils. . . ." Even when the closeup revealed a string of saliva as she moved her head from the hand it was resting upon, she agreed with Logan that the delicate moment "showed great emotion" and ought not to be sanitized by editing it from the film.

Logan put Monroe's performance in an intricate series of frames that had the effect of concentrating more attention on the impact of her character's personality than had been attempted by previous directors. At the beginning of *Bus Stop*, she is viewed in the frames of two windows. The first sight of Cherie is self-consciously cinematic and virtually voyeuristic in revealing the interior of her life. As Virgil (Arthur O'Connell) watches from his window in the boarding house, Cherie is already positioned on the ledge of her dressing room window with her right knee bent and her high-heeled shoe extended so that the pointed toe touches the side of the window frame. She is hot, weary, and fans herself; she seems almost ready to drop as her hand falls downward in a limp gesture. She is looking down disconsolately as cowboys crowd into her private moment, petitioning her for a dance. The camera cuts from Virgil watching her, to Bo (Don Murray) admiring himself in all his freshness in the mirror of their boarding house room, to Cherie sitting again on the window ledge—this time harassed by her boss, who asks her why she is not inside "where you belong." He shakes her and tells her to go to work and throws her on a chair. As Virgil enters the saloon, she is pictured in front of the mirror crying and complaining about the boss who has called her an ignorant hillbilly. Her hand is cupped to the left side of her face as she looks down and then up to her friend, Vera. Cherie scratches the back of her head, then hides her face in her hands, and then scratches the back of her head again as she explains to Vera how she has been "trying to be somebody." Then she puts her face in her hands again, places her hand to the right side of her face, and completes the repetitive cycle of hand and head and face gestures begun on her left side, a chronic cycle that she maintains with delicate consistency throughout the movie. Monroe's constant repositioning of her hand and head and face, and Logan's relentless reframing techniques, complement each other brilliantly in defining Cherie's fatiguing searching for an identity.

When Cherie talks about River Gulch, "the little town where I was born," she puts a finger to her lips in a foreshadowing of her lifted spirits that result from her fingering of the map that traces "the history of my life." Her eyes open wide as she tells of her dream of reaching Hollywood and Vine, and she dresses herself in her dreams as she picks up her saloon costume—the one she will wear when she sings "That Old Black Magic" and expands on the magical impact of the movies that gave her a "direction" in life. In these brief moments of getting ready for the saloon crowd, Monroe is able to move her character deftly through memories of childhood, adolescence, and adulthood—many of which are reflected in her changing expressions in the dressing room mirror. As Cherie gets into her dress, she conveys the feeling that she is getting into her life, which she almost seemed to have relinquished in the first shots of her.

Joan Mellen has pointed out the obvious connections with Monroe's biography, but of special importance are Cherie's dreaminess and her exact plotting on the map of her journey to movie stardom, which parallels Monroe's calculated and determined route to her career. Although Cherie desperately wants to escape from Bo, her cowboy lover who believes he has found his "angel," she hesitates momentarily when she learns that a *Life* photographer will be present at her dreaded marriage. As it had for Monroe, the camera has almost a perverse fascination for Cherie, fixing itself in her consciousness even at a time when her appearance before it will cause her pain.

As beguiling as these comparisons between the actress and her role are, and as surely as Monroe must have experienced them—"you cannot possibly tell where to draw the line between you and your part," Stanislavsky insists—it is not fair to say the actress was playing herself. Cherie shares none of Monroe's informed commitment to her art or her talent and is unsophisticated when compared to the thirty-year-old woman who played her. At best, Cherie might have represented a former self to Monroe, the one who was a star-struck young girl, already a kind of cliche to Stanley Flink, when she walked into the office of *Life* magazine in 1950 and presented her portfolio to him. Even at her worst, however, Monroe could never have given a performance as poorly delivered as Cherie's pathetic "Old Black Magic" number.

Monroe keeps just the right balance between Cherie's meager skills and her naive certainty. This is best illustrated when Cherie achieves her own lighting effect during her song. She confidently yet awkwardly kicks a switch on stage that puts a spotlight on her, emphasizing the shabby gaudiness of her costume. She sings a song in a bad imitation of Hildegarde and has tailored her figure out of parts taken from other performers, the scraps sewn together from a very limited theatrical wardrobe. She is hopelessly off key and seemingly oblivious of the cowboys who ignore her in their rowdy conversations. Several light bulbs suspended over the small band that accompanies her accentuate the tackiness of the scene. Yet in her own light Cherie shines. Somehow she has managed to enclose herself in her own world, and her features are animated with the conviction of a good performance—so much so that it is believable when Bo, the young cowboy on his first big trip off the ranch, is captivated by her angelic luminosity. She does command the stage with her presence, performing above the darkened crowd that Bo does not notice until he has trouble hearing her song and whistles, warning the cowboys to be quiet. Her singing is dreadfully embarrassing, but there is a crazy zest in the way she spoils the rhythms of the song lyrics and an endearing warmth in her Ozark drawl, as she makes do with her drooping long black gloves and swings her arm and scarf, sweeping Bo up in the emotions of his discovery.

Bo's recognition of her enforces her stilted extroverted gestures as the cowboy crowd quiets and she winks at him, absolutely delighted and mischievously smiling like a kid who has been allowed to continue her mimicking of adult behavior. She tugs at her long gloves, trying to keep them up, like a child struggling with an improvised costume. All of her gestures are elaborately staged: "I hear your name" and "only your kiss can put out the fire," she sings as she cups her hand to her ear and puts her fingers to her lips. There also seems to be a momentary reference to Monroe's own cheesecake days when she half closes her lips and eyes in comic sultriness, as though she were finally shedding all the silliness of her former selves.

Cherie is not just another one of Monroe's dumb blondes; there is a difference in the writing and the performing of this character and her successors. Like Elsie Marina, Sugar Kane, Amanda Dell, and Roslyn Taber—the women Monroe plays in her last four films—Cherie has suffered disappointments in her efforts to defy the world's intractability. Cherie has her dreams of Hollywood stardom, but she seems much older, sadder, and—if not wiser than Bo—certainly more cautious and skeptical of the promises made to her. She is more of a whole person, less of an unblemished character, not so unreal as The Girl or Pola or Lorelei Lee. She will not have the world on Bo's masculine terms and will not be cowed by "all that lovin' stuff" that other men have handed her. She allows herself to be roped by Bo not because she is stupid or somehow innately helpless but because she has been quite literally knocked out by her nightclub life, by defeats that Bo has yet to suffer. His untested energy is what overwhelms her. This is apparent when he tries to rouse her from bed; physically she is incapable of competing with him, but she never gives in to him completely. Instead, she uses the ploys of the physically weak: she tries to escape or to distract him. At the same time, Cherie has avoided the crudity of backstage life. She betrays none of the bitterness Monroe herself apparently expressed on some of her movie sets. Cherie has not cultivated the cynicism that would arm her against a rapacious world. Her face often registers bewilderment and the vague pain of confusion, as does her characteristic gesture of putting her hand to the side of her face as if to search for the source of her distress or to soothe her delicate nerves. In Bo's clutches she sometimes behaves like a startled animal. There is something very fresh in Monroe's acting in these scenes (perhaps inspired by Strasberg's insistence on the actor's creation of a role from scratch), for Cherie's emotions are primary, unguarded, and Monroe plays them with great finesse.

In his review of *Bus Stop*, Arthur Knight comments that there is no evidence of "the calendar girl." Indeed, in some scenes Monroe and her director deliberately diminished her physical presence to give Cherie what one reviewer calls "a little girl lost quality." For example, in one scene in the roadside diner and bus stop, Cherie is photographed in her chilling uncertainty against a large, vertical black stove that stands imposingly behind her with its pipe running up to the ceiling. She has just come in from the cold to escape from Bo, who is sleeping on the bus, and for warmth and comfort she clutches the front of her flimsy monkey fur coat with her left hand and with her right hand holds the collar close to her neck. She is near panic and is baffled by Bo's stolid pursuit of her. She is trying to hold herself together, and she looks waiflike and abandoned and caught in a moment of frightful transiency that is emphasized by the stands of cheap paperbacks and postcards that flank her on her left and right.

How is it possible to believe that Cherie is an "angel" after so many shots of her wasted appearance? Oddly enough, her skimpy, ragged clothing invests her with an irresistible genuineness; divested of any resplendent costumery, Monroe makes Cherie's pale countenance ethereal—"incandescent," as Knight puts it. After Bo has been beaten by the bus driver, Carl (Robert Bray), who defends Cherie's right to resist Bo's advances, the camera moves in on Monroe's character in the closeup that so excited her. After his humiliation, Bo has softened, has seen how roughly he has trodden upon Cherie's feelings and meekly begs her pardon. His humble apology awakens in her the tender emotions that were stirred once before when he first declared his love for her. In tight closeup she declares to Bo with the whole force of her being: "I'd go anywhere in the world with you." She throws away her map, thus abandoning her illusions about Hollywood. Bo has relinquished his about her as well, for he finally accepts her confession that she is not an "angel," not the virginal figure he had made of her. Paradoxically, it is at this point, with their illusions destroyed, that Cherie looks most like Bo's vision of an "angel." Bo's gaze into her face is swallowed up by the white depth of her skin. Her face covers the screen and suddenly the rare ideality that has made Cherie so vulnerable and yet inviolable is fully revealed. Bo will take her back to his ranch just as she is because she still speaks to his sense of beauty and perfection.

Bus Stop has a sentimental ending, to be sure, but it avoids having Monroe lapse into the passivity of her earlier roles. It is clear to Virgil, the old friend who has guided Bo to manhood, that Cherie will take care of Bo as much as he will protect her. In the final scene she emerges as Virgil's equal when she insists that Bo allow Virgil to go his own way: "If he don't want to come, you can't make him." It is, however, not just Cherie's words but the authenticity of Monroe's whole characterization that is moving. Notice at the end of the film how sensitively Cherie's hands hold the wedding ring box Bo has given her, and how her hand is tentatively laid on his shoulder, indicating her nervous realization of her attachment to him. Behind her diffidence is a lifetime's worth of disappointments that her simple human gestures have been disregarded. Monroe makes palpable the risk Cherie feels she is taking with Bo. When he first offers her his coat, she looks at it in a surprised and uncertain manner, and then she leans back against him and smiles securely, her head tilted back and her eyes opening in recognition of what she has won. She enjoys enveloping herself in the big coat, in its warmth and softness, easing herself as well into this new relationship. Then she completes her comfortable feeling by turning her head to the right side of the coat with her mouth open and her eyes closed as she did with the left side. Bo draws the coat closer around her and she brings her hand to her neck, also tightening the coat around her in a firm gesture radically different from her scared hunching inside her flimsy costume coat in the bus stop, and from the constricted movements of her hands to her jaw to her brow to the back of her head throughout the film. She draws Bo's hand to her and around her, and then, after closing her eyes and luxuriating once more in the coat, she ties her scarf around his neck, for now they are truly united. Monroe's gestures, like the whole film, are organic. Superb acting, the full building of a character, make the corny conclusion convincing.

Monroe's great effort on *Bus Stop* was, as Logan affirms, "some kind of peak in her emotional as well as intellectual life." It is as if she made the movie set into a disciplined, innovative Actors Studio, and as if Logan helped her make good on Strasberg's ennobling and liberating advice to another actress: "Be your own Stanislavski." "I was twenty-five before I really understood what the whole creative process of acting was," Anne Bancroft has remarked. Monroe might now have said the same of herself at thirty.

8

The Poet of Her Aspirations
(December 1950–July 1956)

After all I have come up from way down.

When exactly did Marilyn Monroe become aware of Arthur Miller and of the special relevance of his writing for her? She had read his novel *Focus* (1945) before their first meeting on a movie set in December of 1950, and she seemed prepared in the same week to engage his deep sympathy on their second encounter at a Hollywood party. After that evening of considerable conversation and silent rapport, she told Natasha Lytess, "It was like running into a tree! You know—like a cool drink when you've got a fever. You see my toe—this toe? Well he sat and held my toe and we just looked into each other's eyes almost all evening." He talked about his next play, and they shared their admiration for Lincoln, and later Miller recommended she read Carl Sandburg's Lincoln biography. She hinted at her need for a hero and observed that she never even had a father to admire. Had Miller, coming to her just after Johnny Hyde's death, played the father for her, touching only her toe while he seemed absorbed in the tale of her whole life?

Miller behaved like a secret sharer of Monroe's dilemma, and in a long letter written shortly after their second meeting he urged her to keep her own counsel: "Bewitch them [the public] with this image they ask for, but I hope and almost pray you won't be hurt in this game, nor ever change. . . ." Perhaps she was attracted to his seemingly selfless identification with her problem; here was a man who was not after her sexually and who did not dispute her integrity. He had seen her whole, objectively, and she responded to his quiet, soothing presence very much like Maggie in Miller's *After the Fall*, who commends her husband Quentin for having once looked at her "out of your *self*." In other words, Miller had not responded to her as a stereotype, a projection of his fantasies, but instead had accepted her on her own ground and seemed fully aware of the stereotyping that could destroy her (he had already created Itzik, the character in *Focus* who "should never have allowed himself to accept the role that was not his").

Miller became one of the guiding lights of her life as they continued to correspond in the next year. One of her friends recalled that on visiting Monroe's apartment in late 1951 she recognized, to Monroe's surprise, a snapshot of the playwright hanging over the actress's bed. Monroe conveyed the impression that she and Miller were greatly attracted to each other. Similarly, Natasha Lytess and Sidney Skolsky report that the actress committed herself to pursuing the playwright someday. He was "the kind of man she could love," Monroe excitedly told Lytess.

It is easy to see why Miller, the person and the playwright, so attracted Monroe. Shortly after Monroe and Miller's marriage, James T. Farrell called Miller "the poet of the frustrated, the poet, therefore, of her own aspirations." She may have empathized with the hero of Miller's only novel, *Focus*, who insisted that he "was not what his face meant to people, he simply was not." In the novel, Lawrence Newman is typed as a Jew because his glasses somehow affix him to the image his society has of Jews. Like Newman, Monroe came to see herself as an outcast desperately seeking the approval of the majority culture—appealing to its sense of melodrama in the Shirley Temple, Little Orphan Annie, versions of her life—while rebelling, as Newman eventually does, against its appropriation of her figure.

Even more so, Miller's renowned drama, *Death of a Salesman* (1949), spoke directly to Monroe's own desperate search for a satisfactory identity. Like Willie Loman, she had to sell herself. She shared his obsession with personal attractiveness, with being "well liked," which came out of his terrible uncertainty: "I still feel—kind of temporary about myself." How she must have sympathized with the accusation that he was a "fake," that he had no "character." She could easily see herself in this small, immature man who never quite grew up, who was self-centered, a dreamer, who wanted to "add up to something," who saw himself as singular, who was both ludicrous and grand in his attempt to invent himself. As Lee Strasberg observed, "Marilyn Monroe was a dream of Marilyn Monroe." Her faith that "anything's possible, almost," expressed in her *Life* interview, is echoed by Willie's exclamation that "the greatest things can happen," that the world can be conquered through the force of personality. And when that idea of stardom was diminished for him, he found a way of displacing his disappointment in himself by putting the burden of success on his son, Biff, who was "going to be magnificent! . . . Yes, outstanding, with twenty thousand behind him." Similarly, in her years with Miller, Monroe would shift back and forth between her dreams of personal success and mass appeal to a hope for progeny; children were part of what Clifford Odets termed her desire "to make herself more humanly productive."

Resembling a character emerging out of Miller's own imagination, she demonstrated to him "the potential for greatness," and Miller sought to protect and nurture her talent after having been struck by her dedicated attack on the role of Anna Christie. "She had a real tragic sense of what that girl was like," Miller told Guiles. In other words, he realized that like one of his major characters she was unwilling to accept complacently society's characterization of her.

Monroe found in Miller much more than the somber, taciturn personage who rarely smiled in public, who preferred, like Joe DiMaggio, to look stonily at the cameras and to concede none of the attractive facets of personality observable in the private man. She admitted to Alan Levy that at first she had something of a "pupil-teacher" relationship with Miller, and it is tempting to imagine her giving birth to herself under the playwright's direction. She would be literally trying to live by Stanislavsky's declaration that "in the creative process there is the father, the author of the play; the mother, the actor pregnant with the part; and the child, the role to be born." In her marriage to Miller, the professional and personal sides of herself would coincide. New roles would be conceived for her, including that of mother with the birth of their child. She had become her own Stanislavsky indeed.

While working on a scene from *Of Mice and Men* with her close friend Ralph Roberts, Monroe remarked that developing a role to full expression was like carrying a child to its complete term. Acting was a way of articulating her continuity with life itself, with the desire to further it, to enrich it, just as Stanislavsky had pointed out: "Our type of creativeness is the conception and birth of a new being—the person in the part. It is a natural act similar to the birth of a human being." To marry Miller must have seemed like nothing less than an organic imperative.

By all accounts, Monroe was deeply in love with Miller and was hardly marrying him simply because he provided the theme by which she could live and work. There was a boyish charm about him for all his august reputation in the theater. He spoke simply, directly, and without condescension. He had a love of nature and of vigorous outdoor life that made him similar to her previous two husbands. Although he was often withdrawn and shy—rather like DiMaggio in this respect—he could also be very demonstrative and was not afraid to show his affection for her in front of close friends like Norman and Hedda Rosten, who warmly welcomed Monroe into their home in the company of the photographer Sam Shaw during the early days of her life in New York. Miller was unaffected and equally at ease with all kinds of work, from writing plays to repairing machinery. For a woman who felt herself of the people Miller had the right sort of demotic temperament; he was a Lincoln to whom she could relate on many different levels.

In the same way, Miller appears to have been captured by Monroe's intriguing many-sidedness, her sincerity, honesty, and earthiness. He enjoyed her "enormous sense of play, inventiveness—and unexpectedness—not only as a wife but as an actress." He had taken her for a "serious actress" and "adroit comedienne" even before he had met her, but it was the person—not the actress with great potential for playing tragedy—whom he loved. Miller had come to his generous estimate of Monroe cautiously, making absolutely sure that his first marriage could not be saved before he began to court her discreetly. By early 1956 Mary Slattery Miller had separated from her husband in acknowledgment of an estrangement that had begun several years earlier, perhaps even before Miller's first meeting with Monroe. He had been seeing Monroe in the homes of friends since her arrival in New York in late 1954. He was a hesitant lover, judging by her delicate, patient pursuit of him. She put no overt pressure on her reluctant suitor, probably because she realized that he was experiencing an especially difficult time not only with his personal life but also with his career. He was beginning to feel an impasse in his writing that many biographers of Monroe try to connect with his passionate interest in her.

By the Christmas season of 1955, the playwright was in love. By late February 1956, as Monroe was leaving New York for her work on *Bus Stop*, he was feeling ebullient about his feelings for her, and was acting like a "kid in love," as one of his friends puts it. There may have been a few discreet meetings of the lovers during the making of *Bus Stop*, and by late May or early June, as Monroe returned to New York from Hollywood, Miller was in Nevada near Pyramid Lake awaiting his divorce decree, and calling her to discuss the possibility of marriage.

By the middle of June, a divorced Miller introduced Monroe to his parents, but the couple continued to deny rumors of their romance. Not only were they trying to preserve their private lives, but there is every indication that until his public announcement—which greatly surprised Monroe—Miller was not absolutely certain he would marry, in spite of her willingness. He was enmeshed in efforts to regain his passport, denied in March of 1954 because of his alleged sympathies with Communists. When the playwright was called to testify before the House Un-American Activities Committee (HUAC) in late June, he agreed to discuss his political history, but he refused to identify other participants in his political activities. He was under threat of being charged with contempt of Congress; if convicted, he was liable to serve a year in prison and pay a $1,000 fine. Monroe publicly stood by Miller even though her studio suggested her career could be ruined if she did not persuade him to be cooperative with the congressional committee by "naming names." She steadfastly refused to be intimidated and told Alan Levy, after her divorce from Miller, that the playwright "introduced me to the importance of political freedom in our society."

Monroe easily identified with Miller's stand against an establishment that could crush the individual, and no doubt she quickly made the connection between what she considered to be the unwarranted authority of the studio and the state. In many ways, she was an instinctive critic of society and recognized herself in Miller's dissent. Like him, she had a healthy skepticism of government, a distrust that Rupert Allan vividly remembers when he relates her reaction to a *New York Times* article that reported the downing of an American plane over the Soviet Union. Allan was inclined to accept the U.S. government's explanation that the plane had not been on a spying mission. "Oh, I don't know," she countered. "I don't trust us."

The press portrayed Miller's and Monroe's plight as a human interest story. Editorials in England and France protested the abusive treatment of one of America's most distinguished writers. Shortly after this public outcry, the State Department quietly issued Miller a passport so he could accompany his bride to England to make *The Prince and the Showgirl* and to observe the production of his new play, *A View from the Bridge*.

In newsreel footage taken just before their wedding, Monroe and Miller appear charmingly at one with each other. Monroe is shy, and Miller is quietly confident. Neither of them has much to say for the cameras, as if they have reluctantly vouchsafed a fleeting glimpse of a happiness they would rather share alone. Indeed, Monroe rarely faces the camera and seems almost ready to slip into the privacy of their passion, for she has eyes only for Miller. She is constantly looking up at him and nuzzling her head into his neck and holding on to his arm. She is very physical with him in an unconscious, dreamy way that is briefly interrupted when her eyes widen to take in the question the interviewer has asked her. She has put herself alongside Miller in every sense of the word—that seems to be the logic of her bodily movements, in sync with him, who looks as solid as the tree he once reminded her of. He cannot so easily forget he is being filmed as she does, although she almost makes him do it in those split seconds he spends away from the camera gazing down at her in the utter ease of their mutuality.

As in her marriage to DiMaggio, the world clamored for pictures, the press pestered Miller about the details of the wedding. Like DiMaggio, he compromised with his sense of privacy and promised press conferences in order to preserve a modicum of peace, but the couple managed to elude reporters by quickly marrying in a courthouse and then again on July 1 in a Jewish ceremony at the country home of Miller's agent and friend, Kay Brown.

Norman Rosten, an old friend of Miller's from their University of Michigan undergraduate days and now—along with his wife Hedda Rosten—one of Monroe's closest confidants, puzzled over Monroe's conversion to Judaism. It seemed so unnecessary. Miller was not Orthodox, not even particularly religious. There had been no pressure on her from his parents to convert. Rosten, who was at the wedding ceremony, observes that "she participated with touching seriousness. Those who had secretly laughed at or mocked her desire to adopt the Jewish faith were moved to silence." Yet he could not help wondering at the "unreality of her conversion. Was it another game for her? A psychic toy?" As Rosten knew, the partial answer was that she wanted to be an intimate member of Miller's family; she wanted to share its tradition just as she had shared its trouble by staying with Miller and his parents just after his HUAC testimony. Edwin Hoyt points out that she took an avid interest in DiMaggio's Catholic faith and family, although Catholicism does not seem to have been as compelling for her as Judaism. It is inviting to adopt Rosten's notion that her conversion was like the trying on of another role—not in the superficial sense of seeking a diversion but in a very solemn way of tying herself to a religion that might strengthen her sense of belonging. Many of her successful friends— Skolsky, the Strasbergs, Milton Greene, Norman Rosten—were Jews. She may have associated her feelings of persecution with the history of a suffering people, a minority that had survived.

Milton Greene's photographs of the Jewish wedding appeared in the July 16 issue of *Life* with a brief description of the ceremony and of the couple's plans to spend a brief period in Roxbury, Connecticut, before Monroe's trip to England with Miller to begin work on *The Prince and the Showgirl*. Shots of a veiled Monroe smiling, of Miller grinning, kissing, and embracing his bride, of some of his friends and family present in a casual, folksy, outdoors setting, suggest much warmth and genuineness all round. Rosten remembers it as "a giddy, delirious day," with Monroe saying "I do" in "a clear if shaky voice" and receiving "dozens of kisses from some twenty-five friends, relatives, and a few reporters."

There was a clarity, as well, in her demeanor, an openness and freshness that evidently dominated the days of her betrothal to Miller. Friends found that she had made an abrupt break with her past, set aside her defenses and the wisdom she had acquired. She strove for, in Guiles's words, a "purified state" that some of them feared might leave her terribly vulnerable and open to destruction. Paula Strasberg interpreted Monroe's crystalline sensibility much more positively: "She's beginning to have new experiences, good ones. It's part of growing up, and perhaps the first time she's allowed things to happen to her. She's like a clear vessel—whatever you pour into her will show up." In spite of Strasberg's confidence, her metaphor, in retrospect, appears exceedingly delicate and indicative of a brittle Monroe whose composure could be easily shattered. In reflecting on his marriage Miller remarked in 1969 that even routine matters could "offend or undermine her." In certain moods "she was like a smashed vase. It is a beautiful thing when it is intact, but the broken pieces can cut you." It is striking that in trying to concretize Monroe's fragility Miller should create a metaphor favored by R. D. Laing in his description of the schizophrenic who "may say that he is made of glass, of such transparency that a look directed at him splinters him to bits and penetrates straight through him."

In July of 1956, Monroe gave no sign of going to pieces. On the contrary, she embodied the lifted spirits of the moment; she was, in Rosten's view, "more beautiful than ever, in a way more unreal." She was "more ethereal, more poignant." She was "really ecstatic. She gave off luminosity like the Rodin marble; she was the girl in 'The Hand of God.' It was the culmination of a dream and carried with it the danger of all dreams." In these last words, Rosten may be speaking in hindsight. Of the wedding ceremony itself, he says, "It was a fairy tale come true. The Prince had appeared, the Princess was saved."

9

The Prince and the Showgirl
(January–October 1956)

*—you know when you get grown up you can get kind of sour, I
mean that's the way it can go . . .*

When Sir Laurence Olivier arrived in America in February of 1956 to join
Monroe at the press conference announcing their plans to costar in the
film adaptation of Terrence Rattigan's play, *The Sleeping Prince*, it was
inevitable that Olivier—perhaps the greatest actor of our time—should
be greeted as visiting royalty. Monroe was much less certain of her
reception:

> Some people have been unkind. If I say I want to grow as an actress, they look at my
> figure. If I say I want to develop, to learn my craft, they laugh. Somehow they don't
> expect me to be serious about my work. I'm more serious about that than anything.
> But people persist in thinking I've pretensions of turning into a Bernhardt or a
> Duse—that I want to play *Lady Macbeth*. And what they'll say when I work with Sir
> Laurence, I don't know.

She had met Olivier very briefly about four years earlier but was not
sure he would remember her, so the question of his attitude toward her
was another source of insecurity. She also bore special responsibility for
this project, since her production company had purchased the play and
selected Rattigan to write and Olivier to direct the screen version. For
some of the press and the public, surely, she was being pretentious in
surrounding herself with such conspicuous talent.

At the end of January, when reports began to appear about the
forthcoming film production, the tone of the press was already set in
such a flippant way that Monroe would find it impossible to be viewed
seriously. For example, on January 30, *Time* quoted Olivier on his eagerness to make the picture with her: "I regard her as an actress and a

comedienne of the first order. . . ." *Time's* punch line, however, implied that he was more interested in being seduced: "Who would resist an approach from Miss Monroe?" She would have agreed with him that sexuality was the basis of her appeal, so long as that sexuality was seen as emanating from her intelligence and craft; the bond between these three aspects was what was missing in press summaries of her performances.

Even before Olivier's appearance in New York City, Monroe had misgivings about the course Milton Greene set for the film, for in January, immediately after learning of Strasberg's mild expression of approval, he asked Sir Laurence to be the director. Greene acted hurriedly, anxious to secure this distinguished actor, without thoroughly consulting her. Perhaps she regretted losing the possibility of meeting her costar on equal terms now that he possessed an additional title to hold over her on the movie set.

Of course, Olivier agreed to direct the film with no intention of lording over Monroe. Indeed, he readily accepted the suggestion of his wife, Vivien Leigh, his costar in the London production of *The Sleeping Prince*, that Monroe would be perfect for the part of Elsie Marina, an American showgirl. He recalls Monroe keeping him and Rattigan waiting for an anxious hour before their first meeting, but that on her appearance "she had us all on the floor at her feet in a second." He was deeply impressed, as though he were the one visiting royalty. He echoes Josh Logan's praise of her when he avers that "she was so adorable, so witty, such incredible fun and more physically attractive than anyone I could have imagined apart from herself on the screen." Evidently she was making every effort to please him, even if she had some doubts about their collaboration.

They appeared together at the press conference and seemed to do everything possible to help each other. Olivier was elegantly dressed in a dark suit, white shirt, and dark tie and was complemented by Monroe in her black silk dress and black silken cape, which she removed to reveal two slender straps on her naked shoulders. The expected ohs and ahs followed, of course, and twenty minutes of picture taking ensued while reporters started asking questions. According to one eyewitness, three-quarters of the questions "were fired at Marilyn," but Olivier began to play his role as director. In command of the microphone, he slowly and deliberately rephrased the reporters' questions so that she could craft her responses carefully. Several times he replied for her until she gradually gained the courage to answer for herself, with considerable wit and aplomb. Presumably one part of Monroe drew sustenance from following Olivier's lead, but another part of her may already have

Figure 14. Arthur Miller, Marilyn Monroe, Laurence Olivier,
and Vivien Leigh, 1956
(*Courtesy Movie Star News*)

been storing up resentment at his preemption of her replies. He was gallant in his protection of her, but she was capable of twisting his gentlemanly behavior into the schizoid's dread of being disrupted and divided from others. Olivier uses this psychological term in his recollections of her personality, a term Greene also favors in summing up his view of her behavior. She could not compete with this Englishman's profound self-assurance and may very well have come to feel he was using it against her all along.

By the middle of July, when Monroe departed with her new husband for the making of *The Prince and the Showgirl* in England, she was capturing the same kind of public enthusiasm and international press coverage that had attended her marriage to Di Maggio and their trip to Japan. But with an uncomfortable Miller at her side and with an important movie about to be made, she seemed somewhat subdued—at least by the ebullient standards she had set for herself in earlier years. British reporters sensed a sourness in her reserve, not a maturity in her guardedness. After all, she was known for her eagerness to please. Since she was not cheerfully forthcoming, the press grilled and ridiculed her about her intellectual interests, her fondness for Beethoven and Dostoevsky. She was able to humor reporters only with self-deprecatory repartee:

> "Are you really studying acting?"
> "Yes. I'm serious about it."
> "What inspired you to study acting?"
> "Seeing my own pictures," she said, smiling gaily.

In a quieter, private moment, she had a different kind of conversation with a British reporter, Tom Hutchinson. He remembers her perceptive comments about Franz Kafka's *The Trial*, in which Josef K. is arrested for a crime against the state that is never explained to him: "It's like we all feel, this sense of guilt. I know they say it's the Jewish thing with Kafka—that's what Arthur (Miller) says anyway—but it goes beyond that. It's about all men and women. This sense that we have fallen or something. I suppose that's what they mean by Original Sin."

Reading Kafka must have confirmed her sense of strangeness, of foreignness, of breaking rules she did not know existed. She was uneasy in Olivier's charge, for he was on home ground and working with a cast and crew whom he could address as old friends, seated around a table on the first day of shooting. Monroe, in Norman Rosten's view, was the outsider, the one needing to prove herself. She would have to "get accustomed to their way of doing things," Olivier remarked. His manners were impeccable, yet his "slight smile" and change in tone when addressing her were annoying. With others, he was a fellow professional; with Monroe, he was careful and elementary, thus emphasizing her status as neophyte. Olivier's behavior seemed patronizing and her guard went up, Rosten concludes. The Strasbergs, the Greenes, and Miller—all of whom respected Olivier enormously— corroborate Rosten's impression that Monroe felt demeaned. Each of them would make mistakes in handling Olivier that would contribute to Monroe's disaffection. The Greenes and Miller were too deferential to the director, a mortal sin in Monroe's view. Increasingly isolated and bitter, she depended on the Strasbergs for moral and artistic support. The Strasbergs conceded Olivier's genius but undermined his authority by calling his performance artificial and by catering to Monroe's worries. In his view she had far too many helpers, so that he had to run through considerable interference to get to her. For all of them the film became an ordeal to finish as Monroe's distrust of her director grew and her health deteriorated.

Much has been made of Monroe's outraged reaction to Olivier's direction: "Be sexy." She called Lee Strasberg at his London hotel to express her resentment. She was no sex machine, and Olivier was ignoring her sensibilities as an actress. He had almost no interest at all in her method of making contact with her role. Indeed, on many occasions he voiced criticism of Strasberg's teachings, since he conceived them to be "deliberately antitechnical." The Method dictated "an all-consuming passion for reality, and if you did not feel attuned to exactly the right images that would make you believe that you were actually *it* and *it* was actually going on, you might as well forget about the scene altogether." For Olivier, acting *was* pretending.

Yet Olivier used more of the Method than one might suppose from his public attacks on it. Indeed in his autobiography he concedes the usefulness of Stanislavsky's principles, and Shelley Winters has given an example of his employment of the Method in a stage role. Conversely, many Method actors have conceded Olivier's point about the need for strenuous training in voice, movement, in the actor's whole technical apparatus, and for faking feelings that the actor cannot reach for in his own life or that are not properly motivated in a script. It is unlikely that in the actual process of acting Olivier and Monroe were quite as mismatched as they thought, but in their perceptions of one another's failings each was adamant, with Olivier evincing more honesty and self-awareness than Monroe, later admitting: "I just don't think I tried terribly hard to get on with her."

Failures of perception were fatal for Monroe, since she was quick to read the nuances in *all* of Olivier's behavior one way. He found her strangely lacking in humor, perhaps because she was unwilling to joke about the one thing she took most seriously, her acting. He may have been joshing her when he said "be sexy" or stupidly insensitive as to how she would take such a comment. Either way, she could not forgive him for it.

Olivier was apparently unaware that Monroe's closest friends were critical of her behavior. Hedda Rosten, who accompanied Monroe on the trip to England, remembers being very dubious about the application of the Method to the light, comic part Monroe played; Monroe's devotion to character motivation seemed fussy and excessive to Rosten. Paula Strasberg, according to her daughter, agonized over Monroe's unprofessional behavior and shouldered much of the blame for it. Milton Greene angered Monroe by trying to dilute the amount of gin she requested with her tea at 9:00 A.M. before appearing on the movie set. "I would have to feed her the uppers she wanted. They came in a different color in London, and she'd think I was faking, changing the pills." Miller— like Greene—seemed to act as Olivier's conscientious surrogate in trying to get his wife to the studio on time and in generally getting her to fulfill her commitment to the film. These acts she came to interpret as her husband's betrayal of her, especially after she discovered his misgivings about her recorded in a journal he thoughtlessly left open on a table.

Monroe had driven Miller to desperation with her insomnia, incessant pill taking, sluggish, drugged days, and nights of worry and inactivity. In his journal he let his disillusionment show, and she was crushed. She went weeping to the Strasbergs, and rather incoherently tried to convey how devastated she felt about Miller's loss of confidence in her. There is considerable dispute about what he actually wrote, but there is no doubt in Norman Rosten's mind that by the end of 1956 "a change was discernible in Marilyn. The tone of the marriage had changed." Close friends sensed something "new and mysterious" between husband and wife, Rosten recalls.

Nevertheless, Monroe keenly appreciated her husband's professional appraisals of her talent and began in England to ask him to judge photographs, a task more suited to Greene. Miller also began to question the propriety of Greene's handling of her business affairs and pointed to instances where Greene acted precipitously. For Greene, the worst of it came when Miller tried to rewrite certain scenes in the film and kept Monroe away from the set reading reviews of his new play, *A View from the Bridge*. Finally, an exasperated Greene urged Miller to "*Be a husband!*" and stop interfering with the production.

Miller responded by losing patience with Greene. Midway through the film, it was clear to Monroe's business partner that he had been effectively compromised by her husband. By cutting Greene off from Monroe, Miller probably did not anticipate that his wife would shift more of her frustrations onto him and lose some of her admiration for him because he had tied himself so closely to her career. As with so many of her relationships, she began to suspect that he had become her servant only to satisfy himself.

Olivier by his equivocal temperament exacerbated the extremely delicate conditions in which Monroe struggled to create her screen characters. On the one hand, he went out of his way to consult Josh Logan and Billy Wilder on the best way to handle Monroe, but on the other hand, he was not willing to take their advice that he would simply have to put up with her vagaries. He either ignored or forgot Josh Logan's advice to work closely with Paula Strasberg but to bar her from the movie set. He preferred complaining to Greene or Miller rather than forthrightly addressing his costar. When he complained to Logan that Monroe was rude to him, that she walked away when he tried to instruct her in how to read a line, Logan replied that he had never had that problem because he had never attempted to tell Monroe how to say her lines. In short, Logan and Olivier were fundamentally different directors, with the latter having almost no confidence at all in the integrity to which the former deferred. There are conflicting accounts of Olivier's treatment of Monroe during the shooting of the film. Some observers found him always gentlemanly while others report some nasty scenes with Monroe. What seems indisputable was his determination not to coddle her, not to go against certain principles that were his pride as a director and actor, or as he put it to one of the cast: "There are one or two things I *will* have right."

One eyewitness account of Monroe has her "too dumb and uncultured and obsessed with herself" to be able to cooperate with Olivier. Similar to Nunnally Johnson's earlier characterization of her work on *We're Not Married*, this criticism is nonetheless hard to credit in the main, given Monroe's alert preparations for *Bus Stop* and Hedda Rosten's observation of Monroe working on *The Prince and the Showgirl* with great concern as to how her role fit into the entire production. Conflicting versions of her awareness and intelligence stem in part, it seems, from her traumatic approach to the camera that sometimes made her close up and fumble even the simplest lines and actions. One observer attributed her failure to follow through to a "quite unconscious but basic resistance to acting." At any rate, it seems that, as on the set of *Bus Stop*, she was "practically paralyzed with nerves." This extreme nervousness, which Lee Strasberg tried to assure her was characteristic of many actors, sometimes made her seem inept, withdrawn, and resistant to direction.

Absolutely none of Monroe's tentativeness showed up on screen, and this came as a surprise to Dame Sybil Thorndyke who, at first, felt Monroe was "so small scale" but who came to call her the perfect film actress, since she came alive on celluloid in a way unrivaled by her fellow actors. There are an economy and a celerity in Monroe's performance as Elsie Marina that are particularly noticeable in comparison to her busy, fretful portrayal of Cherie, a portrayal that is a precise measurement of Cherie's frustrations. Elsie Marina, on the contrary, is able to speak and move freely without seeming knotted up and fatigued. Monroe embodies Elsie's spiritedness by minimizing the cramping gestures to the head and the body that were so appropriate for the introverted Cherie. Instead, almost all of Elsie's movements are outward, sometimes lateral, so that she glides effortlessly from side to side, continually foregrounded for the viewer. In such moments, Elsie is elegant and graceful and more aware of her surroundings than previous Monroe characters who hug themselves in displays of a much cruder exhibitionism.

Although *The Prince and the Showgirl* is extraordinarily faithful to Rattigan's play, it seems that Rattigan was taken with Monroe's personality and shaped the film's structure around it. She, in turn, was able to use her role to provide perspective on her earlier characters. For example, as in *Bus Stop*, Monroe's character is soon defined by mirror shots, by her self-examination in a mirror and her dressing up to meet the Grand Duke (Olivier) who is coming backstage after the performance of a play in which she has a very small part. Mirror scenes occur in *Don't Bother to Knock*, *Gentlemen Prefer Blondes* and *The Misfits*, and all of them have to do with a groping, wayward, sometimes delighted dressing of herself for others. Elsie Marina, like Roslyn Taber in *The Misfits*, is characterized by her tardiness. The film copies an incident that occurred at the Monroe-Olivier press conference in New York by having Elsie's shoulder strap break as she meets the Grand Duke. Thus the impression of a somewhat disheveled personality is created.

Elsie does not lack confidence, however. It is true that she is surprised by the Grand Duke's interest in her and that she uncertainly fusses over what to wear at their meeting—as Monroe did in preparing to meet Olivier in New York—but she is quite sure of her values and represents them robustly. Because her role in the play that the Grand Duke has seen is very small, she is surprised that she has excited his attention. Nevertheless, she is not intimidated by his rank or flattered by his attentions, for she has a very strong sense of self-worth that comes out in her lectures to him on democracy and family feeling. She is working class and ignorant in many ways because of her lack of exposure to a larger world, but the film never condescends to her or makes

Figure 15. Marilyn Monroe in *The Prince and the Showgirl*, 1957
® 1957 Marilyn Monroe Productions, Inc.
(Courtesy The Museum of Modern Art/Film Stills Archive)

sport of her simplicity. On the contrary, as Foster Hirsch observes, she is revealed to have great dignity.

Elsie has been invited to what she thinks is a party given by the Grand Duke when in fact he has planned a private assignation. Her befuddlement as to his intentions, and her slow acclimation to the royal chamber and its furnishings, are humorously acted out in her awkward but successful efforts to avoid colliding with the serving men who are bringing in supper. She sidesteps, darts forward and backward, and swerves around them in maneuvers that are a warmup for her avoidance of the Grand Duke's amorous advances. Her limberness will contrast starkly with his stiff, hardened opinions and figure. As soon as she realizes that she will be his evening's sole entertainment, she is bent on leaving and tells the English foreign service officer who has arranged the meeting that she knows only too well the outcome of such seductive suppers for two. Like Cherie before her and Sugar Kane after her, Elsie had been disappointed by men and is determined to avoid their sexual gambits. She stays only when the Englishman promises to extricate her immediately after she finishes dining with the Grand Duke.

Elsie seems constitutionally incapable of calling the Grand Duke by the appropriate royal title and finally gives up, saying, "the hell with it." She is riled by his dismissive comments on democracy and speaks up for the popular will in just the way Monroe herself would (although in this case Rattigan was not influenced by Monroe, since the Elsie Marina character in *The Sleeping Prince*, named Mary Dagenham, had already been conceived with this populist bias). Monroe fit the role because she represented a certain kind of American sensitivity to the individual which, in its extreme form, provokes Elsie to worry about the fate of an imprisoned politician, Wolffstein—just as Monroe pestered Miller and Rosten to offer Indonesian prime minister Sukarno refuge when she learned that he was in grave danger of being deposed.

The inattentive Duke, more concerned with concluding some business of state on the phone than with dining with Elsie, is subject to her astute mimicking of his European brusqueness as she begins to eat and drink for both of them. As she loses her inhibitions, she mocks the conventions of royalty—at one point ridiculing the way everyone backs out of the room in deference to the Grand Duke by sinuously retreating out the door only to pop in the room again to invite his admiration of her exit: "Pretty good, huh?" Even after he decides it is time to seduce her, she handles him expertly by noting that his performance is cliched and his romancing is pedestrian. In the play, Mary Dagenham brushes off his pass by jabbing him hard in the stomach with her elbow and jumping out of the chair provided for her. In the movie, Monroe's Elsie is more broadly forceful and much funnier when she uses an arm to sweep him aside and against a wall. This is a gesture of immense strength and is indicative of Elsie's unwillingness to adopt the genteel manner of deflecting a pass. Instead, she automatically accepts the Grand Duke's gambit for what it is—much to his chagrin—and good-naturedly responds, "And better luck next time." This honest directness, a part of the Monroe persona in many films, amiably enhances the way Rattigan conceived the American girl in his play.

All of the physical business of Elsie's role, which endows her with great spontaneity and hardiness, also makes it difficult for the Grand Duke to dominate her. Although he succeeds in awakening her romantic interest, and in stimulating her to banish and perplex the Englishman who tries to make good on his promise to interrupt the tête-à-tête, she stresses that she has made a conscious choice to fall in love with him, a choice that she demonstrates by vigorously aligning his face with hers in order to kiss him. There is a hint of melancholy in Elsie's voice, however, a latent vulnerability in her warning the Grand Duke to "watch out" because she is going to fall in love with him. What she means is that she will loosen her guard, and she knows that such a full expression of her emotions will exhilarate but ultimately sadden, perhaps even sour, her. From past experience she realizes that the love they share will be transitory. Comically, Elsie does "fall" for the Grand Duke by passing out from drinking too much vodka before he can have his way with her. Thus she remains lovely, undefiled, and integral in her peaceful, innocent repose, which serves as a transition to the film's consecration of her inviolability in the coronation scenes that follow.

This day, in 1911, at the crowning in London of George V, is Elsie's dream day and Monroe's apotheosis, for at the heart of the film Olivier exposes the figure of the actress and her character in extreme closeups that are bathed in light in much the same way as Logan caught the shimmer of her soft, ethereal face. During the coronation procession, the Grand Duke's severe demeanor begins to lighten into a smile as he allows himself to react to Elsie's freshness and vitality. In the cathedral she gazes upward in awe and is herself portrayed as a fit object of adoration, for her face is framed in a stained-glass window so that she appears angelic, positively holy. Monroe's popularity is here transformed into veneration; she is presented, indeed as an icon, a focus of worship—as Ken Russell realized in *Tommy* when he created the cathedral scene with Monroe acolytes and other faithful. Thus the cameras finally consecrate her and point to the moment of her own coronation.

Logan waited until near the end of *Bus Stop* to attempt such a daring elevation of Monroe's person, so that his closeups summoned to the foreground all the details of her performance and all the allusions to her as an angel. After the opening long shots of her through two window frames and the later scenes of her running from Bo's smothering embraces, the final closeups, tenderly played, are beautiful resolutions of the contradictions in her character, of all her human and ideal qualities. In *The Prince and the Showgirl*, Olivier makes the strategic error of elevating Elsie too soon, so that Monroe is forced to play her character for several more scenes beyond her spiritualization. There is no slackening in Monroe's performance, but she is working against the film's logic. Similarly, Olivier has waited too long to make his Grand Duke fall in love with the showgirl, even though he is wonderfully adept at showing how his character giddily throws off all the formal constraints of his high position.

The rest of the film has difficulty sustaining interest in spite of some wonderful scenes in which Elsie takes charge of the Grand Duke and eventually has him patch up his quarrel with his son, the heir to the throne of Carpathia. In a foreshadowing of *Some Like It Hot*, the ultimate seduction scene in *The Prince and the Showgirl* has Monroe in command of the man, looking him over, gazing at him below her, and feeding him the same lines and adopting the same ploys he has used in an effort to manipulate her. Indeed, Monroe's Elsie takes on the roles of diplomat, politician, and power broker as she goes back and forth bargaining between father and son. This reversal of expectations—what was once just a momentary jest in *Gentlemen Prefer Blondes*, where "dumb" Lorelei gets the better of her future father-in-law in an argument—is carefully built into the structure of this film. Monroe's mischievous wit is shown to full advantage in Elsie's strategy, while the man—in this case even a superbly polished Grand Duke—can seem as clumsy as the nebbish Richard Sherman in *The Seven Year Itch*.

Several critics have been captivated by the movie's poignant ending. The Grand Duke finally confesses that he loves Elsie, and *she* takes him in her arms. He has made arrangements for her to follow him to Carpathia, where he must rule another year and a half before his son assumes the throne, but she declines his invitations and prefers to wait until he can leave his country to join her. It seems unlikely that the couple will be reunited in spite of their depth of feeling for each other, and Elsie may be responding to the unreality of a match between a prince and a showgirl. At any rate, the camera shows the Grand Duke exiting through the doorway of the embassy's entrance while Elsie stands to one side of the first doorway, watching him depart through what was her entranceway at the beginning of the film. With the camera trained again on her, at the door of the drawing room with her eyes

Figure 16. Laurence Olivier and Marilyn Monroe in *The Prince and the Showgirl*, 1957
® 1957 Marilyn Monroe Productions, Inc.
(*Courtesy The Museum of Modern Art/Film Stills Archive*)

closed, she slowly backs out, opening her eyes to survey the whole scene of their mutual seduction. Then there is a long shot of Monroe's back from the point of view of the drawing room looking outward to the entrance that depicts her in solitude framed by the two doorways, walking quietly out into the world. The focus, as Joan Mellen notes, is not really on Monroe's behind but on her sad feelings. She is isolated in the double frame but is not as disconsolate as Cherie in the double framing Logan employs near the beginning of *Bus Stop*.

Milton Greene used to cheer up Monroe when she became soured on her screen roles by invoking the possibility of working with Chaplin. Janice Welsch observes that, like Chaplin's Tramp, Monroe "functions in a world between comedy and tragedy and stimulates her audience to both laughter and pity." Similarly, both characters enter relationships and bring love into other people's lives but ultimately remain alone themselves. They set the world afire with their exuberance and yet end up with something less than whole lives. They are in constant search of some final fulfillment.

At the time of its release, reviewers of *The Prince and the Showgirl* did not see any similarity between Chaplin and Monroe and did not see the film as marking any development in her career. Although it received some good reviews, most of them were mixed or negative, and it has never been a popular or critical success. Bosley Crowther noted that Rattigan "has not let his story do much more than go around and around and then come [to] a sad end. . . . Furthermore—and this is disappointing—his characters do not have enough to do to allow a diverting demonstration of their elaborate acting skills." Foster Hirsch suggests that *The Sleeping Prince* remains good light comedy with sparkling dialogue, but the movie, "with its confined drawing-room setting and its artificial storyline, looks unmistakably like a theater piece transported uncomfortably to an alien and resistant medium." He concludes that "the material never quite manages to move comfortably within the film frame." Even so, Hirsch is quite right that Olivier and Monroe "play beautifully together, and the obvious difference in their style of performance enhances the thin material," for they carry on a duet between the rigid, masked Grand Duke and the pliable, unreserved Elsie. "Significantly, Olivier is dressed up for his part while Monroe wears a simple white dress that reveals every curve and bulge in her figure." Olivier masterfully holds everything to himself whereas Monroe just as skillfully gives everything of herself away. If *The Prince and the Showgirl* is not a cinematic success, since it seems uneasily suspended between stage and screen conventions that the two performers, for all their superb acting, cannot surmount, it still serves as a crucial transition between

Bus Stop and *Some Like It Hot*, the two films that most fully bring out the comic myth of Monroe's persona.

It is doubtful, however, that the actress felt a sense of completion, for as she was leaving England in November she apologized to cast and crew and blamed her bad behavior on ill health. Olivier suspected he was not as effective as Logan and Wilder in stimulating her talent, although in his recent autobiography his views of her acting and the film are somewhat gentler and more generous.

When Josh Logan visited Olivier and Monroe during the making of the film, he found them feeling betrayed. Olivier blamed Logan for not giving him sufficient warning of her intractability. Monroe mistakenly believed Logan had been responsible for cutting one of her most movingly acted scenes in *Bus Stop*, one that she proudly wanted to show to Miller. The loss of the scene was too painful for her to bear, Logan concludes. *The Prince and the Showgirl* was to have been a film, like *Bus Stop*, in which she would express more of her real self, of her talent, than ever before. How could she trust Olivier when Logan, who seemed to understand her so well, had sabotaged her performance? She told Logan, "I was never so angry in my entire life, and I'm just as angry now as I was then!" and banged the door of her dressing room in his face.

Through all of her trials, Monroe clung to Miller, who stayed the course with her, even if he was not quite as strong or as loyal as she hoped. Back in the United States they would try to make the marriage go another way, toward family and semiretirement for Monroe until the right role was available. They had rushed from their romance and marriage to the stresses of her complicated working life. It was time to recover their harmony as lovers and to find the habits of living by which they could hold each other in comfortable regard. It was time to have the home life Monroe had always missed.

10

Home Life
(October 1956–August 1958)

I was never used to being happy, so that wasn't something I ever took for granted. I did sort of think, you know, marriage did that. You see, I was brought up differently from the average American child because the average child is brought up expecting to be happy—that's it, successful, happy, and on time.

After returning from England, Monroe and Miller settled in a cottage at Amagansett, Long Island. Except for a short vacation in Jamaica in January of 1957 and brief periods in New York City, where Monroe maintained her Manhattan apartment, Amagansett served as their principal residence until the early spring of that year, and they returned to it in the summer after spending several busy months with a new home, a two-hundred-acre farm in Connecticut adjacent to the one Miller sold while they were in England. Making a successful marriage with Miller seemed to be Monroe's sole ambition, and with him she revealed her uncertainties and tried to remedy them. She had fundamental fears about the nature of existence and her place in it, even though she appeared to be so full of life herself and was so stimulating to Miller, whose vision of things seemed quickened and sharpened by her sensitivity.

He began to write with her in mind, to explore what might be called a metaphoric expression of his experience of Monroe. Not only the woman herself but what she suggested to him about a variety of female characters made a significant difference in his creative work. He was not writing her biography in a literal sense, but he was extending his awareness of her, of her mythic possibilities, in remarkable ways that moved toward the development of a whole person, one who was only sketched in by her movies. He proceeded very cautiously as a writer and was disrupted by many false starts and by several projects, including plays, that he could not complete. The care he took of Monroe certainly occupied much of his time, but it also seems that he was struggling for a new point of view, unsure of how it would emerge later in both fiction and drama connected to her character.

Miller's short story, "Please Don't Kill Anything" (1960), centers on a figure readily identifiable as Marilyn Monroe and derives its inspiration from his many months of happiness with her in Amagansett, when they were free to concentrate fully on each other and to indulge each other's vagaries. The tenor of their relationship is suggested by the wonderfully whimsical photograph of them on the beach in the summer of 1958, caught up in what looks like gales of laughter, leaning against each other, shoulder to shoulder, mutually supportive. The first third of "Please Don't Kill Anything" renders nearly all of its beach scenes from the unnamed woman's viewpoint; always, what is important is what she sees, what shocks her. She makes others follow her line of sight, her waves of emotion.

The woman is startled by fish struggling in a net hauled to shore by fishermen. She is virtually immobilized in the midst of the helpless fish, but she insists on witnessing the reality of their demise: "I'll watch it. I'm watching it," she says in obvious dread. Sam, her companion and Miller's fictional surrogate, tries to placate her by throwing several of the fish rejected by the fishermen back into the sea.

Miller beautifully dramatizes Monroe's compulsion to make the world whole again so as to compensate for her own rejection. As Norman Rosten says of her, "the survival of an unprotected shrub on a windy hillside, through rain and frost, is to her a source of trembling joy. She knew her own battle to survive and could appreciate the triumph in nature." One of the fishermen is actually embarrassed by the woman's pointed questions, and he lies when he assures her that he puts the rejected fish back into the sea.

This closeness to nature while feeling estranged from the ordered world of human affairs typified Monroe and partially accounted for her hostility to predatory authority, to anything that regimented, that trapped human beings, and denatured them. She much preferred to rely on her intuitive faculties and fellow feeling than to be guided by rational explanations that regulated and, in her view, stifled creativity and ultimately life itself. In the story, Sam senses his woman's desire for reintegrating the world: "as he threw the slimy fish in one by one he saw each fish separately, each straining for its quart of sea, and he was no longer ashamed." Sam is forced to see the world as a succession of individual cases, not as a single mass, undifferentiated and therefore unsalvageable. She is undeterred by his sensible point that all life feeds on life, one fish on another, because "she had in her head a clock which was telling her that every second counted." Similarly, Monroe was not persuaded by Miller's or Rosten's assurances that Sukarno could look after himself, that they had no connection with his political problems, because she saw him as an individual who needed immediate help, not logical explanations of inaction. She was moved by fervent sentiments similar to those expressed by Alexei Karamazov in Miller's favorite novel, *The Brothers Karamazov*: "every one of us is answerable for every-one else, but we don't know it; if we did, we would at once have heaven on earth!" Monroe ended her last recorded interview by pleading for what she considered to be most important: the cause of world peace. "My nightmare is the H Bomb," she told another interviewer in what was not only a refusal to talk about her personal life but a profound fear of the world's destructiveness.

Near the sea Monroe seems to have felt particularly close to other creatures. In her early days at Amagansett, she slept more easily at night and could almost bring her chronic insomnia under control, although she would eventually tire of the seashore and the country—unable to sustain her oneness with nature consistently—and hanker for the urban interludes that liberated her in other ways. Monroe's and Miller's alter-nation between the country and the city—it was to become a regular rhythm for them in the two years following their departure from England—was like her oscillation between the unmatched halves of her character. If "Please Don't Kill Anything" reveals her enormous invest-ment in the perpetuation of life, it also reflects, as Guiles notes, Miller's discovery that she was "becoming obsessively concerned with death and things dying." So much sensitivity to life held within itself a terror of dissolution.

Having a child would increase her sense of a place in the world. Motherhood might provide stability and the promise of continuity. In the early summer of 1957 Monroe became pregnant. Several of her friends remember how she yearned to be a mother, even if it meant, in Rosten's words, "temporarily putting films aside. She desperately wanted fulfillment." She also had the conventional feelings of many parents who compensate for their aggrieved memories of childhood by planning to give their own children a happier, more secure upbringing.

Yet her pregnancy was also troubled by at least one period of depression, and Rosten recalls that she was subject to her usual "sudden shifts in mood. When she's high, a sweet chime of music surrounds her; when she's low, she moves to another plane, withdrawn, private." Ros-ten found her on a porch sobbing one evening during a party, and she would not tell him what was bothering her. She cautioned him to "make believe I just was out here powdering my nose or something," so that her husband—against whom she apparently harbored no quarrel— would not get upset.

Several weeks later, on August 1, 1957, she suffered a miscarriage and was rushed by ambulance to the hospital. She acted cheerful when Rosten visited her, but he was certain of her disappointment. "The love goddess, the woman supreme," could not have a baby. She was devastated. "There was something wrong with her, inside her, a defect, an evil," he surmises. Mailer and Summers give a literal emphasis to Rosten's speculation on Monroe's state of mind by passing on reports that she had several—perhaps more than a dozen—abortions that ruined her insides and made her unfit for childbirth. Life had suddenly stopped in her, and she may have felt at fault because she postponed motherhood so long, had not wanted children earlier, and was preoccupied solely with herself in an immature way that Fred Karger first identified in expressing his doubts about her as a proper mother for his child.

Miller attempted to cheer his wife with the announcement that he had conceived a way of adapting his short story, "The Misfits," into a screenplay featuring a female character, Roslyn, who would be perfect for Monroe. How she must have felt heartened to be the inspiration of a serious script—at least that half of her wedded to acting. At home in Amagansett, however, her euphoria quickly wore off. Unable to sleep, she steadily increased her daily dosage of Nembutal. She found a brief reprieve in the pills, which, as Miller observed late one afternoon, were going to kill her. She was having difficulty breathing and was slowly suffocating herself with one pill too many. He would have to witness several of these episodes when her depression became so deep that there was nothing he could do to rouse her. On more than one occasion, he was forced to call a crew from a nearby clinic to revive her.

Was Monroe deliberately trying to kill herself? In addition to Natasha Lytess's report of a suicide attempt and various other accounts, some of which are surely apocryphal, there is Norman Rosten's recollection of a dialogue with her after having her stomach pumped of its pill overdose (Miller was not present) at 3:00 A.M. in her New York apartment:

> It's all quiet; private doctor, no publicity.
>   My wife enters the room. After a moment I follow in the dim light. I hear someone sobbing quietly. I whisper, leaning over the bed, "It's me, Norman. How are you dear?"
>   "Alive. Bad luck." Her voice is rasping, drugged. "Cruel, all of them, all those bastards. Oh Jesus. . . ."

She doesn't say who. She has tried this before and will try it again.

The way Rosten writes it there is no doubt of her deliberate attempt to end it all. On an earlier occasion she lightly referred to her suicidal emotions and connected them with her insomnia. Rosten made a pact with her stipulating that if either of them "was about to jump, or take the gas, or the rope, or pills, he or she would phone the other." He was joking, but he took the agreement seriously nevertheless and expected to get a call from her one day.

Rosten provides examples of Monroe's poetry that elaborate on the tension of a life suspended precariously and stubbornly between its dichotomies:

> Life—
> I am of both your directions
> Existing more with the cold frost
> Strong as a cobweb in the wind
> Hanging downward the most
> Somehow remaining
> those beaded rays have the colors
> I've seen in paintings—ah life
> they have cheated you

Another version of the same poem emphasizes both life's fierce upward pull on her like "leaping hot fires" and its pull downward to what Rosten supposes is death. Her incomplete poems precisely replicate her idea of herself as a fragment of life; she is as unfinished and as unpolished as her verse. "Strong as a cobweb in the wind" is suggestive of both her delicacy and her stamina, that "somehow" endure, remain, as a projection of nature. The image of beaded rays is elusive—indeed the last three lines are enigmatic, and Rosten offers no help with them, perhaps because they reflect Monroe's private symbolism or a part of the poem she did not deign to develop. It may be significant, however, that the referent of "they" in the last line is ambiguous, so that—as in her vague cursing after her pill overdose—it is impossible to know how it is that life has been cheated. In other words, both her destructive and creative actions are truncated.

The origins of Monroe's abortive poetry can only be guessed at, but the themes of forlorn anguish and the doubleness of all her experience are unmistakable. The same themes pervade her drawings done on Fire Island in the summer of 1955, two of which Susan Strasberg saved:

> In one, with quick, round lines, depicting a feline, sensual grace and movement, she had done a self-portrait. The other was of a little Negro girl in a sad-looking dress,

one sock falling down about her ankles. I thought that was a self-portrait, too, of Marilyn's hidden self.

Norman Rosten has four of Monroe's drawings that elaborate on her introverted and extroverted sides: (1) a lonely-looking little girl with a tiny face and a flowing gown; (2) a simple sketch of a figure hunched over perhaps in pain with the caption "I'd die if I could"; (3) a singer with prominent breasts and behind; (4) an old woman studying her hand. Faces are almost never prominent or clearly drawn. Figures count for almost all of the artist's interest, and they are rendered with great energy. Monroe's self-portrait in Sam Shaw's book is drawn in flamboyant, broad strokes, with breasts, hips, arms, and legs swinging out in wide curves that suggest a flaunting of her body. It is much harder to read the little face, since the eyes and lips are dark blots dominated by the mass of hair that ascends vigorously from her small head. The caption for the self-portrait—"What the Hell, that's life!"—may be her way of shrugging off disappointment by expressing her vitality.

On the one hand, Monroe could look and feel like the personification of health; on the other, she could have that down-in-the-mouth hopelessness that made everyone want to help her. In her drawings she pictured herself as both the victim of her doubts and the vanquisher of her troubles. This kind of paradoxical appeal is perhaps what prompted one psychiatrist to write to her in this humorously contradictory fashion: "I am sure that there is *NOTHING* wrong with you. Please let me know whether I can be of assistance."

Monroe's drawings, her acting, her movies, her public appearances were all extensions of the self that perhaps, for a time, retarded that inner contraction of character that made her feel so tiny, so inconsequential and abused—like the little Negro girl she drew—and so old, or at least aging—like the insular old woman preoccupied with her hand. The bushels of fan mail she showed to Rosten were a way of reaffirming she had a self to exhibit—at least one she could dress up and enlarge like her drawing of the little girl with the tiny face and flowing gown.

Between the extremes depicted in her poems and drawings, the actress sought equilibrium. Several of her friends remember the autumn of 1957 as having been a particularly joyful period in her life. She and Miller spent weekdays in the city and weekends at the farm in Connecticut. In Sam Shaw's New York City photographs in the October 1, 1957 issue of *Look*, there are scenes of Monroe and Miller preparing for a ride in their convertible, driving through the financial district, stopping for a snack at Battery Park, stretching their legs beside East River Drive, absorbed in each other's eyes against the background of a bridge and expressway, walking together hand-in-hand on the sidewalk. Other photographs show Monroe by an elevator at Tiffany's, surrounded by a crowd on the sidewalk, reading a newspaper next to a couple seemingly oblivious of her presence, rowing a boat in Central Park, and eating hot dogs at an outdoor restaurant on 112th Street, a street where Miller had lived a while when young. The photographs create the impression that she has given herself over to him as he points out interesting landmarks and gazes outward on the city. They have achieved balance and equality in their lives.

The city was also the place where Monroe could play at being other selves, where she could disguise or reveal herself at will. Norman Rosten recalls that neither he nor his wife recognized Monroe when the photographer Sam Shaw first introduced her to them. With "no makeup, hair short and careless and wet" she looked like "a pretty high school kid," and Norman told her that she would not be recognized at a party they were to attend a few hours later. Sure enough, no one believed that this woman could be a film star, and Rosten wonders if she had stepped "into the reality of her true self." Certainly she was attractive to the partygoers, but he could not tell exactly what drew them to her, whether it was "her voice, the half-shy, half-curious way she looked at people, her sudden warmth, that quick infectious laugh?" She enjoyed herself and did not seem at all displeased by what Rosten calls her anonymity in Brooklyn. She could have fun with herself and with others when it came to trying to fathom her identity. She made a game of teasing the crowd, practiced elaborate rituals of self-disguise, picked outlandish clothing to wear, and hired huge limousines with shades that invited curiosity. In effect, she was challenging strangers to say "I know who you are!" speculates Rosten.

The actress had an oscillating notion of identity, so that she would do things, so to speak, by halves. She had a fluid, even volatile, idea of herself. She was molded to the moment in the same way as Dmitry Karamazov, Dostoevsky's supreme example of the manic-depressive personality whose histrionic sense of himself fluctuates above and below the normal ego's more or less stable lines of behavior.

The reminiscence of Lena Pepitone, Monroe's personal maid, sensationalizes her mistress's violent mood changes, but something essential in Monroe's extremes of feeling is rendered in this description of Pepitone's first coming to work for the actress in October of 1957:

> [Monroe] turned several full, slow circles, using both wall mirrors to scrutinize every angle.

"You have a beautiful figure," I complimented her. I had the feeling she was looking for praise.

"Thank you," she replied sincerely. "My ass is way too big." She glanced again at her rear and grimaced. Her slightly bulging stomach didn't seem to bother her. "They tell me men like it like that. Crazy, huh?"

"It's sexy," I answered, and we both laughed.

"I like you," Marilyn said. She returned to the closet and rummaged through those endless racks of blouses and pants. "I need something to wear today." She yanked out about ten blouses, held them up, then threw them on the floor. "I can't stand it!" she yelled.

At best, this dialogue is an approximation and more likely just a dramatization of what Pepitone remembers from the rhythms of days with Monroe, but the rhythms seem right, since by nearly all accounts there was hardly a day when Monroe did not go up and down the scale of her many selves.

Monroe, in Pepitone's portrayal, is almost all at once regal, innocent, glowing, vulgar, unwashed, overweight, bored, "near desperation," and "a beautiful mess." The mirrors that line several walls of her apartment, and even a table top, repeatedly reflect the joy and despair she took in her selves. She is always viewing herself, as in her drawings, as a figure who is dressing or undressing herself in endless, isolated permutations. As in Truman Capote's remembrance of her, she sometimes seems to identify absolutely with the mirror image and sometimes is able to measure off a distance between herself and her reflection. "Can I really be as good as [the Strasbergs] say?" she questions herself, staring in the mirror. "What are you doing" Capote asks Monroe as she confronts a dimly lit mirror. "Looking at Her," is Monroe's reply. Unfortunately, she was rarely able to bring her multiple personalities together to produce a single, complex state of consciousness, a fullness of self that she perhaps felt only while acting. This may be why Pepitone recalls the following words echoing through the New York apartment for the entire time she was with Monroe: " 'I'm learning to be a serious dramatic actress.' . . . She said it with dead seriousness, too. In fact, it was the only thing she ever said without sort of laughing at herself."

Yet it was not enough for Monroe to go from classes at the Actors Studio, to sessions with her psychoanalyst, and back to her apartment, where she would play—over and over again—her favorite Frank Sinatra records, dance and dress in front of her mirrors, and nurse her sense of self-pity and abandonment in songs like "Every Day I Have the Blues." She found solace in these songs and in her social life with the Strasbergs and the Rostens. With these people—especially in their kitchens—she could indulge in homely pleasures, feel neighborly, and surround herself with a small community of friends. Miller admitted his communication with Monroe was sometimes short-circuited, a point that Pepitone emphasizes by depicting him as lacking the ability to draw Monroe out of her anxieties—although Pepitone is hardly the best witness since she saw very little of the couple's truly private life.

Monroe seemed to know so little about making herself happy apart from her husband, her friends, and her roles. She could not please herself, for she lacked "a firm core of ontological security"—to apply R. D. Laing's terminology. Her behavior resembled Laing's view of the schizoid's lack of "an over-riding sense of personal consistency or cohesiveness," and therefore she spent most of her time simply trying to keep herself intact, or, as Laing puts it, "the ontologically insecure person is preoccupied with preserving rather than gratifying himself: the ordinary circumstances of living threaten his low threshold of security." Her life with Miller was as solid and dependable as any she ever had, and yet the very matter-of-factness of it upset her, drove her to her mirrors to live—sometimes like the schizoid—in a world of her own. "It's you I hate to lose," "Every Day I have the Blues" says, and Monroe may have had the schizoid's worry that, in Laing's words, "the world of his experience comes to be one he can no longer share with other people."

In spite of all their shortcomings, movies were still a bona fide way for Monroe to share at least part of herself with other people, and Miller seemed to appreciate them in that way, for he urged her to face the cameras again in the hope that she would come to herself in the concentration required to perform for them. He was particularly anxious to go forward with his screenplay of *The Misfits*, a draft of which he finished some time in the spring of 1957, and which he would continue to work on for the next year. In the meantime, she decided to do the role of Sugar Kane in Billy Wilder's *Some Like It Hot*, which would be ready to shoot in the summer of 1958.

Miller's counsel carried more weight than ever, since Monroe publicly announced on April 11, 1957, her intention of breaking with Greene. She accused Greene of "mismanagement and seeking personal glory." She felt he had misinformed her about contracts and had made secret commitments. Their partnership was legally dissolved in April of 1958, after two years of working for the critical acclaim that still eluded her. *Bus Stop* and *The Prince and the Showgirl* were creditable projects, but she measured him against the grander goals he had promised to achieve. He was bewildered by her bitter disappointment, since he had devoted himself exclusively to her career. Miller would find himself in a similar position a few years later when her fondest hopes for their marriage and *The Misfits* collapsed.

From the spring of 1957 to the summer of 1958, however, Monroe and Miller were busily involved in a joint career. She could still imagine that they were creatively inseparable, as cast and crew of *The Misfits* managed to be assembled in what must have seemed like a magical order. John Huston, her ideal director, enthusiastically agreed to direct the film. Clark Gable, her romantic childhood image of her father and a Hollywood king, had welcomed the opportunity to costar with her. Her good friend from the Actors Studio, Eli Wallach, would be another costar, and Montgomery Clift, whom she felt was like her in many ways, completed the male trio revolving around her. She asked Frank Taylor, an old friend of Miller's who had been one of the first to hear the author read his screenplay, to be the film's producer. With the interim prospect of working with Wilder, a director she admired enormously, Monroe believed she had the elements that could coalesce into a unified person and career. The Strasbergs were heartily in favor of Miller's strong script and were shrewdly preparing her for one of her greatest performances in *Some Like It Hot*. She also held on to the hope of another pregnancy. Perhaps her self-fruition was not so far away after all.

11

Impersonations and Repetitions
(August 1958–June 1960)

*What am I afraid of? Do I think I can't act? I know I can act but I
am afraid. I am afraid. I am afraid and I should not be and I must
not be.*

On August 4, 1958, the first day of shooting *Some Like It Hot*, Marilyn
Monroe arrived on the sound stage with her usual assortment of associates that included, according to Guiles, not only her husband but her
own "hairdresser, make-up man, press representative, a maternal dramatic coach confidante, and untitled others." Billy Wilder does not seem
to have minded her menage, for he realized she was a genius when it
came to building upon her Marilyn Monroe image. He had worked
closely and amicably with Monroe and Natasha Lytess on *The Seven Year
Itch* and felt the actress had developed a wonderful comic performance,
a part of which had to be completed during her wrenching separation
from Joe Di Maggio. To be sure, there were times when she held up
production by forgetting lines or showing up late. She was susceptible
to sudden illnesses and prolonged periods of agonizing insecurity. But
the huge success of their previous project and his fundamental faith in
her talent sustained Wilder in what were to be the most miserable days
of his movie making career.

Of the three main roles in *Some Like It Hot*, Monroe's was actually the
smallest, yet she knew that the quality of her performance and its strategic placement were absolutely crucial to the film's success. Wilder knew
it too and carefully consulted Monroe and Miller about the role and
obtained her acceptance of it before he and his collaborator, I. A. L.
Diamond (screenwriter of her earlier film, *Love Nest*) finished the screenplay. Monroe was also courted by her costars, Jack Lemmon and Tony
Curtis, who were most charming in the early stages of the planning and

filming. Rupert Allan remembers Monroe telling him how especially solicitous Tony Curtis was. He would drop by her dressing room every day to pay her elaborate compliments. She was flattered by his attention, which was diametrically opposed to his remark later on (in a screening room) that kissing her was like kissing Hitler.

Jack Lemmon remembers that at their first meeting she came over to him and grabbed him and kissed him. He could not imagine feeling "more wonderful." Like Olivier at his initial encounter with the actress, Lemmon was delighted by her sweetness and charm. He was also impressed by her thorough knowledge of the parts he had played and by the critiques she made of each one. He was "stunned." She had him "right in the palm of her hand," he confesses. So they got along "beautifully," and he admits he "really loved Marilyn very much." She had enormous respect for Lemmon's talent, Rupert Allan recalls, and she explained to Allan her suspicion that Curtis's meanness derived from her favoring Lemmon.

Working on *Some Like It Hot* should have been a deeply satisfying experience for Monroe, since cast and crew and her whole entourage began with such total commitment to the picture. She appeared to like Wilder personally and was as pleased with their earlier effort on *The Seven Year Itch* as he was. The role of Sugar Kane was written expressly for her with a finesse that was missing from all of her previous parts save Cherie. Wilder was quite willing to work with both Miller and Paula Strasberg when they had suggestions for improving Monroe's role. It had been two years since she had worked on a film, and now she had an independent production, with a share of the profits—exactly the kind of deal that justified her return from semiretirement.

Monroe's friends say she wanted to work; she loved the part. Ralph Roberts, John Springer, and Rupert Allan cannot recall her ever discussing any misgivings about the role. Lena Pepitone, on the other hand, portrays an actress acutely distressed about having to play another dumb blonde, and Arthur Miller characterizes Sugar Kane as "a tasteless and characterless ingenue which she had to invest with some life so that it was real. . . . She had so assiduously worked on this small worthless role, and she couldn't get a part worth working on. . . . Underneath it all, it was to her something of an affront."

Monroe's behavior on and off the movie set suggests ambivalence; almost in spite of herself she struggled to attain a superlative performance. Perhaps she shared Miller's view, expressed after all the acrimony involved in working with Wilder, that her role was of "no consequence. That part was a triumph of her comedic inventions. She had made something out of nothing." Nearly every step forward in her acting seemed to require a step backward, a rehearsing of previous mistakes. She was mastered by a compulsion to repeat even as she slowly edged toward her best work. On *Some Like It Hot*, distrust, paranoia, and frustration peaked. Indeed, she seemed to suffer from a sense of dislocation that ultimately estranged her from her closest companion, advisor, and lover, Arthur Miller.

The ensemble playing of all of the main actors is so superb—they have a way of matching each other's brio and bravado perfectly—that it is hard to believe the production was beset by delays in filming many scenes. Take after take exhausted actors, especially Curtis, while Monroe stumbled over dialogue. One brief scene, in which she was to enter a hotel room, search through dresser drawers, and ask "Where's the bourbon?" took fifty-nine takes as she continually flubbed her one line with such attempts as "Where's the bonbon?" Wilder even took to taping the single line to the inside of the dresser drawers, but nothing helped her, and she seemed oblivious to the strain she was putting on everyone.

Sometimes Monroe had extreme difficulty accepting even elementary directions or taking the simplest scenes at face value. For example, Wilder wanted her to act surprised when a concealed whiskey flask drops out of her dress onto the floor of the train as she is rehearsing a song with the band. Monroe thought her character should be frightened—presumably of losing her job, since she had been warned about her drinking. She halfheartedly tried to do the scene his way. When he cut and asked for more surprise, she immediately went to Paula Strasberg and for fifteen minutes discussed the scene while a humiliated Wilder waited for her return. She was refusing to act what she did not feel—a perfectly reasonable reaction in a Method acting class but terribly destructive to movie set discipline. Jack Lemmon, exceedingly tolerant of her halting performance, identifies what he calls a "built-in alarm system" that would "go off" in the midst of a scene that was not working. She would come to an abrupt stop and "stand there with her eyes closed, biting her lip, and kind of wringing her hands." Eventually she would sort out the problem without considering the reactions of "the director, the actors, or anyone else." For Lemmon, this proved to be a difficult but fascinating way of acting.

Lemmon's sympathetic interest in Monroe's method is reminiscent of Logan's and of Don Murray's understanding of her self-centeredness. Both could see, like Lemmon, how deeply she wanted to know her characters and how her acting had to be all of a piece; all of it had to come organically out of herself—even the smallest gestures and seemingly innocuous expressions. Sugar Kane could easily have been just a stereotype, a figure in a farce, but in the playing of her Monroe generated a substantial personality, a wholeness that transcends caricature.

Right from the beginning of her work on Sugar Kane, Monroe was concerned with really believing in the character. She wanted to know how she could play a woman who could be so intimately involved with two female impersonators and not discover their true identities. Since the film is a farce, and since many other characters are also deceived by Joe and Jerry, the question might seem irrelevant. But to Monroe there had to be some compelling reason for Sugar's identification with Jerry/Daphne and Joe/Josephine. Lee Strasberg solved Monroe's problem by reminding her that while men always wanted to be close to her she often had difficulty getting to know women. Now, in the film, two women liked her and wanted to be her girlfriends. Strasberg recalled that his explanation settled her doubts. As Jack Lemmon perceived, "she had a good sense of comedy, but she had to bend the character to herself." Every approach to her character Sugar was an approach to herself; she was making a profoundly personal investment in her role.

After seeing the first day's rushes of her opening scene, in which closeups singled her out among a band of female musicians as the heroine, Monroe and Miller realized that not enough had been done to distinguish her personality from the others. They suggested to Wilder what needed to be done, and, as a result, Sugar Kane is first seen in a sleek black outfit carrying her ukulele and stepping hurriedly and nimbly in very high heels along the same train platform that Daphne (Lemmon) and Josephine (Curtis) had cautiously and somewhat unsteadily crossed moments earlier. Her entrance is accompanied by a raucous and jazzy horn solo that amplifies the sexy agitation of her walk and sounds the male note of interest in her vocalized by Daphne's male half, Jerry, who watches her move on tiny heel and toe points that almost shake and lift her off the ground. He exclaims that it's like "jello on springs." At this point she has already swerved away from the shaft of steam that has hit her rear, and Jerry is studying her, swinging his shoulders in imitation of her mobility, and perfecting his Daphne in ways that will later entice the male millionaire Osgood (Joe E. Brown).

The shot of steam is a comic device, a bit of physical humor particularly appropriate in a farce, but it also signals the first male thrust at Sugar Kane. Later Jerry/Daphne pinches her in the water after they have arrived in Florida—a trick s/he says s/he picked up (from Osgood) in the hotel's elevator. Finally, there is the steam on Joe's glasses in the seduction scene when Sugar has knowingly made him hot. Also, the blast of steam neatly diverts Joe and Jerry from their previous concern: at a stroke, as it were, they are no longer simply running away from the hot pursuit of Spats Columbo and his gang. They are now chasing Sugar, who is as innocent and unsuspecting as they were when they became witnesses to Spats's Saint Valentine's Day Massacre of the stoolie Toothpick Charlie and his gambling associates.

For the film to be able to withstand so many parallels between male and female experiences without seeming just a clever contrivance, the first scene with Sugar has to carry a special charge, catapulting the characters and the audience into an outrageous new realm in which male and female role reversals are not only accepted but welcomed. As Jerry playing Daphne, Lemmon is instrumental in taking on many of Sugar's characteristics; that is, he learns from her how to be a woman even while as a man he desires her. He also takes on aspects of the movie persona Monroe had developed in earlier films. For instance, in the course of commenting on Sugar's vibrating walk, he blurts out, "It's a whole different sex." The stupid sincerity of his observation is pure Monroe, pure Sugar, in its endearing daffiness. As Stephen Farber observes, Lemmon and Monroe are a team, "two great big dumb innocents, throwing themselves at life with verve and abandon." At the same time, Lemmon as Jerry/Daphne is never entirely feminized, for the actor also parodies the comic mannerisms of Joe E. Brown (Osgood) — especially Brown's wide-open, fulsome, aspirated laugh, so that Brown romances his counterpart in the same way that Lemmon latches onto Monroe as the female complement to his character. Similarly, Tony Curtis is both the suave male lover impersonating Cary Grant and the sisterly Josephine, who comes on like Jane Russell — "big and sassy" the bellboy calls him/her. Curtis as Joe restrains Jerry's predatory eyeing of Sugar just as Russell as Dorothy in *Gentlemen Prefer Blondes* tries to tone down Lorelei's vulgar appraisal of men.

That Sugar's experience parallels Joe's and Jerry's is made explicit when she speaks to Joe's female half, Josephine, explaining that she is running away from male bands — particularly male saxophone players (like Joe) who have exploited and rejected her. Her first song, "Running Wild," is a frenetic equivalent of Joe and Jerry's escape from the violent male world of Chicago. In fact, "Running Wild" provides much of the momentum for the film's train sequence. Sugar strums her ukulele and steps in circular yet forward fashion down the aisle in imitation of the locomotive's spinning wheels which are periodically pictured during the train trip. When the music stops, the band leader notices the bullet holes in what Jerry calls his "bull fiddle," so that the reasons for his running away are recalled. When Sugar's liquor flask falls to the floor, Jerry covers for her as he has always done for his arch male chauvinist partner, Joe, when he has been in a jam with a woman. But Jerry also acts as

Daphne, as one woman protecting another, just as Joe will later act as Josephine, Sugar's female confidante, advising her that no man—not even himself—is worth her suffering. Similarly, Sugar will adopt many of Joe's lines in portraying herself as a debutante suitable for marriage to his mockup of a millionaire and in going after him with an assurance she has never expressed before. Indeed, the film is full of these repetitions and reversals of behavior in which males and females impersonate each other and identify with male and female experiences without either sex becoming totally dominant.

Some Like It Hot presents a world of comic dualism in which Monroe's persona of the dumb blonde is acknowledged but also displaced, since it is Jerry as the blonde Daphne who wins the millionaire, whereas Sugar settles for the reality of poor Joe. There is a sadness in Sugar—she calls it being blue—and a neurotic quality (she drinks too much and frets over the repetitiveness of her experience) that distinguishes her from Lorelei, Pola, and Monroe's earlier female impersonations. Like Elsie and Cherie, Sugar seems older than Monroe's previous blondes, disheartened by male duplicity, and determined not to make the same mistakes again:

> You fall for them and you love 'em—you think it's going to be the biggest thing since the Graf Zeppelin—and the next thing you know they're borrowing money from you and spending it on other dames and betting the horses. . . . Then one morning you wake up and the saxophone is gone and the guy is gone, and all that's left behind is a pair of old socks and a tube of toothpaste, all squeezed out. . . . So you pull yourself together and you go on to the next job, and the next saxophone player, and it's the same thing all over again. See what I mean? Not very bright? . . . I can tell you one thing—it's not going to happen to me again. Ever.

Monroe delivers these lines with as much disappointment in herself as in the men who have exploited her. Bitterness is mixed with self-criticism as she catches the recurring rhythm of her experience in a voice that is edged with fatigue but finally buttressed with determination and a reserve of energy. Like Monroe herself, Sugar seems an excellent candidate for psychotherapy, caught in her own contradictions and repetitions, a helpless person bent on helping herself. Somehow the actress manages to speak with the voice of experience and of injured innocence.

Although there are a certain number of lines that qualify Sugar as a dumb blonde, she is aware of her limitations and has a self-consciousness that suggests some maturity. Indeed, the brilliance of Wilder and Diamond's dialogue is that it encompasses Sugar's paradoxical appeal so simply, directly, and believably. Of male saxophone players Sugar remarks: "I don't know what it is, but they just curdle me. All they have to do is play eight bars of 'Come to Me My Melancholy Baby'—and my spine turns to custard, and I get goose-pimply all over—and I come to them." Monroe manages to be ignorant, helpless, sad, resigned, and sexually suggestive by mixing her matter-of-fact delivery with a chronic plaintiveness that is somehow not tiresome but attractive. There is nothing put-on about her speech. She keeps just enough lilt in her voice to suggest vitality while saying how depressed she gets over her compulsiveness, and then hits her head as if either to knock some sense into it or to chastise herself. However one interprets her gesture, her whole stance in the ladies' washroom reveals an avowal of her limitations. In *The Seven Year Itch*, The Girl also frankly confesses that she gets "goose-pimply all over," but she lacks Sugar's sense of having been abused. The Girl is not dissatisfied with her toothpaste commercials, and she does not feel squeezed out, like the tube of toothpaste left behind by Sugar's lovers.

For Sugar, Joe, and Jerry, Florida is, in a way, the end of the line; they are all trying to escape former selves and all trying to fashion a life that will not simply be a repetition of past mistakes. For Joe and Jerry, a repetition of the past would literally mean death; Sugar, on the other hand, senses a psychic death, a further diminution of her person if she continues to work for male bands. Yet it is two males, impersonating women, who, in effect, save her from herself—just as she, in a sense, rescues them from the destructive aspects of their maleness, of the murderously masculine world epitomized by the gangsters. Joe, as Josephine, tries to dissuade Sugar from joining the drinking party in Jerry/Daphne's train berth, a party that began with Sugar's simple wish to thank him/her for protecting her by pretending to have dropped the whiskey flask that would have cost her her job. At the same time, of course, both men are desperately figuring out ways to seduce her. Their predatory attitude very gradually changes as they are put in her place. Thus Sugar says to Jerry: "If it hadn't been for you, they would have kicked me off the train. I'd be out there in the middle of nowhere, sitting on my ukulele"—to which he replies: "It must be freezing outside. When I think of you—and your poor ukulele. . . ." As he empathizes with her, he recapitulates her experience as his own—which in a way it is, since before getting on the train he had been out in the cold with his bull fiddle looking for work.

Brandon French terms *Some Like It Hot* "a good-natured dream of sexuality as a sliding scale from male to female." Her phrase making is particularly apt, considering the way Lemmon modulates his voice between high and low pitches so that it often cracks somewhere between male and female registers. Similarly, Curtis drops his voice an octave on the word "really" when he learns Sugar goes for male saxophone players, and Sugar roughs up her voice to say "some like it hot" when she describes the jazz the female band plays. This variety of voice and music—from Sugar's coy boop-boopy-doop song to the mellow bass and brassy horn solos—provide contrasts of character not equaled in any of Monroe's other films.

Unlike Monroe's previous leading men, Lemmon and Curtis are forced to warm up to her before they can try to possess her. Jerry, as a woman, has to allow Sugar to snuggle up to Daphne without making advances. His restraint puts him in a fever, and Sugar tries to rub the chills out of him. Similarly, Joe discovers that Sugar will not be responsive to his usual male saxophone-player ploys, so he behaves like a girlfriend, sharing his lipstick with her, and like a mother, offering tender, supportive suggestions. In his impersonation of a millionaire, he remains passive and cool, preferring classical music to jazz, and inviting Sugar to help him recover his potency. In these hilarious scenes, Sugar is, indeed, the source of energy as well as the fulfillment of male sexual fantasies. She is a character who is on terms with Monroe's past screen personas, but she is also more maternal. She is more suggestive of life's vibrancy than they ever were.

Once Sugar thinks she has found her millionaire on the beach, one who is "quiet, bespectacled, intellectual" like The Girl's ideal man in *The Seven Year Itch*, she manipulates him in the same way Joe has handled women. Like Joe, she even uses Jerry/Daphne as her straight man/woman when she wants him/her to support her pretensions:

> SUGAR: This is my friend Daphne. She's a Vassar girl.
> JERRY: I'm a *what?*
> SUGAR: Or was it Bryn Mawr?

The more Joe puts on his act as aloof millionaire, the more Sugar plays her part as high society girl, so that her naive parody of a debutante is the exact equivalent of his simple burlesque of the rich. One caricature, in other words, begets another.

This coupling and recoupling of characters—Sugar with Daphne, then Sugar with Josephine, then Sugar with the millionaire—is also an escalation of impersonations that reaches a crisis when Jerry/Daphne decides to expose Joe by dashing back to their hotel room with Sugar before Joe can return from the beach to change back to his Josephine getup. When they arrive, however, Josephine is already in a sudsy bathtub—like the one in *The Seven Year Itch*—singing Sugar's song, "Running Wild." Both figuratively and literally, Monroe's male costars assume her role, and it is the role playing itself that is actually exposed when Sugar leaves the room and Josephine/Joe/Shell Oil millionaire all emerge from the tub, for the figure has Josephine's wig and makeup, the millionaire's blazer and white pants, and Joe's formidable anger as he makes Jerry back away and dumps his yacht cap full of water on Jerry's head. Thus Joe douses Jerry's rebellion against him, so that they are no longer rivals for Sugar's love. Now a new act is created in which Jerry as Daphne will woo the millionaire Osgood and help Joe win Sugar by getting Osgood out of the way while Joe entertains Sugar on Osgood's yacht.

These plot changes prepare for a reversal of emphasis that puts Monroe's character in charge of the action—as in *The Prince and the Showgirl* when Elsie begins to dominate the Grand Duke by using the very same seductive tactics he had used against her. Midway through the film the Grand Duke feigns love-struck humility to engage Elsie's sympathy and then reveals a genuine ineptness and awkwardness as she turns his tricks against him. Similarly, Joe feigns sexual immaturity—he calls himself Junior—and an ineffectualness that proves to be somewhat true when he has trouble with the gears on the small boat that he has to drive in reverse to get out to the yacht. He also fumbles around the yacht, opens the wrong doors and generally acts as blindly with his glasses on as Pola acts with hers off in *How To Marry a Millionaire*. Indeed, it is Sugar who finds the appropriate room for their tête-à-tête. It is at this point that Monroe takes over the whole film.

After Junior relates his woeful tale about the causes of his impotence and the futile attempts to revive his sex drive—including sessions with Dr. Freud and a trip to the Mayo Clinic—Sugar asks him if he has tried American girls. Like Elsie, she is presented as having a pure sexuality that will arouse even the most jaded sophisticate to an elemental and profoundly moving passion. Sugar is all over Junior, pressing her flesh against him, running her fingers through his hair, kissing him tenderly then heavily from several different angles. As in the major love scene with Olivier in *The Prince and the Showgirl*, Curtis's character reclines against plush pillows as Monroe softens him up, using her hands to half hold and caress him, to shape him to her desires. Her head is above his, and he has to look slightly upward to follow her cue—as does Lorelei's lover boy in *Gentlemen Prefer Blondes*. Then Junior's glasses slide down his nose and are eventually removed as all his pretense of cool formality slips away. In response to her first kiss, he kicks his leg abruptly upward into an erection reminiscent of Wilder's sexual signaling in *The Seven Year Itch*. After her second kiss, he loosens his collar. Finally, Monroe encircles him with her arms in the full heat of her kisses and pushes him further down into the pillows almost smothering him with love. Surely the audience is enjoying Monroe, not Sugar, at this point, though the actress does nothing out of character. It is just that scenes like this one — and like "Diamonds Are a Girl's Best Friend" — have a magnificence to them that is not strictly necessary for the development of Sugar's or Lorelei's personalities. That Curtis continues to parody Cary Grant only adds to the audience's awareness that its enjoyment of movie stars and movies is played with here.

Wilder avoids the danger of making the scene an excessive vehicle for Monroe by swish panning to scenes with Daphne and Osgood dancing, the lead switching between them, in a perfect matchup with Joe and Sugar who have also alternated in their pursuit of each other. In fact, Osgood and Daphne bring together the dominant and recessive traits continually exchanged between the main characters in this film, so that male and female qualities are as inseparable as the dance itself. One scene naturally leads into another as sexuality in this film is portrayed as an endlessly variable dance. For example, Junior/Cary Grant's remark that Sugar's passion has caused a tingling sensation in his toes, recalls her rubbing of Jerry/Daphne's feet in the train berth, so that the earlier scene is just a warmup for her erotic ministrations to her millionaire.

Sugar is fragile and poignant — afraid of catching Daphne's cold and lamenting that she will never love again — but she is also robust and redemptive, a "New World" woman, as Sinyard and Turner say. Guided by her compelling candor and unpretentiousness, Joe sheds all his old roles and confesses his true sex by kissing her on the bandstand even though he is still dressed as Josephine. It is the perfect way of exposing and accepting his contradictions and of saving Sugar just when she thinks her bogus millionaire has departed to marry a rich woman. Her song, "I'm Through with Love," as many critics have noted, shows Monroe at her best. She puts heartbreak in the lyrics and sings on the verge of emotional collapse, a collapse that the actress — in weak physical and emotional health throughout the shooting of the film — undoubtedly felt for both herself and Sugar, who is the last of the four main characters to reach the small boat that will take them to Osgood's yacht. Osgood has been married twelve or thirteen times — he's not sure and his mother keeps count — so he has been even more disappointed by women than Sugar has been by saxophone players in six male bands. When Osgood refuses to be dismayed by Jerry's sudden revelation that he is a man and contentedly offers the closing line of the film, "Nobody's perfect," he might as well be speaking for everyone in the boat — especially Sugar, who accepts her lover, faults and all.

It is amusingly appropriate that Osgood, the character with the big-

Figure 17. Tony Curtis and Marilyn Monroe in *Some Like It Hot*, 1959 From the UA release *Some Like It Hot* ® 1959 Ashton Productions, Inc. (*Courtesy The Museum of Modern Art/Film Stills Archive*)

gest mouth, should have the last word. He speaks for a generosity of temperament that is immensely tolerant of a farcical world. His words arise naturally out of *Some Like It Hot*'s good humor, in which no one is truly demeaned—least of all Monroe—though everyone is shown to have his or her limitations. No one can perform as Monroe's superior for very long in this film, and without her it is hard to see how it could have had nearly as much drive. There is, for example, her full certainty that she is inspiriting when she reacts to Junior's description of the impact of her kiss. "It's like smoking without inhaling," he says regretfully. "So inhale!" she urges him as she infuses him with another kiss. The utter relaxation of her voice and the ease with which she commands him to let go of all inhibitions are inimitable. As Wilder said after Monroe's death, "a whole category of films has been lost with her gone." This is not to minimize the astute performances of the other actors, especially Jack Lemmon, whose versatility in voice and gesture are without parallel. But Monroe is the model for Jerry and Joe, she arouses the action, the steam has to point at her.

Shooting of *Some Like It Hot* ended on November 6, 1958, and Wilder held a dinner party to celebrate. Monroe was not invited. He had been cautious with the press during filming, but shortly afterwards he allowed his disgust with her to show. She had seldom worked a full day on the set, and because of her the production had gone several weeks past its scheduled end and had exceeded its budget by about half a million dollars. He took his revenge in a series of sarcastic statements. He was the only director who dared to cast her in two of his films. The Screen Directors Guild should honor him with a Purple Heart. His appetite was improving, and he no longer suffered from the back pain that plagued him throughout the filming. His insomnia had vanished, and he could now look at his wife "without wanting to hit her because she's a woman." He was "too old and too rich" to have to undergo the ordeal of directing Monroe again. Two years later there would be something like a public reconciliation between Wilder and Monroe, but immediately after finishing the film both of them were enraged, and Arthur Miller felt called upon not to mediate—as he had done with Olivier—but to support his wife in a series of vehement telegrams.

Miller noted the director had been informed by Monroe's physician that she could not work a full day because of a pregnancy that she learned about when starting the movie, and he implied that Wilder was to blame for her second miscarriage that began "twelve hours after the last shooting day" in November. She had begun the picture "with a throat infection so serious that a specialist forbade her to work at all until it was cured," but she continued her efforts on the film out of her sense of responsibility. Now that the picture was going to be such a success — in large part because of her performance — Wilder's attack was "contemptible," and he was "an unjust man and a cruel one."

Wilder sent a telegram replying that reports of Monroe's conduct "would have been twice as vicious" had he not spoken up, and while he was very sorry about her miscarriage, he totally rejected "the implication that overwork or inconsiderate treatment by me or anyone else associated with the production was in any way responsible for it. The fact is that the company pampered her, coddled her and acceded to all her whims." He insisted on her inconsiderateness and pointed out her inability to understand "anybody else's problems." The cast and crew, he asserted, would testify to her "overwhelming lack of popularity." And then in a covert reference to her heavy drinking from a thermos of vodka and orange juice on the set he closed out his telegram by suggesting that if "you had been . . . subjected to all the indignities I was, you would have thrown her out on her can, thermos bottle and all."

Miller followed up with one more telegram defending Monroe's admittedly shaky discipline. He suggested that Wilder was riled by her unwillingness to be obedient, and that gifted actors, as long as they were doing their best, ought to be allowed to take their own route to an extraordinary performance. Having defended Monroe as both his wife and a great artist Miller withdrew from the argument.

Wilder sent a final, facetious apology, offering to "acknowledge that good wife Marilyn is a unique personality and I am the Beast of Belsen but in the immortal words of Joe E. Brown quote nobody is perfect end quote." Wilder's humor barely masked an almost insane anger generated on the set of *Some Like It Hot*, an anger that Miller may have also experienced. According to Guiles, Wilder witnessed one of Miller's "killing glances" at Monroe and "wondered if perhaps Arthur didn't dislike Marilyn more than he did." The director's reference to the concentration camp, Belsen, recalls Curtis's comment about how kissing Monroe was like kissing Hitler. In response to an assistant director who knocked on her dressing room door to tell her that cast and crew were ready for her, Monroe screamed, "Fuck you," and went on reading from Tom Paine's *The Rights of Man*. Later Wilder made a joke out of this too, saying, "Maybe she doesn't consider that directors and assistant directors have rights. . . . Or maybe she doesn't consider us men."

Although Monroe's next film, *Let's Make Love*, had almost a calming impact upon her, it was an anomaly in what was otherwise a pattern of increasing anger that most likely had been suppressed or displaced in earlier stages of her career by periods of depression. She was always capable of making remarkably swift transitions from fury to joy — or to a variety of emotions between those extremes—but displays of anger in her last years multiply. On the advice of her psychiatrist, she called Wilder's home to reconcile their differences. Audrey, the director's wife, answered the call and said her husband was not at home. So Monroe, stammering slightly, decided to speak with her. The actress, evidently under tension, struggled to express her feelings. After only a few inconsequential words, she lost control over herself and began screaming, denouncing the director, in his wife's words, as "the worst son of a bitch who ever lived." Monroe wanted Audrey to "tell him he can just go and fuck himself, fuck himself, fuck himself. . . ." Then she paused, regained her composure, and wished Mrs. Wilder well. Years later, in a part that was edited out of her *Life* interview, Monroe called Wilder "paranoid on celluloid." She seemed to be joking, but it is difficult not to surmise that, like Wilder, she was half camouflaging her hatred. In 1968, he attempted to deflate her legend as a victim and martyr: "I am appalled by this Marilyn Monroe cult. . . . I have never met anyone as utterly mean as Marilyn Monroe."

The actress's wrath may have forced Miller to be uncharacteristically defensive with Wilder. He was accusatory in her accents, almost as though he were trying to maintain their bond by identifying with her sense of injury. Anything less than an expression of his total commitment to her she probably perceived as a rejection. Viewed in this light, he was also desperately combating her collapsing faith in herself; all she seemed to have left was her fight with others. Rosten recalls that in this period she was much taken with the hero of Joyce Cary's novel, *Mister Johnson*, who "represented to her the spirit of innocence killed by the 'bad guys.' Marilyn would say it was 'them' against 'us' everywhere. The story with its tragic ending left a deep impression upon her." It is at precisely this time that Monroe began to lose much of her hope in Miller. Rosten remembers that "their evenings with friends were often played out in a facade of marital harmony. Miller was more and more living with her in the third person, as it were, an observer."

In early November of 1958 the divide deepened between Monroe and Miller with the loss of her second baby in the third month of pregnancy. She had been elated to be pregnant again and had enjoyed performing well during the beach scenes on *Some Like It Hot* because the sunshine and fresh air would be "great for the baby." She took special precautions to avoid needless movement and tried to retire early every evening. When this little life was once again stilled in her, she felt deeply inadequate and lost her equilibrium. According to Lena Pepitone, Monroe transferred her disappointment to Miller and unreasonably accused him of somehow having cheated and deprived her of her "last chance." She felt all used up.

The marriage held together—in part because Miller hoped to save it with *The Misfits*, in part because Monroe could not easily relinquish a helpmate and lover thoroughly bound up in her career. He would yet have a hand in choosing her next leading man, Yves Montand, and in rewriting dialogue in *Let's Make Love*, which was a commitment to Fox she decided to fulfill before making *The Misfits*. Miller would have to fail her again before she could imagine life without him.

In the winter of 1958–59, Miller and Monroe stationed themselves in New York City, where Monroe continued to study with the Strasbergs and to make new friends, many of whom she first met in the Strasberg home, which served as a secure environment for actors and actresses keen on coping with the rigors of performing. As Estelle Parsons observes, Lee Strasberg "creates an atmosphere that forces you to open and draw the terrors out. This then creates a safety for you and you're comfortable with him. I've been terrified to work for Lee but afterward I felt like a great artist—highly exalted." There is no question that Monroe shared this faith in the way he could father talent, and so she communed with people in the same orbit of expectation.

A new friend she made at the Strasbergs was to become one of her dearest companions in her last years. Listening to Ralph Roberts speak reverently about her today—and catching the light in his eyes as he describes their first meeting—is to capture the affectionate exuberance he and other friends often absorbed from her presence. Even before he knew exactly who it was he was meeting at the Strasbergs, he was taken with her glow. If she had felt "used up" after the loss of her second baby, her recuperative powers were awesome, for Roberts's description of that first meeting makes her seem like the principle of life itself, so that (later in the summer of 1959) one can imagine her saying to Hans Lembourn: "You said one day that life subsists by its own inner contrasts. If that's true, I'm the most alive person in the world!"

There is very little reason to suppose that Roberts is exaggerating, since many other people, like Gloria Steinem, have similar recollections of Monroe. Ellen Burstyn speaks of a photograph of Monroe at the Actors Studio shot in available light in which she shines against the darker background of other faces, and Miller, in the December 22, 1958, issue of *Life* would pen a tribute to her no less idealized than Roberts's. Beyond her presence, what Roberts seems to remember most was her esthetic appreciation of life. They took many long walks together in Brooklyn, in which she took an observant delight. They would occasionally act a scene together, talk over what turned out to be a mutual admiration of Todd's *The Thinking Body* and discuss her curiosity about art. At one point, she even took a "Famous Artists Painting Course," Copyright 1953, a copy of which, bound in a large red book with her name stamped in gold on the cover is in Roberts's possession.

Roberts was an actor who was making most of his living as a masseur, and in that capacity he would prove especially important in alleviating the actress's tensions. In some ways, she found it easier to confide in him than in others because he was something of an alter ego. Roberts has a commanding physical presence, and yet he is quiet and gently spoken. He measures his words carefully and speaks slowly, sometimes hesitantly, as Monroe herself would often do. His sensitivity and vulnerability must have been particularly endearing to her and may have become increasingly apparent as the two actors worked on a scene from *Of Mice and Men.* Roberts played Lennie, a role perfectly suited to his robust frame and mild demeanor. Monroe played Curley's wife, a beauty especially proud of her hair and desperate to gather the attention of men in her deadly dull environment. For some time, Monroe and Roberts struggled with the sense of the scene, with the frustrated woman who wanted slow-witted but sensitive Lennie to understand her. Monroe kept feeling that they were not getting it right, that contact between the characters—and between actor and actress—was somehow never quite established. Suddenly it occurred to her that that was exactly how the scene should be played—or, as she put it to Roberts, "the fact that we aren't communicating is what it's all about." Monroe's earnest striving for insight makes up a large part of Roberts's poignant memories.

She never turned her powerful ability to be disappointed against him as she did against Miller, a fact Miller explains by calling Roberts one of those "neutralized persons" who never actually had to make a life together with her. Unlike Miller, Roberts never had to function as her hero. On the contrary, he was her coworker, and his services to her were therapeutic. Miller, however, was part of her plan of rehabilitation, a Lincolnesque figure helping to heal the deep divisions within herself. After *Some Like It Hot*, Miller was still prepared to play that role by directly using his power as a writer for her glorification.

Miller's writing about Monroe countered the public's perception of her as solely a symbol of sex; his language attempted to rescue her from becoming a cliche. He did not so much directly refute the popular conception of her as a passive, pretty package, as a mass-produced commodity of sensuality; instead, he emphasized images and metaphors that made her appear active, spontaneous, and creative. In the December 22, 1958, issue of *Life* he published a brief text to accompany Richard

Avedon's photographs of Monroe impersonating past movie stars, in which her ability to enter completely into the artistic aspects of her assignment is apparent. Instead of just looking like movie stars of times past

> Marilyn came onto the set . . . and a record player was started. Songs of the '20s burst forth. Marilyn aimed an experimental kick at a balloon on the floor. She said she was ready. Avedon yelled, "Go!" and she pursed her mouth around her cigaret [in a Clara Bow pose], kicked a balloon, shot the fan out forward—and she made a world. I suddenly saw her dancing on a table, a hundred Scott Fitzgeralds sitting all around her cheering, Pierce-Arrow cars waiting outside, a real orchestra on the stand, the Marines in Nicaragua. We all found ourselves laughing.
>
> Her miraculous sense of sheer play had been unloosed. Suddenly she was all angles, suddenly the wig had become her own hair and the costume her own dress.

In watching her work her metamorphoses from Theda Bara to Clara Bow to Jean Harlow, Miller was most taken by her ability to render different personalities—become alternative selves—and yet remain identifiable as Monroe. The creation of these doubles of herself was somewhat like the droll use of masking and mimicking employed in *Some Like It Hot*, except that here the actress was in control and could measure herself, one to one, against Avedon's still camera rather than having to contend with Wilder's motion picture. Later, *The Misfits* would nearly rip away her mask by coming very close to a literal presentation of the off camera Monroe who had no one to mimic but herself.

Miller continued to work on the draft of *The Misfits* through the early months of 1959, while Monroe hardly seemed heartened by her success in *Some Like It Hot*. The film became an almost instant popular and critical favorite, and she looked magnificent at the premiere on March 29. But in the lobby of the Loew's Capitol Theatre on Broadway she spoke with her childhood stammer and seemed to lose some control over her public persona. In May she was gratified to receive the David Di Donatello statuette from Italy and a crystal star from the French film industry for her performance in *The Prince and the Showgirl*. In June she underwent surgery meant to facilitate another pregnancy, but that summer was a considerable strain for her and Miller, and the last half of the year was spent with no great purpose in mind.

In the winter of 1959–60, as she approached the filming of *Let's Make Love*, Monroe roused herself in the company of her costar Yves Montand and his charming wife Simone Signoret, who was the perfect model of the serious actress Monroe wanted to become. Signoret had all of Amy Greene's polish and sophistication, and she was a professional comfortable with her work, sharing stories about it with Monroe without the slightest condescension. As Signoret puts it, they became friends and neighbors, occasionally cooking dinner together, having their hair done as they reveled in the hairdresser's anecdotes about working with Jean Harlow, and enjoying a harmonious home life. Signoret discovered that Monroe had no stories to tell about her film work but instead talked about Avedon's series of photographs for *Life* as one of the highlights of her career. Signoret and Montand were providing the kind of backstage culture Monroe had always missed, and she readily fit into the foursome assembled in adjoining bungalows in February of 1960 for the shooting of *Let's Make Love*.

Miller admired Signoret's and Montand's production of his play, *The Crucible*, and all four shared basically the same political views. Signoret respected Monroe's courage in standing beside Miller during his congressional testimony in spite of threats from her studio. Miller, with his deep sympathy for the underprivileged, and Monroe, with her acute memories of childhood poverty, easily identified with Montand's working class background and his struggle for both his principles and his profession. He first caught Monroe's attention in his highly successful one-man show on Broadway, where he exemplified an elegance she was still striving to attain.

Aspects of Montand, the man and the actor, paralleled characteristics in both Miller and Monroe. By the same token, he may have represented those qualities in her husband the actress still wanted to admire: an earthiness and intellectuality that epitomized her democratic values and emotions. A recent article on Montand's return to New York City for a one-man show describes his appeal in terms that apply equally well to Monroe: "throughout his whole life he has attracted working people and intellectuals alike."

As Sidney Skolsky, who spent several evenings with Signoret and Monroe, saw it, Miller got stuck in the humiliating process of rewriting a poor script according to the producer's deadlines: "while Miller's stature was shrinking, Yves Montand's was growing in Marilyn's eyes. And, ironically, Montand was drawing Marilyn closer to him by leaning on her for assistance with his English. That she could offer him help, and that he sought her assistance so openly and unaffectedly, was particularly gratifying and perhaps reminded her of the time when Miller had relied heavily on her.

An affair between Montand and Monroe began in earnest after a mid-March break in shooting caused by an actors' strike. Miller had decided to take advantage of the interval in the production by traveling to Ireland to consult with John Huston about the script for *The Misfits* and by visiting locations in Nevada that would be used for the film.

Shortly thereafter Signoret was called to Europe to fulfill a professional commitment. In early June, when filming of *Let's Make Love* was about half finished, Miller decided to travel East to be with his children, whom he had not seen in a long time. He could not have missed his wife's increasing reliance on Montand, and although his ostensible reasons for leaving her were good ones, it is difficult not to suppose that he was, in some sense, clearing out, making it easier for them to have each other if that was their wish. If Miller was not exactly abdicating his responsibility for keeping her intact, he seemed to be confessing his helplessness. Or was his departure an act of selflessness, a giving in to his recognition, expressed to Fred Guiles, that Montand made her happy?

This was not Monroe's interpretation. She believed her husband abandoned her, and she needed the passionate liaison with Montand to survive, especially since she had begun to criticize Paula Strasberg for paying "too much attention to her daughter, Susan." Dr. Greenson, who heard all of these complaints, found himself playing the role of "supportive acting coach." Although Monroe wanted "to go straight on the couch for a session of Freudian therapy," the psychiatrist decided upon a less intense inquiry into "the facts of her day-to-day life."

Greenson must have realized that Monroe was not prepared for treatment that forced her to examine her own motivations. She preferred to find fault in others, in her husband, whom she termed "'cold and unresponsive' to her problems, attracted to other women, and dominated by his mother." She attacked Miller with "venemous resentment," pointing out that he neglected his father and was not "nice" to his children. Greenson was not to believe Miller's side of things, Monroe cautioned, but when the psychiatrist did meet her husband, he saw him as a father figure "rapidly coming to the end of his rope." Greenson advised Miller to give his wife unconditional love; she could accept nothing less. Greenson believed Miller genuinely wanted to help Monroe but was not able to control an anger that expressed itself as a rejection of his wife. Ironically, Greenson himself would eventually come under similar strains as the actress demanded his undivided attention and sympathy. No single man, it seems, could satisfy her, since she was looking for an ideal father who could be all things to her.

In her few remaining years, Monroe would revel in a pattern of promiscuity that suggests lack of sexual fulfillment and a preference for a succession of men who might momentarily serve as ideal types, substitutes for the loving relationship she could not sustain with Miller. As parts of her past were revealed in sessions with Greenson, she came to dwell more and more on the image of herself as an orphan and a waif, and Greenson—perhaps more than he realized at the time—had to perform the exhausting role of healing father.

The affair with Montand was more fulfilling than the film they were making. From the first day's rushes she knew *Let's Make Love* was not going well, and she complained to Greenson that she did not like her part. The pedestrian script did nothing to test her talents or to enlarge her screen persona, for Amanda Dell is a shadow of Monroe's full self, a cloying cliche almost all sweetness and light. Like most of her films, *Let's Make Love* lags behind her off screen self. In *Some Like It Hot*, for example, Sugar was twenty-five while Monroe was thirty-two. In *Let's Make Love*, Amanda attends classes at night to get a high school diploma and to learn about what people are referring to; Monroe took extension courses at UCLA several years earlier. In the first stages of her career Monroe deliberately shaved a few years off her age, but by 1959, on a trip promoting *Some Like It Hot*, she emphasized her maturity—although the press still used her lines as jokes: "a charming pitchman, Marilyn tells Chicago reporters, 'I'm a big girl now—I'm 32.' As newsmen looked puzzled, she said she meant years old."

In *Let's Make Love*, there is a sentimentalization of Monroe's persona that is not tempered by the raucous humor and cynicism of *Some Like It Hot*. As Amanda Dell, Monroe has little to play against, and her voice flattens out. Her gestures and facial expressions—except in her songs—have very little range, and she comes remarkably close to seeming dull. Monroe's face never kindles with the sudden joy she shows in *Some Like It Hot* after Daphne claims the whisky flask. Sugar beams with the glee of a child who has been spared a spanking or of a kid who has found a pal who will stick up for her. Her face vibrates with happiness; the emotion suffuses her skin with highlights. In *Let's Make Love*, Amanda's face is pasty by comparison.

Monroe worked very hard at getting her routines in *Let's Make Love* right, and her professionalism is evident, but the musical sequences do not advance the action or deepen her character as they do in *Some Like It Hot*. Instead, there are weak echoes of her earlier production numbers. Thus "My Heart Belongs to Daddy" is comparable to "Diamonds Are A Girl's Best Friend." She uses the same finger motion to call men to her in both scenes, and there is the sexual wink, the hip swing, and allied manuevers that are meant to evoke the ambiance of a Marilyn Monroe film. She is all persona here, an impersonation of an impersonation revolving around itself—just as Monroe swings and circles around a small, dimly lit stage that closes her in. The sets, the acting, the direction—all are on a diminutive, redundant scale.

Montand's acting, unfortunately, is no help to her. As the billionaire, Jean-Marc Clement, pursuing Amanda Dell, loving her for her freshness and her ability to "forget herself," he is stiff and awkward. He is supposed to be, so that Amanda's motility will be especially striking. But Montand has none of the charming clumsiness that Cary Grant suavely insinuates into similar roles. It was Montand's first part in an American film. His poor English made him uncomfortable, and he may not have fully grasped the comic tradition out of which the screenplay developed.

Off the screen Monroe was usually docile in Montand's presence, and on screen she is rather easily mollified when she discovers that his character, Jean-Marc, has deceived her. True, it is part of Monroe's persona to behave generously, but there is some grit in Cherie, Elsie, and Sugar; they do not like to be pushed around. Amanda's resistance is exceedingly brief; she is the equal of her predecessors only in those scenes where she exhibits the poise of a mature woman dedicated to her craft. And if she is sometimes naive—dumb seems too harsh a word to use for a character with her keen sensibility—she is not foolish like Jean-Marc, Joe and Jerry, the Grand Duke, and Bo, all those men who blunder about in their masculine mania to have everything on their terms. "Money doesn't mean anything to me," Amanda avers in an accentuation of feelings Monroe also held. The male coarseness of a world of gain repels the female who is famous for all she has to give.

During the early stages of production, before she left for Europe, it was evident to Simone Signoret that Monroe did not like her job very much, and along with Montand she attempted to keep the actress in good cheer while Miller was away in Ireland with stories about their theatrical past. After one late night session of tale telling, in which Monroe gave Signoret the impression of "a kid who's delaying the moment for lights out," Monroe failed to show up at the studio the next day. At first, Montand and Signoret were simply concerned to get her back to work, then they and everyone at the studio became scared as Monroe refused to acknowledge efforts to contact her and acted as though she were dead to the world. With considerable irritation Montand slipped a note under her door denouncing her capriciousness in hopes of rousing her to work. After a full day and evening of her disappearance, Miller phoned from Dublin explaining that his wife had called him to confess that she was "ashamed" and did not know what to do. At Miller's instigation Signoret knocked on Monroe's door and suddenly she had in her arms "a weeping girl, who kept saying, 'I'm bad, I'm bad, I'm bad. I won't do it again, I promise!'" All was forgiven and it even became a joke with them: "She phoned Dublin so that Dublin would phone her next-door neighbors."

In retrospect, Signoret regards that "lost day" somberly, seeing in it an alarming resemblance to Monroe's actual death, an event that did not surprise Signoret when she first heard it announced. She wondered when Monroe "had started to be angry with herself in that silence, that false death." The actress seemed paralyzed, unable to make contact with the outside world, and feeling absolute despair about reuniting the broken ends of her life. As Fred Guiles remarks, her life seemed more and more like "a series of endings."

The threefold repetition of "I'm bad" and the promise not to "do it again" sound remarkably childlike, but, like all children, Monroe would "do it again," would feel she had disappointed others by not meeting her obligations, by not acting like an adult. Earlier, on the set of *The Prince and the Showgirl*, she had sent for her New York psychiatrist, Dr. Marianne Kris (an expert on child psychology), after learning of Miller's disillusionment with her. In this case, she was angry with herself and out of control on her "lost day," which was expressive of her lost life, or of a life late in arriving. She articulated her biography as a Freudian fate sealed in childhood. Freud stresses that "loss of love and failure leave behind them a permanent injury to self-regard in the form of a narcissistic scar, which . . . contributes more than anything to the 'sense of inferiority' which is so common in neurotics," who are unable to accept themselves. In May 1961, Dr. Greenson wrote of Monroe to one of his colleagues, expressing how appalled he was at the "emptiness of her life" and at her almost total lack of objectivity. Even when he saw signs of improvement, her "narcissistic way of life" troubled him, and he wondered how deep and lasting her recovery would be.

Monroe knew that somehow her anger had to be contained or she would surrender to the madness that had put her mother and grandmother in asylums. After completing *Let's Make Love* in June, she moved almost immediately in July to the set of *The Misfits*. Like a zombie, she was dragging all of this discontentment along with her; she was in despair about her ruined marriage, about her career, and maybe about the inconclusiveness of all her therapeutic efforts. It would take more than *The Misfits* — meant to be the film of her life — to revive her to even a semblance of wholeness.

12

The Film of Her Life
(July 1960–January 1961)

Gable said about me, "When she's there, she's there. She's there to work." . . . I now live in my work and in a few relationships with the few people I can really count on.

The Misfits originally had been scheduled for shooting in the fall of 1959, but Monroe's agreement with Fox to do *Let's Make Love* and Clark Gable's performance in *It Happened in Naples* put off planning for *The Misfits* until the spring of 1960. Then the actors' strike during the filming of *Let's Make Love* and other production delays meant that Monroe would not be available for another role until the middle of July. As a result, there was hardly a break in her work between the two films. With just a few hectic days in New York spent on costume fittings and test photography for *The Misfits*, she rushed to Reno, Nevada, where a cast and crew of over two hundred waited her appearance on the set of what had been intended as the masterwork of her career and the fulfillment of her life. Unfortunately, she and Miller had waited too long to consummate their joint vision. Their marriage was dying, and both of them were forced to engage in a furious struggle against each other to maintain their integrity as persons and professionals, an integrity that once seemed as indivisible as the marriage itself.

All the elements of the production—the original screenplay by a major American writer, the best director for it, John Huston, and the perfect casting—provoked Frank Taylor, the producer of *The Misfits*, to call it "the ultimate motion picture." "If anything happened to one of our players, I don't know what we'd do. Each of them, Marilyn, Clark, Monty Clift, Eli Wallach, Thelma Ritter, *is* the person they play," he insisted. The line between art and life was perilously thin. Everything about this independent, austere movie—characters, locations, stunts, and story—had to be as authentic as possible, deliberately antithetical to machine-made, studio-faked extravagances like *Let's Make Love*. On *The Misfits* there would be no closed set, as there had been on *The Prince and the Showgirl*. James Goode was permitted to write a diarylike version of the filming, Magnum was allowed to field a group of photographers on the set, numerous friends and acquaintances of the cast and crew visited, as did other celebrities and the press. It was as if the makers of *The Misfits* wanted an intimate contact not only with the Western environment they were depicting but with the larger world outside the movie set.

Wallach, Ritter, and Clift described the normal difficulties of film making they were trying to overcome: no rehearsal before the first day's shooting starts, the lack of ensemble playing between actors who do not know each other's work habits, the distractions of the lights and the crew requiring a concentration more intense than that used in preparing plays, and the minute adjustments the actor must effect to given the essence of a character. This constant commentary on movie making while they were making the movie represented a virtual catalogue of the disruptions and disarrangements of Monroe's replicated life.

Montgomery Clift, in particular, felt the self-reflexive quality that informed his as well as Monroe's role. In a naked admission of the lifelike nature of film (which sometimes attaches itself to the actor's vulnerable person in a way he cannot shake off), Clift commented: "Someone said, 'My God, it's exactly like you.' Now it's just a question of can I do it? It's a wonderful part, and if I don't do it justice I'll shoot myself." Miller denied having written the character specifically for Clift, but like Gable and Monroe, Clift would inhabit his role, making it look like a fusion of art and life.

Huston abetted the actors in achieving an organic bond between themselves and their characters by shooting *The Misfits* in chronological sequence, an unusual and most expensive way of filming that furthered the natural growth of their characters. Monroe had never had the opportunity to develop a role in continuity, except in *Don't Bother to Knock*, in which Roy Baker, the director, followed a rehearsal format resembling that used for a stage play. Huston was well known for his subtle, unobtrusive handling of actors, and ever grateful for his faith in her performance in *The Asphalt Jungle*, Monroe could be hopeful their collaboration would reveal new dimensions of her talent as it had ten years earlier.

At the same time, Monroe had grave doubts about the script and was angry about Roslyn's "wishy-washy" character. Lee Strasberg told Fred Guiles he could hear Monroe's accents in Roslyn; even some of Monroe's expressions found their way into Roslyn's dialogue. On the twentieth anniversary of Monroe's death Miller recalled on ABC TV's *Good Morning America* program the contradictions in Roslyn that resembled Monroe's. He was admitting that, in effect, he had put his wife under a microscope. Monroe may have suspected him of scrutinizing her like a specimen, a specimen struggling in his experimental script (eventually published as a cinema-novel) for more than two years. Now Roslyn became the final point at issue: her handling would determine how the marriage would end.

Like the nameless woman in Miller's short story, "Please Don't Kill Anything," and like the Marilyn Monroe of his *Life* tribute, Roslyn Taber in *The Misfits* declares her reverence for the permanence of things: "I can't stand to kill anything." "She claps her hands to her ears" in surprise and profound dismay over the impending capture of the mustangs, just as the woman in "Please Don't Kill Anything" "put her two hands up to her cheeks" in shock over the sudden capture of fish that are gathered into the fishermen's net. In *The Misfits*, we once again see the world as a woman sees it, but in this case Roslyn's modes of perception—and what they stand for metaphorically—are explored and to some extent modified by a complex drama of human relationships only hinted at in the *Life* tribute and briefly sketched in the short story.

In one sense, Roslyn's all-encompassing vision turns her into a vibrant nature symbol, and even into a tender metaphor for life itself. She moves in sensitive solidarity with plants, animals, and people; she offers herself as an exuberant and generous unifying principle of the kind Miller lightly touches on in *Life* when he praises the manifestations of Monroe's beauty and spirit in what might be called her natural, everyday self, "playing with the dog, redoing the cleaning woman's hair, emerging from the ocean after a swim, or bursting into the house full of news."

Roslyn is a "golden girl [who] comes bursting out of the closet." Gay tells her, "You just shine in my eyes." Guido remarks on how she lights up his house and how she has the "gift of life." As her cowboy companions get to know her, she virtually becomes their source of light, their point of reference, as when Gay tells her, "Honey, when you smile it's like the sun comin' up." The metaphors arising out of seemingly casual speech are meant to render the men's growing sense of discovery that Roslyn has, in Guido's words, "that big connection. You're really hooked in; whatever happens to anybody, it happens to you." Most of these metaphors shift from the concrete impressions the males have of her person to rather abstract, even mystical, yearnings. By achieving oneness with her, each would fill the emptiness he feels in his lack of relation to family, to society, to the world at large, where he is regarded as a misfit. Roslyn's gift is to minister to each man equally—even if the help she offers is only a simple heartfelt "hello" to Guido at a time when he feels most alienated from himself and others, to Perce a gentle mothering that allows him to probe his disaffections, and to Gay a resolute but pliable sense of her own femininity that persuades him to accept, in a manner similar to Sam's in "Please Don't Kill Anything," the other half of the world, the female side he has always dismissed from his world of permanence and self-containment.

These males ignore and sometimes even fight against Roslyn's adamant defense of life's sacredness. Their contrary urge is to make life a test, as in Perce's rodeo riding and the roping of the mustangs. But she enforces her will to free the captured misfit mustangs, a family (a stallion, four mares, and a colt) not unlike the misfit family of three men and one woman she joins together. She does so not by arguing her beliefs, but by fully responding to life in a manner that justifies the metaphors the males use to describe her. For example, when Perce rides his bull, Roslyn does not hear the crowd roaring and she is only partly involved in observing him hang on for his prize—for his life really. Her sense of the scene is more organic. She feels the "earth shake as the bull pounds out across the arena." She feels the thunder of its weight and the "resounding answers from deep below the ground." "She nearly goes blind" as her world shakes and seems to fall to pieces.

If Roslyn's eyes can seem "larger than life" in the breadth of their vision, and if she seems capable of joining "the sun and earth in staring at" Gay, there is a sense in which she exists not before but after the fall. In her own way, she is just as solitary as the other characters, and her organic grasp of life has not been allowed to develop. She tells Gay, who gardens for her in an Eden of their own making, "I never really saw anything grow before." She has never had possession of herself until, for a sudden moment, she feels his love and is no longer afraid: "it was like my life flew into my body. For the first time."

Roslyn searches for the meaning of life, which often eludes her. Many of her statements are questions and tentative probings of relationships. She has failed at marriage once, and she seems caught in some indeterminate, mystifying stage between childhood and adulthood (Miller suggests something like this about Monroe in *Life*) that provokes Guido to comment: "One minute she looks dumb and brand new. Like a kid. But maybe he [her first husband] caught her knockin' around, huh?"

The finest expression of Roslyn's quest for wholeness occurs when "she flies into a warm, longing solo dance among the weeds, and coming to a great tree she halts and then embraces it, pressing her face against its trunk," as Monroe had hugged a tree in Sam Shaw's photograph of her in Connecticut in 1956. Roslyn seeks to steady herself in the grip of nature and in the presence of its creatures, for she also "presses her face against" the dog who quivers during the mustang hunt just as she quivers when she first realizes that the horses will not only be captured but killed and used for dog food. The dog and the tree save her from solitary suffering. So does the dance toward the tree, her metaphor for life's permanence—as Miller himself had once been for Monroe, when she said meeting him was "like running into a tree."

Roslyn's moment of self-fulfillment, her embrace of the tree, is reminiscent of one of Monroe's own lyric fragments, "To the Weeping Willow":

> I stood beneath your limbs
> and you flowered and finally clung to me
> and when the wind struck with . . . the earth
> and sand—you clung to me

The tree in Monroe's poem is both symbol and fact, her friend Norman Rosten points out, for it had been "planted under her watchful eye at her country place." Similarly, Gay's garden is cultivated under Roslyn's appreciative gaze. Like Monroe's unfinished poem, *The Misfits* takes its tone from the fruition of human and natural relationships, with the female character acting as the erotic magnet drawing the world together.

There are Edenic moments in *The Misfits* when the characters try to make the desert bloom, when Roslyn goes "all out" and seems equal to enjoying life in its fullness, when Gay blesses her for making him feel as if he has "touched the whole world." But these innocent, metaphoric apprehensions of existence are tempered by Roslyn's worries, by her sense of being lost, and by her need for help because she does not know where she belongs. She seeks guidance from Gay but cannot reconcile herself to his gentle, paradoxical insistence—so like Sam's in "Please Don't Kill Anything" and probably like Miller's as well—that, "Honey, a kind man can kill."

The filming of Roslyn's unreconciled state was Monroe's most arduous assignment. On July 21, during the shooting of her character's first appearance, the temperature in the bedroom setting reached a hundred degrees, with Huston, his crew and their equipment crowded together with the actress. After Isabelle (Thelma Ritter) is seen calling Roslyn to hurry up, the camera concentrates on a mirror Roslyn uses both to make herself up and to memorize the lines she will say in applying for a divorce. Isabelle is rather like the strong-minded but extremely sensitive female coaches and confidantes Monroe relied on. Isabelle, like Natasha Lytess, Paula Strasberg, and Hedda Rosten, is a woman from an earlier generation helping her young charge compose herself. Already, Monroe had to have been acutely conscious that this film was limning her life in a new dimension—not simply by making her character late and by giving her trouble with lines, but by revealing the struggle of going through a rehearsal and replication of self. Roslyn, like Monroe, wants to articulate herself authentically: "I can't remember this. It's not the way it was," she says. She resists putting on a face and a dialogue in what might be called this "behind the scenes scene," which in Huston's capable direction gives the lie to earlier backstage and powder room scenes in *Gentlemen Prefer Blondes* and *How to Marry a Millionaire* where Lorelei and Pola are happily content with putting on the roles they play. Instead, Roslyn resents her scripted self, and is shown to be on the verge of a hysteria and an exhaustion akin to Cherie's frail fretfulness in *Bus Stop*. But Roslyn seems much older and more mature than Cherie and more disillusioned; for once there is less of a gap in age and temperament between Monroe and the character she plays. How much Monroe's own physical fatigue contributed to this scene is hard to gauge. When James Goode asked her whether she would discuss how much energy her acting took, she replied, "No, because I didn't start with any."

As with Cherie, Elsie, and Sugar, experience has taken its toll on Roslyn and she is wary, but Roslyn is alone in expressing her worry over the ambiguity of human relationships and her doubt that any genuine communication is possible. She *knows* she is a misfit and she reacts somberly to the atmosphere of Reno, the divorce capital, that is heavy with failure. In part, Roslyn's languid demeanor at the beginning of the film may be an indication of how the divorce has numbed her and made her temporarily incapable of the outgoing emotions and gestures usually associated with Monroe's screen personas, and this is also perhaps why some critics find Roslyn rather remote and amorphous. Only in the course of her awakening life is she able to pin down the troubling issues that have made her back away from full involvement in the experiences of others and in an understanding of herself.

Somehow Roslyn has escaped most of the cynicism and self-pity Guido (Eli Wallach) harbors in himself, and the mirror shot in her first scene reflects a rudimentary purity, complicated by disappointment, but expressive nevertheless of an innocence highlighted for the first time when she sees Gay's (Clark Gable's) dog, Tom Dooley. Her affection for animals animates her. Her eyes appear completely open for what seems like the first time in this transitional scene between her divorce and her new life with Guido, Gay, and eventually Perce (Montgomery Clift).

When Gay tells Roslyn she shines in his eyes, he is, to be sure, complimenting her, but he is also commenting, however inadvertently, on her reflective capacity and on his power to measure it, a power film points up by isolating the glint in his eye. In the film of *The Misfits*, it is inescapably apparent that Gable is courting Monroe, and his compliment, not Gay's, confers upon Monroe her status as cynosure of the screen. In the cinema-novel, on the other hand, Roslyn's consciousness controls such scenes as the one at the rodeo, where the very ground shakes in accord with her trembling concern for Perce.

In their first big closeup, when Gable leans over to kiss Monroe, and she responds by confessing she does not feel "that way" about him, Gable's easy assurance that in time she "just might" is inextricably tied to his movie persona, to the "King" of Hollywood who for so many years carried his roles with a bluff, hardy confidence. The aplomb with which he receives Monroe's mild rebuff seems tinged with sly humor over her demurrer before the most romantic masculine figure the movies have produced, the father-idol of his costar. Although Gable and Monroe looked to performances in *The Misfits* to prove their prowess as actors, not just personalities, and although neither of them does anything to disturb the consistency of their characters, Gay and Roslyn, the sensation of actors moving in tandem with their screen personalities is undeniable.

It had been Monroe's lifelong dream to play opposite Gable in the movies, but the prospect of performing with him also put great pressure on her to be perfect, a pressure he unfailingly and gallantly tried to relieve by taking every opportunity to encourage her—in one instance kissing her after an especially well done scene. John Huston says that in private Gable was nonplussed by her unprofessional behavior, but in public he was always deferential to her and extremely protective, as if he were willing to impersonate the father-lover she saw in him for the sake of her emotional health and of the tender scenes in *The Misfits* that mirrored the core of her desire to be his consort. As Thelma Ritter pointed out, "this picture is a little unlike any I've done before, because it depends on the personalities and the relationships of the actors. . . . We stage actors don't get this kind of jazz. They'd say, 'What's she playing?' There's more emphasis on the stage on roles, not personalities." Actors in *The Misfits* could not simply escape into their roles and become their characters; in fact, the film depended on the clash and coordination of personalities and not just on "playing" as stage actors would have it.

From the middle of July to nearly the end of August, Monroe and her three male leads struggled with the cumbersome first half of the

Figure 18. Marilyn Monroe and Thelma Ritter in *The Misfits*, 1961
From the UA release *The Misfits* ® 1961 Seven Arts Productions, Inc.
(Courtesy The Museum of Modern Art/Film Stills Archive)

script that required Gable, Wallach, and Clift to vie for the honor of charming her. Each man had to have his chance to dance with her, to woo her, and she had to receive them openly without encouraging their advances, to probe their reasons for their lovelessness, and to nurse their sensitivities. At the same time, she was in their care as they showed her how they lived in accord with the West's freedom of space, its frontier mentality. Although the careful approach to personalities provided fine shadings of character, to Monroe *The Misfits* may have seemed curiously irresolute and Roslyn too elastic, given the enormous demands upon her compassion and her loyalty to each man. Huston and Miller constantly conferred on changes in the script and sometimes debated wording and camera work. In spite of all the considerable advance planning, the shooting in continuity, the fine cast and crew, the picture lost coherence, and each day was devoted to tinkering with the disordered pieces.

Monroe was reaching the center of the film where Roslyn, Guido, and Gay accompany Perce to the rodeo in exchange for his agreement to join them in the mustang hunt. Monroe had to play Roslyn's hysterical fears for Perce's life, followed by a very demanding five-minute scene — the longest take Huston had ever filmed — with Clift just after his injury at the rodeo. All the different aspects of Roslyn's appeal would be necessary to soothe Perce's wounded body and spirit.

Increasing her intake of Nembutals in the evening, Monroe relied ever more heavily on Ralph Roberts's morning massages and on the ministrations of others who tried to walk her into wakefulness and prop her up with coffee. At night in Miller's presence she would sometimes get hysterical, and he would try to calm her with innocuous conversation, but in the middle of the night she would often lose control and rage at him. Close to a breakdown himself he was persuaded by Nan Taylor, the producer's wife, to take a separate room. A prolonged fit of anxiety kept Monroe away from the set on August 27 and led to her complete breakdown, officially announced on August 29, when she was flown for medical care to Los Angeles. The whole production shut down, and shooting did not resume until her reappearance on the set September 6.

At Westside Hospital in Los Angeles Monroe was gradually given milder medication in place of Nembutal. She was visited by Miller, Huston, the Strasbergs, and numerous other friends, including Joe DiMaggio, who began to emerge as one of her dearest supporters. Nearly ten days after her collapse, she visited him briefly before returning to Reno to finish *The Misfits*. To Huston, in the hospital, she seemed to have made great progress. He was encouraged because she was bright and alert and feeling ashamed of her behavior on the picture. He could see that she was aware that drugs were destroying her, and she asked his forgiveness. He remembers reassuring her.

In spite of some setbacks, her acting was stronger upon her return, and she had more control over herself. Just before her breakdown she had to do retakes of the rodeo scenes, since her reactions to Perce's dangerous stunts were exaggerated in what was perhaps a sign of her impending neurasthenic collapse. There was a new calm in her treatment of Miller—on one occasion they even went on a walk together, and on another Miller danced with her to demonstrate the kind of action he had in mind for one scene. They were not intimate—not even for the sake of public appearances—but the contest between them abated and would not revive until the final tense days of filming.

Monroe resumed work on the five-minute scene with Clift. In speaking to Clift as Perce she was perfectly in tune with herself as Roslyn. Like Roslyn, who complains that her husband was not "there," Perce regrets that his mother, after her remarriage, could not "hear" him. He puts his head in Roslyn's lap to ease the aches of mind and body. She responds to his garrulity, prompted by his drinking and dancing, by trying to quiet him and to smooth over all the rough edges he has acquired in proving himself. Just as Gable as Gay acts as her father-lover, so Monroe as Roslyn acts as mother-lover to Clift as Perce, as W. J. Weatherby sensed when he noticed Monroe behaving "like a concerned mother hen" while the reporter spoke with Clift.

Frank Taylor called Monroe and Clift "psychic twins," and Weatherby observed that Clift "was sensitive to any vibes from or around Monroe." They shared their insecurities, their drinking and drug problems, and treated each other very affectionately from their first shy meeting some time after the completion of *Bus Stop*. As one of Clift's biographers, Robert La Guardia, puts it, "Marilyn could bitch and laugh and feel as uninhibited as she wanted around him." Clift responded in kind, first as himself, then as Perce revealing to Roslyn fundamental misgivings about himself: "I . . . I don't understand how you're supposed to do." On the set of *The Misfits*, Clift spoke to James Goode of the actor's need to "uncallous" himself; the long scene with Monroe accomplishes just that, for it portrays an exquisite exfoliation of Perce's hardened self—the one who does not mind the bruising rodeo stunts and who accepts the harsh world of male rivalries. This supreme blending of the actor with his art is what Monroe was always seeking and what she and Clift manage between them in a setting suggestive of their characters' fragmentary careers: "they emerge behind the saloon. Trash, a mound of empty liquor bottles and beer cans, broken cartons, are littered about. . . ." In the moonlight—the cameraman Russell Metty was actually shooting day for night—Roslyn and Perce articulate the miscel-laneousness of their betrayed lives. "Maybe all there really is is what happens next, just the next thing and you're not supposed to remember anybody's promises," Roslyn speculates.

It is impossible to say how many times Monroe and Clift obliterated the thin margin between their on and off screen selves while working on their five-minute scene. That more than usual was at stake is clear from the closed set, from Gable's keen interest in being present—he was not even on call to act that day—and from the rehearsal time used before filming. At first, both Clift and Monroe had trouble with their dialogue; then after several takes they finished the scene without missing any lines. Monroe complimented Clift on his performance, was herself reas-sured by Miller, and checked with Paula Strasberg just as Huston decided the scene should be repeated. Two more takes were spoiled— one by Monroe (who thought she had shifted Clift's bandage out of place) and one by Clift who had trouble with a line. Goode reports that she "clutched him to her in compassion for his mistake." In the next take, she missed a word. Near the end of the day tension mounted as two more takes were ruined before the final, perfect scene was shot. Compared to the multiple takes of much shorter scenes, this long, beau-tifully modulated exchange between Clift and Monroe was performed with extreme economy and grace.

Clift might have been thinking of this outstanding scene when he commented after Monroe's death that "working with her was fantastic . . . like an escalator. You would meet her on one level and then she would rise higher and you would rise to that point, and then you both would go higher." She evidently responded to Clift's sincerity as an actor with an ingenuousness of her own rarely apparent to other actors—even to those like Jack Lemmon who admired her but who noted her "tendency to act at instead of with you." Clift would not have con-curred with Lemmon's conclusion: "you just got so far with her, and then you could feel a curtain drop—and you didn't go beyond that. I suspect nobody in the world really understood Marilyn."

The second half of *The Misfits* profited immensely from Monroe's recovery and resilience; both the shooting of the film and the pacing of its scenes quickened from the moment when Roslyn feels the dog shiv-ering and begins to inquire into the purpose of the mustang hunt. Like Monroe herself, who at this time became, in Guiles's words, "alive to her surroundings," Roslyn explores her environment with renewed intensity. As her questions become more pointed, the cowboys must confront their own complicity in decimating their dreams of a frontier past, in which mustangs were used to settle a wild country and not to feed dogs, the tamed animals of a modern consumer culture.

Roslyn appears helpless not only to stop the hunt but also to mount an effective objection to it, since, as Gay reminds her, she eats steaks and gives Tom Dooley dog food made of mustang meat. She appears naive and without the courage to accept her own compromises with killing. The momentum of the film is against her, for the men are taking all the risks, and beside them, she seems merely hysterical and belittled in the immense Western landscape. Conceding Gay's victory over the mustangs—"you won," she tells him—she tries to restrain him, but he sweeps her to the ground with his arm. Finally, she breaks out of the frame that Gay, Guido, and Perce have established in the chase sequence by recentering herself at a considerable distance from them. As Nick Barbaro observes: "she is at a totally different depth from the men in the foreground on either side":

> They see Roslyn walking. She is heading across the open lake bed.
> "Roslyn." Gay takes a step, and halts himself.
> She has swerved about. Her shadow sketches toward them. Forty yards away, she screams, her body writhing, bending over as though to catapult her hatred.
> "You liars! All of you." Clenching her fists, she screams toward their faces: "*Liars!*"
> Unnerved, Gay flinches.
> "Man! Big man! You're only living when you can watch something die! Kill everything, that's all you want! Why don't you just kill yourselves and be happy?"
> She runs toward them, but stops as though afraid, and says directly toward Gay: "You. With your God's country. Freedom!" She screams into his face: "*I hate you!*"
> Unable to bear it, Gay mutters: "We've had it now, Roslyn."
> "You sure did—more than you'll ever know. But you didn't want it. Nobody does. I pity you all." Looking from one to another and beyond them to imagined others: "You know everything except what it feels like to be alive. You're three dear, sweet dead men."

Roslyn is almost out of control and voices her bitterest feelings, severing her connection with the cowboys even as her shadow, their conscience, approaches them. In the space she has created between them she performs what almost amounts to an exorcism, an exhaustion of her hostility. At the same time, she is attacking "man" as well as these men who serve a rapacious society. The urge to destroy, she implies, is ultimately suicidal. She turns Gay's remarks about having "had it" into an elliptical comment on their former harmony, and implicates herself, as well, in the tragic insight that "nobody" knows how to have it all, to experience the togetherness she and Gay have lost. In spite of her rage, there is still compassion in her condemnation of "three dear, sweet dead men," with whom reconciliation is still possible.

As Huston films it, the scene is deliberately awkward, since there is a sudden shift, a break in the action betokening a set piece, an unwieldy supplanting of the exciting chase sequence with Roslyn at the frame's center. Her speech ought to be redundant after so many speeches in this exceptionally talkative movie. Yet her words work because they are fitted to a frame *she* is seen to form, however clumsily, and because, unlike all her previous dialogue, these words come up from the pit of suppressed resentment she barely manages to articulate. Her bent-over posture suggests a being who is divided in two by male and female contentiousness, by love and hate of society, and by life and death themselves. In projecting her profound sense of alienation to Gay, to his male companions, to men in general, and to the whole of existence, Roslyn is both triumphant and defeated. She is the ultimate cinematic embodiment of Monroe's double bind.

Huston and Miller were uncertain about how to prepare for the final scenes between Roslyn and her male companions. Gable had not liked the original ending of the screenplay, in which Roslyn feels compassion for Gay who lies on the lake bed defeated by the stallion. Huston, on the other hand, was concerned about clearing up what he perceived as a vagueness in Guido's character, and Frank Taylor wondered whether the screenwriter and the director still had the energy to create the proper ending. The final scene had gone through at least three revisions since March of 1960, and as of the first week of October there were rumors of still more changes — with one version of the ending that "awarded" Roslyn to Perce. When Monroe finally had the opportunity to read the scene that made Guido Roslyn's exlover, she became hysterical, for it threw the whole picture "out of key," she told Paula Strasberg. Gable, who had the contractual authority to reject script alterations, agreed, and Monroe's supporters felt vindicated. Later, Miller conceded that Gable's judgment was sounder than his own.

In the end, Miller was satisfied that he had achieved the appropriate close to *The Misfits*, and Gable concurred. Gay conquers the stallion Perce has cut loose in deference to Roslyn's feelings, but then Gay frees the stallion himself and makes his peace with Roslyn. Gable felt his character was not broken, but he had acknowledged the necessity of finding "another way of life." Miller thought Gay and Roslyn had compromised and recognized reality. Gay would have to come to terms with "a settled existence, and face the struggle between a personal code and social cooperation." Roslyn would have to accept the fact that "the violence in all of us . . . can exist side by side with love." This couple would not live happily ever after, but a certain balance had been achieved in their relationship with each other.

There is no reason to suppose that Monroe viewed the film in such harmonious terms. She never cited it as an example of having reached a dramatic crossroads in the way that she tentatively regarded *Some Like It Hot* as a significant achievement in comedy. Before the filming she quarreled with Miller about his screenplay; after shooting it, she complained about Huston's tampering with the writer's words.

Many viewers of *The Misfits* come away from it feeling the ending has somehow been tacked on, that the troubling ambiguities of Roslyn's relationship with Gay, with the other male characters, and with the world at large have been evaded, even sentimentalized. The ending is also a beginning, however, since Roslyn and Gay have reached a fuller consciousness that precludes seeing them in absolute, unchanging terms. "We see them only in frontal shots and only inside the truck," Nick Barbaro points out. The effect is to emphasize "moving on, trying to find their way home," not "riding off into the sunset to live happily ever after." No doubt this was Miller's and Huston's intention, but Gable's utter calm and sureness of self, and the romantic aura of twilight that bathes him and Monroe mitigate the sobriety of Miller's outlook and Huston's shot selection. Barbaro successfully shows that the ending is not just an affected appendage, but he discounts too heavily the way these movie stars radiate in their roles, thus making the final frames of *The Misfits* verge on cinema cliché.

In late October, when *The Misfits* was nearly completed, Monroe told Miller to get out, which he proceeded to do with the help of Monroe's secretary May Reis, Frank Taylor, and his aide, Edward Parone. In early November Monroe became hysterical and incoherent when a reporter called her with news of Gable's death. Reis, Rupert Allan, Patricia Newcomb, and frequently Joe DiMaggio helped her through the shaky weeks of November. Newcomb had been recommended to Monroe by Allan, who was not able to accompany his distraught friend to New York City. Newcomb supervised the Monroe household, screening calls and generally insulating the actress after her announcement of her separation from Miller.

Late December and early January was a period when she felt compelled to sort out her allegiances; she was making up a new will, thinking of her family ties with her half-sister, Berneice Miracle in Florida, whom she did not know well but with whom she nevertheless felt "family-like." May Reis, now much more than an appointments secretary, was also remembered in the will. Reis had become a trusted advisor of exceptional tact and discretion, and to this day she keeps her relationship with Monroe to herself. Monroe felt some ambivalence about Paula Strasberg, probably because Paula, like Natasha Lytess, had become too visible in aggressively championing her charge and some-what stifling for a younger woman who was used to suspecting those who came to her aid too readily. Monroe had been generous with Paula, supplying not only a good salary but several gifts, so it was Lee—even closer to the nurture of the actress's talent but circumspectly distant from the actual conditions of her employment on movie sets—who was to receive a part of her estate and personal belongings.

The everyday business of living defeated Monroe as she attempted to put her leave taking of it in order. She was back on heavy doses of Nembutal, even pricking the capsules with a pin for faster effect, as Rupert Allan observed; she made no secret of her pill habit or of her craving for oblivion. Pat Newcomb noticed her employer's fascination with "the murky depths of New York harbor" one day and moved "close enough to reach out in case of emergency." Lena Pepitone portrays an ambivalent, sometimes suicidal Monroe, who considered leaping from her New York apartment window and had to be revived from a drug overdose during the Christmas holidays. She spent listless days with a motivation so low that she rarely visited the Strasberg apartment, the source of so much of her inspiration.

On January 20, 1961, in the company of her attorney Aaron Frosch, and Pat Newcomb, Monroe flew to Juarez, Mexico, to obtain her divorce from Miller, a sad public acknowledgment of her dashed hopes on the very day the country was inaugurating a new leader. The date had been selected by Newcomb and John Springer—who had been handling Monroe's publicity on the East Coast since early 1959—in hopes that President Kennedy would get all the headlines.

If Monroe was to survive, she had to find new areas of interest. Miller had opened up the life of politics for her, and she became attuned to all the talk about the new direction signaled by the presidential election year. During the making of *The Misfits*, as cast and crew followed the presidential debates on television, Monroe told W. J. Weatherby that she wanted to see Kennedy win because of Nixon's association "with that whole [Red-baiting] scene." She may have met Kennedy as early as 1951 in the company of Charles Feldman, one of her agents with close connections to the Kennedy family. But her admiration and affection for Kennedy grew as Adlai Stevenson's supporters failed to secure his nomination at the Democratic convention. She watched the inaugural during a two-hour layover in Dallas on her way to Mexico. She was already responding to the Kennedy charisma, to the novelty of a national political figure with the glamour of a movie star. A few weeks before his inauguration, she told a friend about her "date with the next President of the United States." Many people were expecting to participate in an unusual administration, in a New Frontier, that had all the sensational-ism usually attributed to Hollywood. Just as she had missed her moment of rebirth in *The Misfits* and dropped precipitously into the worst depression of her life, Monroe was storing up energy for one more ascension by reaching out, as she had through Miller, to the society outside herself, to the future that Kennedy represented.

13

The Lady of Shalott
(December 1960–August 1962)

And moving thro' a mirror clear
That hangs before her all the year,
Shadows of the world appear.

In a series of intermittent discussions with W. J. Weatherby in New York from late 1960 to some time in January 1961, Monroe latched onto his phrase, a "pattern of selves," to argue against the idea of a single self persisting through an entire lifetime and in favor of "fragmentary, changing natures." In his presence, her moods changed quickly. Her contradictoriness and fatiguing awareness of deeply divided feelings were driving her toward collapse and hospitalization. Weatherby sensed she was struggling for control of herself.

One time, in the bar they used for their talks, Monroe appeared tentative, nervous, and "rather distant," and sloppily dressed. As she had with Margaret Parton, who interviewed her in mid-March of 1961, Monroe skirted her past, refusing to discuss her childhood rape story. On the other hand, she revealed her mirror obsession: "I sit in front of the mirror for hours looking for signs of age." She was attracted to old people, to the sense of completion age may bring: "I want to grow old without face-lifts. They take the life out of a face, the character. I want to have the courage to be loyal to the face I've made." In the next breath, however, she conceded that sometimes "it would be easier to avoid old age." She claimed control over the depiction of her person: "When the photographers come, it's like looking into a mirror. They think they arrange me to suit themselves, but I use them to put over myself." But how much character did she have, she wondered, when she was killing the truth by killing photographs harmful to her public image? Was she in charge of her body or simply infatuated with it? She was not sure. Compared to the beauty of a stage career, her attractiveness on screen seemed ephemeral: "You can go on forever in the theater. The distance, the footlights, the makeup—it all helps create whatever illusion you wish."

In their last few meetings, Weatherby detected a new strain in her behavior, perhaps in anxious anticipation of the mixed reception *The Misfits* would indeed receive in early February. At his mention of a Steinbeck character who commits suicide, "she seemed to draw back in her seat," and asked why the character did it, admitting she had tried it once and was "kinda disappointed it didn't work." She looked depressed and worried she did not have "what it takes" to carry out her plans. She was afraid to be alone. She showed up at their final meeting with unwashed hair and "a faint body odor." All "worked up," she aggressively maintained a "person's privilege" to commit suicide. "I don't believe it's a sin or a crime . . . although it doesn't get you any-where," she said in reaction to Hemingway's killing of himself. She found it hard to trust people, to see that she had made any progress in her life. She speculated on a "weak-minded quality" inherited from her mother and appeared confused, embarrassed and tired—almost totally enveloped in self-doubt and doped up with sleeping pills.

The winter of 1961 was a bleak season for Marilyn Monroe. The lilt was gone from her blurred and weakened voice. She was more depressed than Norman Rosten had ever known her to be. Often she was heavily sedated or in a state of high nervous tension. She saw few friends and put herself, it seemed, at considerable remove from the world. By early February, she was on the verge of total collapse and agreed with her psychiatrist, Dr. Marianne Kris, that hospitalization was necessary.

Dr. Kris accompanied her patient to the Payne-Whitney clinic in New York without explaining its nature as a mental institution. Monroe supposed it would be like other hospitals to which she had retired for secluded rest. Much later, Dr. Kris admitted to Ralph Roberts it had been a terrible mistake sending her patient to Payne-Whitney, for Monroe immediately panicked. A nurse present at Monroe's admission to the hospital ward recalled for Richard Meryman how Monroe froze when she heard "the grim snap of a lock closing behind her." She "stood there endlessly repeating, 'Open that door! Just open that door! I won't make any trouble, just let me out! Please! Open that door!'" A letter she hurriedly wrote to the Strasbergs emphasized her desperate circum-stances:

You haven't heard from me because I'm locked up with all these poor nutty people. I'm *sure* to end up a nut if I stay in this nightmare—please help me Lee, this is the *last* place I should be—maybe if you called Dr. Kris and assured her of my sensitivity and that I must get back to class so I'll be better prepared for "rain" [the Somerset Maugham play planned for television production with Strasberg as director]. . . .
P.S. forgive the spelling—and theres nothing to write on here. Im on the dangerous floor its like a cell. Can you imagine—cement blocks. They put me in here because they *lied* to me about calling my doctor and Joe [DiMaggio] and they had the bathroom door locked so I broke the glass and outside of that I haven't done anything [to?] be unco[o]perative!"

With her family's history of mental illness, it is not surprising that Monroe was frightened and resistant. According to Rosten, she became exasperated with a very young doctor who kept asking her why she was so unhappy. In anger she struck back: "I've been paying the best doctors a fortune to find out why, and you're asking *me*?" To Alan Levy she denied rumors of disrobing and playing "other scenes of high drama in the hospital." She laughed and said she wished she had done so just to have gotten something out of her system. She was proud of having told them to have their heads examined. To another friend she admitted she was going out of her mind and that she even tore her gown off. She later told Patricia Newcomb that "if they were going to treat her like a nut, she would behave like one."

In three days, she was out of Payne-Whitney, thanks to the help of Joe DiMaggio, and was moved to Columbia Presbyterian Hospital, where she spent nearly three weeks withdrawing from her pill habit. She recuperated at home in New York, followed up on her plans to do *Rain* on television, and granted an interview to Margaret Parton, who wrote an admiring, sensitive profile rejected by the *Ladies Home Journal* because its editors believed the journalist had been "mesmerized" by her subject. It was typical of Monroe to come out of her deepest depressions and hysterical episodes full of vigor and intelligence, and just as typical for her self-renewal to be greeted with extreme skepticism.

When NBC refused to accept Lee Strasberg as her director, Monroe canceled plans for *Rain* and accepted DiMaggio's invitation in late March to join him in Florida. The change of scene refreshed her, and she was able to see again her half-sister Berneice Miracle. Naturally, the press was curious about the possible resumption of a DiMaggio-Monroe romance, but they insisted on calling themselves just friends. As with Miller, she needed to draw on DiMaggio's strength—or, as Norman Rosten would have it, "she gravitated toward power. This type of [stern] figure gives you security and absolution." At the same time, she probably tired of DiMaggio rather quickly; his interest in outdoor sports like surf fishing could not command her attention for long, and she returned to New York to resume her career.

March and April were not easy months for Monroe. On March 9 she was photographed in a black mink leaving the funeral of Arthur Miller's mother, with whom she had remained close after the divorce. This was a death in the family for her, as she indicated by taking a seat with the Millers at the services. After returning from Florida she was shattered by a press report that Clark Gable's wife, Kay, said, "*The Misfits* helped to kill him. But it wasn't the physical exertion that did it. It was the waiting, waiting, waiting." According to Skolsky, Monroe took Kay Gable's remark as an indirect reference to her tardiness on the set. Rupert Allan, who was in especially close contact with Monroe during this period, says Kay Gable told him she never made the critical statement and that she remained a friend of Monroe's after her husband's death, and even invited the actress to the christening of Clark Gable's son. But in any case, Gable's death afflicted the actress with great guilt, both Weatherby and Skolsky report. The latter recalls her asking, "Was I punishing my father? Getting even for all the years he kept me waiting?" She was feeling suicidal, and friends persuaded her to close up her New York apartment temporarily. In the late spring of 1961, she flew to Hollywood to rest and to diet in preparation for a gall bladder operation scheduled for late June in New York City. In California, under the supervision of Dr. Hyman Engelberg, her internist, and Dr. Greenson, who now took over complete responsibility for her psychiatric care, she began in mid-July the agonizing process of putting her life back together.

From the spring to the autumn of 1961, Monroe made little progress. Greenson had earlier noted "symptoms of paranoia and 'depressive reaction.' " Now he observed "signs of schizophrenia." In May, he wrote to a colleague that Monroe was still trying to "escape into the drugs or get involved with very destructive people, who will engage in some sort of sado-masochistic relationship with her." He was apparently referring to Frank Sinatra and his Las Vegas friends whose parties she frequented. Greenson was aware that he was speaking like a disapproving father, for he referred to the actress as "an adolescent girl who needs guidance, friendliness, and firmness." Although Monroe emphasized how important therapy was for her, it did not, in Greenson's words, "prevent her from canceling several hours to go to Palm Springs with Mr. F. S. She is unfaithful to me as one is to a parent."

Monroe became frightened, almost terrorized, by her father's attempt to communicate with her, feeling that it was "too late" to hear from him; she then hardened herself against his second effort to reach her. In these six months, she began to see signs of aging. The scar on the right side of her stomach from the gall bladder operation "seemed to shatter her whole view of herself," Pepitone claims. Monroe decided her breasts were getting flabby; she noticed stretch marks on her backside and lines—the beginnings of crow's feet—on her face, and, somewhat later, brown spots on her hands.

From Marjorie Stengel, employed as Monroe's secretary during this period, Mailer draws a picture of his subject's aimlessness. She was uncommunicative and in disarray, rising late, wandering about her New York apartment in a "slightly soiled" nightie, and spending a long time on the phone with Dr. Greenson. Her apartment was nondescript, except for the mirror on the ceiling—her "major touch," Mailer calls it. In the living room "all [was] white": walls, rug, piano, couch, transparent leaves in a vase—even a Cecil Beaton photograph had her in a white gown. This is the white dream home described in *My Story*, the one Gladys promised but could not deliver to her daughter. Except for Joe DiMaggio, friends did not visit.

Across the continent, in November of 1961, Eunice Murray saw Monroe in another apartment, emerging from her six-month ordeal. Dr. Greenson helped her withdraw from barbiturates, and his patient now seemed ready for more independence after months of "round-the-clock" nursing care. Murray, who was to serve the actress—with Greenson's encouragement—in several capacities without ever acquiring a specific title, was immediately fascinated by a radiant Monroe, without makeup and in every way different from the drab described by Stengel. Only the bedroom with "huge floor-to-ceiling mirrors" linked her Los Angeles and New York lives.

In the last year of her life, Monroe traveled between New York and Hollywood without surcease, as if her identity were indeed bilocated. Evidence can be compiled to demonstrate that now she meant New York, now Hollywood, to be her home. She was of two worlds, and most of her friends in one realm had little knowledge of her friends in the other, for she usually liked to segregate her intimates. Norman Rosten, for example, thought it was strange for her to introduce him to Frank Sinatra. Robert Slatzer, who continued to see Monroe since meeting her in the mid 1940s, was unknown to even close friends like Rupert Allan. Recently, Anthony Summers has shown just how complicated Monroe made her life by swinging between circles of friends in show business, politics, and perhaps (through Sinatra) the Mafia. Consequently, radically different impressions of her personality and plans, of her commitments to the East and West coasts—and to the stage and the screen—were common among her friends and acquaintances who are perhaps not fully aware of how much she tended to play the chameleon.

Monroe attempted to pattern her life after her psychiatrist's suggestions. "By late 1961, for Dr. Greenson, Marilyn was both patient and ever present family friend," Summers notes. She "took great offense at the slightest irritation on his part," for, in his own words, he had become one of those "ideal figures in her life" from whom she expected perfection. By February of 1962 she found a house—similar in style to his own—and was trying out his idea of a stable, rooted existence.

With Murray's help, the actress began slowly to furnish and remodel her home. A trip to Mexico, where she purchased furniture and other items for her household, concentrated her mind wonderfully. Murray remembers that her employer was particularly interested in meeting politicians and actually preferred that to invitations to meet members of the artistic community. Fred Field, an American expatriate living in Mexico, saw a great deal of Monroe (she had come with an introduction to him from mutual friends in Connecticut) and remembers her vehement support of civil rights for blacks and of the government in China, and her anger at all forms of Red-baiting. J. Edgar Hoover was singled out as an object of hatred. Judging by her conversations with Weatherby and Robert Slatzer, by her comments on politics in portions of the *Life* interview that were not printed, and by the new material (including parts of an FBI file) Anthony Summers has discovered on Monroe's connections with the Kennedys, it is now clear how deeply and intensely she had intertwined her personal sense of well-being with her absorbing interest in public affairs. The Kennedys, in particular, would set things right; they would finally bring about a more just world of equal opportunity for the abused and for abandoned minorities, among whom Monroe counted herself. She was naive in the extreme, but as Greenson observed, she could not seem to survive without these heroic examples in her life.

In the spring of 1962, the Rostens, visiting Monroe in Los Angeles, were invited to the Greenson home, where Norman immediately sensed her "complete relaxation." With his patient's consent, Dr. Greenson described in general terms his treatment of her. He told Rosten that she was "some years" away from becoming an "analytic patient," even though she needed "psychotherapy, both supportive and analytical." He encouraged her familiarity with his family in order to supply the attachments she had been lacking "from childhood onward."

As Greenson explained to Maurice Zolotow in 1973, he was taking a "desperate measure—because previous forms of therapy had failed." It seems likely that Monroe was suffering from what Greenson called, in a paper published in 1958, "a defective formation of the self image, an identity disorder" that explained why she was "not ready" for psychoanalysis. He may have regarded her as one of his "screen patients," although he does not identify her by name in any of his writings.

A screen patient is anxious about how well he or she communicates. Like such patients, Monroe seemed warm and giving, ready to recite her life history, "despite anxiety or shame." She had been successful, yet she belittled her accomplishments. In spite of her talent, her productivity had been "sporadic and unreliable." Like other screen patients, she was unduly concerned about her popularity and her ability to entertain, prone to severe mood swings and exhibitionism, yet chronically optimistic about her career. Enthusiastic and sentimental, impressionable, suggestible—even gullible—she tended to exaggerate to the point of lying, almost like a swindler, although she was "sensitive, perceptive, and empathic." In fact, as with Greenson's other screen patients, she was "psychologically minded" and could spontaneously come upon important insights but had "great difficulty in integrating these new insights effectively."

Monroe evidently followed a pattern that Greenson detected in his other screen patients. She developed "a strong, positive transference." This technical term, on which Greenson published a great deal, describes the process by which the patient becomes irrevocably committed to the analyst and sometimes "morbidly dependent" on him. In its first stages, transference can be remarkably helpful because, as in Monroe's case, the patient is eager to rebuild her life along the lines the analyst suggests. Unfortunately, in its later stages transference can thwart the resolution of neurotic conflicts because patients identify totally with the analyst and lash out at others, displaying, in Greenson's words, "a markedly different set of character traits at work and at home, with their family or with strangers." Monroe would demonstrate this kind of bifurcation of behavior when she began work, in the late spring of 1962, on *Something's Got to Give*.

Like other screen patients she was not able to assimilate or clearly comprehend her past: "almost all the important people of their past lives are remembered as essentially black or white figures." This "rather disturbed relationship to time" promotes a blurring of past and present, with the past remaining so alive in patients' minds that they project "a youthful quality and their self picture is many years younger than their chronological age." In movies, Monroe was screened in precisely this way; that is, she was literally screened or blocked off from her true age, from a character who should have been maturing. Just like other screen patients, Monroe's characters had to be presented anew. Off the screen as well, each phase of her life was conceived as a beginning, not a continuation of what was already in place. Screen patients, Greenson points out, have to feel fresh and have the ability to "awaken new hopes." But since such personalities cannot be old, and cannot be *seen* to carry a past with them, they are essentially suspended in a nowhere land, like Sugar Kane, whose behavior can be compared to the "imperative, urgent, and repetitive quality" Greenson identifies in screen patients.

Screen patients feel favored, like "the lucky ones," and exhibit "feelings of omnipotence and expansiveness. This occurs in moments of triumph or in rage." At other times, as in Monroe's "lost day" with the Montands, their megalomania may manifest itself as "monumental self-punishment with which no one may interfere." The reason for such drastic psychic alternations, Greenson submits, is that "these people confuse the *wish* to be favorites with the feeling that they *are* the favorite," or "well liked" as Monroe or Willie Loman imagined themselves to be. Frequently such people change their names, undergo plastic surgery, and, in general, hold themselves together by manufacturing self-gratifying visions of their appearance as substitutions for deprivations in childhood associated with "their mothers as unreliable givers." To feel intact, they must be looked at as though they were on stage. At home, where nobody could see her, the actress "might not be able to put herself together very well," Greenson wrote to a colleague. Monroe, he pointed out, thrived on the public perception of her as a beautiful woman, "perhaps the most beautiful woman in the world." Of screen patients, he concludes: "Whereas the ordinary patient comes to analysis because he does not like who he is, these patients come to analysis to find out who they really are." Such phrases echo Monroe's confessions of self-doubt, from *My Story* to her last recorded interview for *Life*.

By the time *Something's Got to Give* went into full production on April 23, 1962, the actress was facing a lifetime of failed enthusiasms. Although both Dr. Greenson and Mrs. Murray (acting now as the actress's housekeeper) believed she was making significant progress, she was feeling profoundly ambivalent about going back to work, for she had not been able to cope very well with her buried paranoia, feelings of persecution, frustration, and rage. It is not as if she avoided dealing with her traumatic memories; rather, such memories, Greenson says of other screen patients, "may serve a screening function for a more severe trauma" the patient is somehow powerless to get at.

Monroe did take certain measures that might relieve her anxieties about her role. Before the shooting date she consulted Nunnally Johnson who was writing the script, a remake of a 1940 comedy, *My Favorite Wife*. Her first words to him, "Have you been trapped into this too?," were a fair indication of her distrust of the studio and of her wariness toward any project it might propose. She was fulfilling her commitment to Fox negotiated during Milton Greene's tenure as her business partner, and it is unlikely she felt inspired by her role. Dr. Engelberg was treating her for a viral infection she may have picked up in Mexico. Her energy level was low, but it rose immediately, stimulated by Johnson's assurance that he had chosen to write the screenplay rather than accept other projects offered to him. When she realized he was not talking to her merely out of a sense of obligation, she became enthusiastic about the film, exploring questions of casting and plot development. He was so taken with her sharp perceptions that he regretted every harsh word he ever said against her and became her unabashed admirer.

Monroe's main worry then became the director, George Cukor, who told Johnson how much he "loathed" Monroe. When Cukor began to revise the script, his actions were tantamount to challenging her hard-won convictions, for this was a script she could *believe* in. The revisions were an attack upon herself, especially since, according to Johnson, Cukor had similarly sabotaged her performance in *Let's Make Love*. The studio did nothing to allay her doubts about the script changes.

Walter Bernstein, the last of six writers to work on *Something's Got to Give*, portrays the studio as catering to Monroe's every whim. She complained that the script had her chasing a man when just the reverse should be true of a Marilyn Monroe movie. Bernstein, who was plainly disgusted with her, does not see that after Johnson's departure she regarded *all* changes as assaults on her personal integrity. Consequently, she took every opportunity to make her image immaculate. Once her artistic vision of the film was violated, she reacted like a politician or a general, making sure her power remained intact: "Sometimes she would refer to herself in the third person, like Caesar. 'Remember you've got Marilyn Monroe,'" she said to Bernstein when she wanted to wear a bikini in one scene. "'You've got to use her,'" she instructed the screenwriter.

Such comments reveal how difficult it was for the actress to jettison her screen personality. If Fox would not use it properly, she would find other ways to get the attention she deserved. On Friday, May 18, she traveled to New York to sing Happy Birthday to President Kennedy Saturday evening. She promised to return to work Monday. She considered her appearance in Madison Square Garden a "Command Performance," Guiles states. That it caused her considerable anxiety is apparent in the taped but not the published transcript of her *Life* interview.

In a paper published in 1974, Dr. Greenson—identifying Monroe only as "an emotionally immature young woman patient, who had developed a very dependent transference to me"—mentions her "major concern about the period of my absence [to attend an International Congress in Europe] was a public appearance of great importance to her professionally." She felt the event ratified her existence and defined her both as a star and as just one of "the people"—as she put it in the *Life* interview. By singing to "the people," she was singing to herself, to her fantasy of watching herself at center stage from way above "under one of those rafters, close to the ceiling." Marilyn Monroe, she was implying, was everyone's dream of democratic success. On tape, she can be heard, again and again, marveling that the sound of her voice did get out. It is as if the child in her feared some stifling of the sexy Happy Birthday song she had practiced for months—sometimes in the presence of Ralph Roberts and others—and planned for in elaborate fittings of a skin-tight dress with "hundreds of strategically placed brilliants [that] shimmered and glittered so brightly that the body beneath was clothed in reflected light."

This last description by Mrs. Murray, who helped the actress with her wardrobe, is reminiscent of the studio's description of the outfit for *There's No Business Like Show Business*. Once again, Monroe was marketing herself as an item of sexual provocation and indulging in the child-like exhibitionism typical of screen patients.

The scene of her singing to JFK is often reproduced in documentaries side-by-side with excerpts from her movies, for the scene was directed to play for the screen. After Peter Lawford's joking introduction of the "late" Marilyn Monroe and her delayed entrance, she glides forward with small steps, adjusting her fur wrap as she approaches Lawford. With one arm she covers her shoulders with the stole and smiles at him, bringing the fur closer to her neck as she greets him. She flicks a finger at the microphone, then grabs it with her hands, raises her arms and hands to make a visor in front of the bright lights, surveys the whole audience, and smiles again. Languidly and suggestively she begins to sing—thus calling forth Kennedy's subsequent joke about retiring from politics now that Miss Monroe had sung happy birthday to him in such a wholesome way. She starts a second chorus of the song by shifting out of her seductive pose, vigorously waving her arms like a conductor and jumping up and down on the stage like the President's most enthusiastic cheerleader.

Politics and show business, on this night, were more closely allied than ever before in American life. After all, the "birthday salute"—as it was called in an advertisement extolling the "most exciting program ever staged!"—included a "Spectacular Array of the World's Greatest Talent." The actress craved this kind of singling out, and her association with the Kennedys completed an ambitious profile of herself initiated by her marriage to DiMaggio and confirmed by her marriage to Miller. She was the screen actress as politician, finding her positions in the public's eye, and allying herself with an administration that prided itself on its high production values.

As with Greenson's other screen patients, Monroe's life had to have a high gloss, and the Kennedys with their Hollywood connections fit comfortably into her endless efforts to polish her image. John Kennedy reveled in Hollywood gossip, and his brother Robert was deeply interested in movie personalities like Monroe and Judy Garland. Their father Joseph had once been active in Hollywood film production, and their sister, Pat, was married to Peter Lawford. The Lawfords, who lived nearby, became close friends of Monroe's, and the actress would see the Kennedys on several social occasions. They enjoyed her wit and seemed bothered very little by the gossip that linked her sexually with both John and Robert. And while Monroe felt complimented by being invited into their company, she was also drawn to Robert's interest in issues of civil rights and political freedom.

The Kennedys were important to the actress because they represented a stage on which to perform that was so much greater than what her current film offered. Returning from her Madison Square Garden performance on May 21, she seemed submerged in what had become the miasma of movie making: "she acted in a kind of slow motion that was hypnotic. Cukor thought now that she would not finish the picture. There was talk of replacing her," Bernstein remembers. Her single sign of vitality was the impromptu nude swimming scene, as if she viewed disrobing for the cameras as a way of stripping the picture of its hackneyed plot and of recapturing the original sheen of her early calendar work.

Visiting her in late May, Rosten found her edgy and irritable. When they made a visit to Greenson's home, the actress was abrupt and even belligerent with the psychiatrist, goading him to interpret a Rodin statue of two lovers she had just purchased. Her voice was shrill and strident, and she repeatedly asked the analyst to tell her what the statue meant. Was the man "screwing" the woman or was it a "fake?" Her interpretation seemed to reflect her own ambivalent feelings: "Look at them both. How beautiful. He's hurting her, but he wants to love her, too." Her words echo Greenson's correspondence with a colleague, in which he dwelled upon "her inability to cope with any sort of hurt" as one of the "decisive factors that led to her death."

Did the statue reflect a gap in herself, what Alexander Lowen calls "a break in the personality, which fixates the individual at a certain pattern of behavior he cannot change?" What cannot get changed, gets repeated, and Monroe's actions recall Freud's use of the term "repetition compulsion" to describe the personality's return "to the situation where it got stuck, in the hopes of someday getting unstuck." It is clear that Monroe was losing patience and approaching the despair of many patients who cannot help themselves and do not see therapy as providing the relief it initially promised.

By June 1, Greenson had left for Europe and Rosten had returned home to Brooklyn. The psychiatrist was perilously close to admitting feeling defeated by her demands upon him. When she "threatened to fall back wholly on drugs, his sessions with her would last four or five hours," Summers reports. Greenson confessed to having become "a prisoner of a form of treatment that I thought was correct for her, but almost impossible for me." In a later letter he confided to a friend that "at times I felt I couldn't go on with this."

Sick again, Monroe missed several shooting days on *Something's Got to Give*. Bernstein suggests she was not the studio's idea of a star: "sprightly and sexy and full of fun. Cukor saw all the film on her. He emerged shaken." By the middle of June, the studio fired her, and she spent her next days first crying, then in a stupor, and finally angrily defiant. Scenes from *Something's Got to Give* in the 1963 documentary, *Marilyn*, reveal a strikingly beautiful, ethereal actress, who sparkles with the maturity of an older woman, although too little is shown of her to be able to test Cukor's claim that "she was so intelligent that she knew she was not good. But, somehow, you couldn't reach her, she was like underwater."

In her last two months, Monroe was facing "the dark tunnel of her career," her good friend Rupert Allan recalls. She was very aware of her age, of the need to make the transition to roles reflecting her maturing appearance and talent. She worked again at Actors Studio – this time on a one-act play, an adaptation of a short story by Colette. Once again her sensitivity impressed the Strasbergs and others, and hopes were high for her stage career until an unsettling mood sent her back to Dr. Greenson in California. In his view, she had come to identify with him as her "white knight," her "protector," her "talisman" serving to avert "bad luck or evil." In his absence, he says, she experienced the "terror" of a "child who has lost her security blanket."

In a final conversation with Weatherby, perhaps sometime in late June, she seemed to be making plans to stay in California, more or less permanently. When he asked her about the Actors Studio, she shrugged for an answer. Her psychiatrist apparently advised her to concentrate on "fun" movies for the time being, and she teased the reporter about her affair with a famous married politician even as she enthused about

President Kennedy as "another Lincoln," about whom she would brook no criticism. She should stick to the movie audience of millions, her politician friend advised her. Negotiations began with Fox for her to complete *Something's Got to Give* in September.

From late June to early August, the actress was under terrific stress, seeing Dr. Greenson almost every day and calling Ralph Roberts, sometimes in the middle of the night, for massages to relieve tensions that had her saying, "I'm about to jump out of my skin." At the same time, George Barris's photographs of her—especially the shots of her on the beach—suggest a sturdy personality. In conversation with Richard Meryman and during photographic sessions with Bert Stern, she let more of herself loose, offering not just a reprise of her career but articulating herself more precisely and creatively than ever before. If her persona demanded repetitions of her successful poses, so that she often operated perilously close to cliche, it is remarkable how much energy remained for one more go at originality.

Monroe's moods were mercurial, Stern recalls. His photographs almost seem to chart the rise and fall of her temperature, of the fever to create. Through Pat Newcomb she requested that he have on hand three bottles of her favorite champagne, Dom Perignon, for the modeling assignment arranged by *Vogue*. He bought a whole case, and in the first session June 23 he kept shooting for twelve hours, which perhaps accounts, in part, for the tired, even drunken look in some of her poses. In one series, she seems narcotized in a playful happiness verging on melancholy. She puckers her lips, bites on a strand of beads, partly covers her mouth with her fingers, puts her hands around her head and neck while her eyelids droop. All of this framing of herself is done as though she were half-conscious—on the edge of either an awakening or a very deep sleep.

Monroe projects an identity that wavers between extreme states even as she is in complete touch with her body. As Greenson put it in one of his letters, "the main mechanism she used to bring some feeling of stability and significance to her life was the attractiveness of her body." She had lost considerable weight, and her breasts are not nearly so prominent as in her early 1950s heyday. It is as if a new decade has shifted concern to other aspects of her body, other areas of the self. There is a thinness in the shoulders, arms, face, and torso that tone down the lushness exhibited in earlier poses. A la Milton Greene, wisps of her mussed hair trail down her forehead, glance past her right eye, and make the left eye seem larger and clearer. Stern stimulated her liking for psychologically intriguing poses. She is wiry, taut, and sharp, but at the same time gauzy, available in outline only as she covers her body with the fabrics Stern supplied.

In some of the photographs she smiles broadly, allowing her upper gums—and her facial wrinkles—to show. The actress plays with a string of beads, clutching part of it to her breast with her left hand, while holding out another part of it with her extended right arm. This pose suggests an alternation between her introverted and extroverted impulses, played here for humor with a more honest edge on it than in "Diamonds Are a Girl's Best Friend." Far more riveting and disturbing is the shot of Monroe with her fingers seemingly penetrating her forehead in great anguish, the tongue askew in her mouth, she seems about to let go or about to summon great concentration.

As each new pose worked itself out—there was very little talking— "we would go a step higher," Stern says, echoing Montgomery Clift. One photograph resembles Monroe's bent-over screaming scene in *The Misfits*: she drops her scarf for "one glimpse, one stolen frame," out of a series of frames masking various parts of her body. In the fugitive frame she looks convulsive and extremely vulnerable, a slight figure—naked, not nude, with her traumas slipping out of her in a setting no longer squared off by the scarf; there is only the tensed fabric of Monroe's own person.

Just as Bert Stern was impressed at how thoroughly the actress prepared for her "last sitting," Richard Meryman marveled at her professionalism in her last interview. She asked to see his questions in advance, thought about them for days, and refused to essay any answer she had not pondered. He noted the excellent taste of the furnishings and art work in her new house, and he responded enthusiastically to her keen intelligence. He saw her in many different guises: a sweet little girl, a low-key hysteric—frightened and not convinced of her abilities— and a perceptive critic of her own work and that of others. Most important of all, however, was her skill at presenting an ideal Monroe. She turned her best side to him, he was sure, going about the interview in a mature, systematic manner. She was pleased with the edited tape, which she saw in print two days before her death. Her words with Meryman are the closest she came to a final testament. He ended the interview feeling somewhat troubled about her seclusion, in which her home functioned as a bulwark. She chose it for its privacy—it was at the end of a cul-de-sac—and sometimes she gave the impression of retreating behind its high walls.

Like the last months of her life, Monroe's last days are filled with contradictory evidence about her physical and mental health. Meryman, for example, recalls that "she looked terrific," but when examined closely her skin was "pasty and lifeless-looking," and her hair "had no body to it, like hair that has been primped and heated and blown a thousand times." Her face "was kind of cardboardy." She was not sleeping well and she was under constant psychiatric care. Her final hours, from some time around 7:30 P.M. to about 3:30 A.M. August 5, when her lifeless body was discovered, are open to endless speculation, even though the Los Angeles District Attorney's office has recently examined the original autopsy report and found no reason to doubt the original finding of "probable suicide" as the result of a drug overdose. Pills that for the longest time failed to supply her with enough sleep now disoriented her. In the past, she had built up a great tolerance for massive doses, but recently she had been able to get along with fewer sedatives. Perhaps she misjudged how much her body could absorb on an empty stomach. She was not drinking, and her death was nothing so simple as an accidental overdose. It was, rather, part of a pattern of self-abuse and self-absorption that she could not overcome.

At her most fragmented moments she inhabited, like the lady of Shalott, an intensely private domain, full of a personal mythology, impenetrable to the outsider, even to her psychiatrist perhaps—if one is to judge by her poem that prefaces Rosten's reminiscence of her. It is about a rootless child with a doll in a carriage that goes "over the cracks" (that break a mother's back?) traveling far away from home. The child in the poem comforts her doll ("Don't cry / I hold you and rock you to sleep"). But the poem ends with a plea for "help" as the child feels "life coming closer / When all I want is to die"). The child and the adult vie for attention as the actress attempts to become her own mother, to give herself the feeling of a mother, the mother she never had, the mother who died, more than once, inside of her.

As in the lives of many suicides, a terrible isolation encloses her every move, an isolation that is broken by attempts to escape from past failures by assuming glorious roles and dwelling on the grand possibilities of the future. There is a feverish desperation in her plans, a fluctuation between physical vanity and self-abuse, and an "outlandish mixture of the profound and the trivial" that, in Leslie Farber's view, is a common characteristic of the suicide. Robert Slatzer's memoir of Monroe, which presents a paranoid actress concerned over the tapping of her phone, resentful toward the Kennedys when they apparently cut off communication with her, but still hopeful that somehow she could take center stage in their affairs, now seems less far fetched because of Anthony Summers's interviews with several Kennedy friends and associates. One does not have to believe in murder conspiracies, or even in the coverup of information about Monroe's last hours, to see that at the slightest provocation this woman with a fragile psyche would begin to feel abused by the Kennedys and fear for her safety as soon as she began to doubt their probity.

Monroe's heavy use of drugs to relieve anxiety made her less and less capable of resuming her search for a sound identity and a substantial role. As late as May 1962 she had sought out Timothy Leary, who gave her a very small dose of LSD. They took a drive and walked by the sea. He remembers it as a "joyous" experience. She appeared contradictory to him, shrewd and "wobbly." On an earlier occasion, she offered him what she called "Randy-Mandys," the "street name for Mandrax, a sedative popular among drug users in the early sixties because it gives a sense of euphoria when combined with alcohol," Summers reports. These temporary stimulants debilitated her, and she could not find the natural dynamic of her life. It became impossible to cope with the frustrations of her career without the lift or the tranquillity provided by her pills. The will becomes paralyzed and the whole personality is susceptible to exhaustion, derangement, and depleting illnesses.

Yet the power of Marilyn Monroe's life, of her myth, remains because her death still left her poised between alternatives, between the telephone and her pills, between her ragged endings and beginnings. There were disturbing contrary impulses, like an obsessive fear of homosexuality in herself, that led to an uncontrollable fury she could not quell even with the help of Dr. Greenson. Surely she was angry with herself and concerned that she could not sustain a loving relationship with a man; she felt less than a whole woman and may have wondered if she was capable of fulfillment with a member of the opposite sex.

Some found the actress too fey, like the fairy Lady of Shalott laboring under a curse, weaving a magic web around herself that was certain to be unraveled by reality. George Cukor called her death "a nasty business . . . her worst rejection. Power and money. In the end she was too innocent." He was apparently referring to the rumors, already rampant, about her affairs with both John and Robert Kennedy. Dr. Greenson, who publicly denied that his patient was involved with either Kennedy, nevertheless told a member of the suicide team investigating her death that on her last evening she sounded "drugged and depressed" because her meeting with one of the "very important people" she had been seeing was canceled. He also noted that she had found it gratifying to have a "a close relationship with extremely important men in government." The relationship was "sexual," and "the men concerned were '"at the highest level.'" Dr. Robert Litman, the suicide team member to whom Greenson gave his report, says that it was clear Greenson was referring to the Kennedys, although they were not named—perhaps, as another suicide team member suggests, because "discretion entered into it." Greenson had been concerned about her romantic involvement but did not feel he could oppose it so long as it supplied such a badly needed sense of her own importance. On her last night she was feeling a letdown. The most beautiful woman in the world, she told her psychiatrist, did not have a date. She was feeling "rejected by some of the people she had been close to," Greenson concluded.

Sooner or later Monroe's mind, like a crystal mirror, would crack. Constance Collier, who briefly served as Monroe's acting teacher, was fascinated by her pupil's "flickering intelligence. . . . It's so fragile and subtle, it can only be caught by the camera." Collier and Greta Garbo agreed Monroe would make an "exquisite Ophelia," perhaps because, like Henri Cartier-Bresson, they viewed her as an "apparition in a fairy tale" with "something extremely alert and vivid in her, an intelligence . . . something very tenuous . . . that disappears quickly, that appears again." "What really counts in film acting is that rare moment—just a flickering," said John Huston, "when through the eyes you get a glimpse of the real meaning of the character. It is not technique or professionalism, just truth. Garbo had it. Monroe had it." Some, like Arthur Miller, believe that with "a little luck" she might have survived, for she had a worldly side and a tenacity, a faith that made her say "you're always as good as your potential," a certainty that never deserted her until that last moment.

In tape recordings of the Richard Meryman *Life* interview, the actress's voice is strong, full-bodied, and active, ringing with laughter. One person can be heard in the laughter, energizing her listeners as well as herself. The woman with this robust laugh was never seen on the screen, this woman momentarily at one with her mature self. The laughter sounds like it comes from the core of her being, the core for which she searched. The laughter justifies her claim that on screen and off she had more to express than her roles permitted. If she went to pieces at the last, she still seems to be calling, entreating her audience to "find me, find me, / complete this form."

Richard Meryman Interview, *Life*, August 3, 1962

"Fame May Go By . . ."

An Interview

Richard Meryman

Sometimes wearing a scarf and a polo coat and no make-up and with a certain attitude of walking, I go shopping—or just looking at people living. But then you know, there will be a few teen-agers who are kind of sharp and they'll say, "Hey, just a minute—you know who I think that is?" And then they'll start tailing me. And I don't mind. I realize some people want to see if you're real. The teen-agers, the little kids, their faces light up—they say "gee" and they can't wait to tell their friends. And old people come up and say, "Wait till I tell my wife." You've changed their whole day.

In the morning the garbage men that go by 57th Street when I come out the door say, "Marilyn, hi! How do you feel this morning?" To me it's an honor, and I love them for it. The workingmen—I'll go by and they'll whistle. At first they whistle because they think, oh, it's a girl, she's got blond hair and she's not out of shape, and then they say, "Gosh, it's Marilyn Monroe!" And that has its—you know, those are the times it's nice, people knowing who you are and all of that, and feeling that you've meant something to them.

I don't know quite why, but somehow I feel they know that I mean what I do—both when I'm acting on the screen or when if I see them in person and greet them—that I really always do mean hello and how are you? In their fantasies they feel—Gee, it can happen to me!

But when you're famous you kind of run into human nature in a raw kind of way. It stirs up envy, fame does. People you run into feel that, well, who is she—who does she think she is, Marilyn Monroe? They feel fame gives them some kind of privilege to walk up to you and say anything to you, you know, of any kind of nature—and it won't hurt your feelings—like it's happening to your clothing. One time here I am looking for a home to buy and I stopped at this place. A man came out and was very pleasant, very cheerful, and said, "Oh, just a moment, I want my wife to meet you." Well, she came out and said, "Will you please get off the premises?"

You're always running into people's unconscious. Let's take some actors—or directors. Usually they don't say it to me, they say it to the newspapers because that's a bigger play. You know, if they're only insulting me to my face that doesn't make a big enough play because all I have to do is say, "See you around, like never." But if it's the newspapers, it's coast to coast and on around the world. I don't understand why people aren't a little more generous with each other. I don't like to say this, but I'm afraid there is a lot of envy in this business. The only thing I can do is I stop and think, "I'm all right but I'm not so sure about *them!*"

For instance, you've read there was some actor that once said about me that kissing me was like kissing Hitler. Well, I think that's *his* problem. If I have to do intimate love scenes with somebody who really has these kinds of feelings toward me, then my fantasy can come into play. In other words, out with him, in with my fantasy. He was never there.

But one thing about fame is the bigger the people are or the simpler the people are, the more they are not awed by you! They don't feel they have to be offensive, they don't feel they have to insult you. You can meet Carl Sandburg and he is so pleased to meet you. He wants to know about you and you want to know about him. Not in any way has he ever let me down. Or else you can meet working people who want to know what is it like. You try to explain to them. I don't like to disillusion them and tell them it's sometimes nearly impossible. They kind of look toward you for something that's away from their everyday life. I guess you call that entertainment, a world to escape into, a fantasy.

Sometimes it makes you a little bit sad because you'd like to meet somebody kind of on face value. It's nice to be included in people's fantasies but you also like to be accepted for your own sake.

I don't look at myself as a commodity, but I'm sure a lot of people have. Including, well, one corporation in particular which shall be nameless. If I'm sounding picked on or something, I think I am. I'll think I have a few wonderful friends and all of a sudden, ooooh, here it comes. They do a lot of things—they talk about you to the press, to their friends, tell stories, and you know, it's disappointing. These are the ones you aren't interested in seeing every day of your life.

Of course, it *does* depend on the people, but sometimes I'm invited places to kind of brighten up a dinner table—like a musician who'll play the piano after dinner, and I know you're not really invited for yourself. You're just an ornament.

When I was 5—I think that's when I started wanting to be an actress—I loved to play. I didn't like the world around me because it was kind of grim—but I loved to play house and it was like you could make your own boundaries. It goes beyond house—you could make your own situations and you could pretend and even if the other kids were a little slow on the imagining part you could say, "Hey, what about if you were such and such and I were such and such—wouldn't that be fun?" And they'd say, "Oh, yes," and then I'd say, "Well, that will be a horse and this will be—" it was play, playfulness. When I heard that this was acting, I said that's what I want to be—you can play. But then you grow up and find out about playing, that they make playing very difficult for you.

Some of my foster families used to send me to the movies to get me out of the house and there I'd sit all day and way into the night—up in front, there with the screen so big, a little kid all alone, and I loved it. I loved anything that moved up there and I didn't miss anything that happened—and there was no popcorn either.

When I was 11 the whole world which was always closed to me—I just felt like I was on the outside of the world—suddenly, everything opened up. Even the girls paid a little attention to me just because they thought, "Hmmm, she's to be dealt with!" And I had this long walk to school—2½ miles to school, 2½ miles back—it was just sheer pleasure. Every fellow honked his horn—you know, workers driving to work, waving, you know, and I'd wave back. The world became friendly.

All the newspaper boys when they delivered the paper would come around to where I lived, and I used to hang from a limb of a tree, and I had sort of a sweatshirt on—I didn't realize the value of a sweatshirt in those days—and then I was sort of beginning to catch on, but I didn't quite get it because I couldn't really afford sweaters. But here they'd come with their bicycles, you know, and I'd get these free papers and the family liked that, and they'd all pull their bicycles up around the tree and then I'd be hanging, looking kind of like a monkey, I guess. I was a little shy to come down. I did get down to the curb, kinda kicking the curb and kicking the leaves and talking, but mostly listening.

And sometimes the family used to worry because I used to laugh so loud and so gay; I guess they felt it was hysterical. It was just this sudden freedom because I would ask the boys, "Can I ride your bike now?" and they'd say, "Sure." Then I'd go zooming, laughing in the wind, riding down the block, laughing, and they'd all stand around and wait till I came back, but I loved the wind. It caressed me.

But it was kind of a double-edged thing. I did find, too, when the world opened up that people took a lot for granted, like not only could they be friendly, but they could get suddenly overly friendly and expect an awful lot for very little.

When I was older, I used to go to Grauman's Chinese Theatre and try to fit my foot in the prints in the cement there. And I'd say, "Oh, oh, my foot's too big, I guess, that's out." I did have a funny feeling later when I finally put my foot down into that wet cement. I sure knew what it really meant to me—anything's possible, almost.

It was the creative part that kept me going—trying to be an actress. I enjoy acting when you really hit it right. And I guess I've always had too much fantasy to be only a housewife. Well, also, I had to eat. I was never kept, to be blunt about it. I always kept myself. I have always had a pride in the fact that I was on my own. And Los Angeles was my home, too, so when they said, "Go home!" I said, "I *am* home."

The time when I sort of began to think I was famous I was driving somebody to the airport and as I came back there was this movie house and I saw my name in lights. I pulled the car up at a distance down the street—it was too much to take up close, you know—all of a sudden. And I said, "God, somebody's made a mistake." But there it was, in lights. And I sat there and said, "So that's the way it looks," and it was all very strange to me, and yet at the studio they had said, "Remember you're not a star." Yet there it is up in lights.

I really got the idea I must be a star, or *something* from the newspapermen—I'm saying men, not the women—who would interview me and they would be warm and friendly. By the way, that part of the press, you know, the men of the press, unless they have their own personal quirks against me, they were always very warm and friendly and they'd say "You know, you're the only star," and I'd say, "star?" and they'd look at me as if I were nuts. I think they, in their own kind of way, made me realize I was famous.

I remember when I got the part in *Gentlemen Prefer Blondes*, Jane Russell—she was the brunette in it and I was the blonde—she got $200,000 for it and I got my $500 a week, but that to me was, you know, considerable. She, by the way, was quite wonderful to me. The only thing was I couldn't get a dressing room. I said, finally—I really got to this kind of level—I said, "Look, after all, I am the blonde and it is *Gentlemen Prefer Blondes!*" Because still they always kept saying, "Remember, you're not a star." I said, "Well, whatever I am, I *am* the blonde!"

And I want to say that the people—if I am a star—the people made me a star—no studio, no person, but the people did. There was a reaction that came to the studio, the fan mail, or when I went to a premiere, or the exhibitors wanted to meet me. I didn't know why. When they all rushed toward me I looked behind me to see who was there and I said, "My heavens!" I was scared to death. I used to get the feeling, and sometimes I still get it, that sometimes I was fooling somebody. I don't know who or what—maybe myself.

I've always felt toward the slightest scene—even if all I had to do in a scene was just to come in and say, "Hi," that the people ought to get their money's worth and that this is an obligation of mine, to give them the best you can get from me. I do have feelings some days when there are some scenes with a lot of responsibility toward the meaning, and I'll wish, gee, if only I would have been a cleaning woman. On the way to the studio I would see somebody cleaning and I'd say, "That's what I'd like to be. That's my ambition in life." But I think all actors go through this. We not only *want* to be good; we have to be.

You know, when they talk about nervousness—my teacher, Lee Strasberg—when I said to him, "I don't know what's wrong with me but I'm a little nervous," he said, "When you're not, give up, because nervousness indicates sensitivity."

Also, a struggle with shyness is in every actor more than anyone can imagine. There is a censor inside us that says to what degree do we let go, like a child playing. I guess people think we just go out there, and you know, that's all we do—just do it. But it's a real struggle. I'm one of the world's most self-conscious people. I really have to struggle.

An actor is not a machine, no matter how much they want to say you are. Creativity has got to start with humanity and when you're a human being, you feel, you suffer—you're gay, you're sick, you're nervous or whatever. Like any creative human being, I *would* like a bit more control so that it would be a little easier for me when the director says, "One tear, right now," that one tear would pop out. But once there came two tears because I thought, "How dare he?"

Goethe said, "Talent is developed in privacy," you know? And it's really true. There is a need for aloneness which I don't think most people realize for an actor. It's almost having certain kinds of secrets for yourself that you'll let the whole world in on only for a moment, when you're acting.

But everybody is always tugging at you. They'd all like sort of a chunk of you. They kind of like to take pieces out of you. I don't think they realize it, but it's like "rrr do this, rrr do that." But you do want to stay intact—intact and on two feet.

I think that when you are famous every weakness is exaggerated. This industry should behave like a mother whose child has just run out in front of a car. But instead of clasping the child to them, they start punishing the child. Like you don't dare get a cold—how dare you get a cold! I mean, the executives can get colds and stay home forever and phone it in, but how dare you, the actor, get a cold or a virus. You know, no one feels worse than the one who's sick. I sometimes wish, gee, I wish they had to act a comedy with a temperature and a virus infection. I am not an actress who appears at a studio just for the purpose of discipline. This doesn't have anything at all to do with art. I myself would like to become more disciplined within my work. But I'm there to give a performance and not to be disciplined by a studio! After all, I'm not in a military school. This is supposed to be an art form, not just a manufacturing establishment.

The sensitivity that helps me to act, you see, also makes me react. An actor is supposed to be a sensitive instrument. Isaac Stern takes good care of his violin. What if everybody jumped on his violin?

If you've noticed in Hollywood where millions and billions of dollars have been made, there aren't really any kind of monuments or museums, and I don't call putting your footprint in Grauman's Chinese a monument—all right this did mean a lot to sentimentally ballyhoo me at the time. Gee, nobody left anything behind, they took it, they grabbed it and they ran—the ones who made the billions of dollars, never the workers.

You know a lot of people have, oh gee, real quirky problems that they wouldn't dare have anyone know. But one of my problems happens to show—I'm late. I guess people think that why I'm late is some kind of arrogance and I think it is the opposite of arrogance. I also feel that I'm not in this big American rush—you know, you got to go and you got to go fast but for no good reason. The main thing is, I do want to be prepared when I get there to give a good performance or whatever to the best of my ability.

A lot of people can be there on time and do nothing, which I have seen them do, and you know, all sit around and sort of chit-chatting and talking trivia about their social life. Gable said about me, "When she's there, she's there. All of her is there! She's there to work."

I was honored when they asked me to appear at the President's birthday rally in Madison Square Garden. There was like a hush over the whole place when I came on to sing *Happy Birthday*—like if I had been wearing a slip I would have thought it was showing, or something. I thought, "Oh, my gosh, what if no sound comes out!"

A hush like that from the people warms me. It's sort of like an embrace. Then you think, by God, I'll sing this song if it's the last thing I ever do. And for all the people. Because I remember when I turned to the microphone I looked all the way up and back, and I thought, "That's where I'd be—way up there under one of those rafters, close to the ceiling, after I paid my $2 to come into the place."

Afterwards they had some sort of a reception. I was with my former father-in-law, Isadore Miller, so I think I did something wrong when I met the President. Instead of saying, "How do you do?" I just said, "This is my former father-in-law, Isadore Miller." He came here an immigrant and I thought this would be one of the biggest things in his life—he's about 75 or 80 years old and I thought this would be something that he would be telling his grandchildren about and all that. I should have said, "How do you do, Mr. President," but I had already done the singing, so well you know. I guess nobody noticed it.

Fame has a special burden, which I might as well state here and now. I don't mind being burdened with being glamorous and sexual. But what goes with it can be a burden—like the man was going to show me around but the woman said, "Off the premises." I feel that beauty and femininity are ageless and can't be contrived, and glamor—although the manufacturers won't like this—cannot be manufactured. Not real glamor, it's based on femininity. I think that sexuality is only attractive when it's natural and spontaneous. This is where a lot of them miss the boat. And then something I'd just like to spout off on. We are all born sexual creatures, thank God, but it's a pity so many people despise and crush this natural gift. Art, real art, comes from it—everything.

I never quite understood it—this sex symbol—I always thought symbols were those things you clash together! That's the trouble, a sex symbol becomes a thing. I just hate to be a thing. But if I'm going to be a symbol of something I'd rather have it sex than some other things they've got symbols of! These girls who try to be me—I guess the studios put them up to it, or they get the ideas themselves. But gee, they haven't—you can make a lot of gags about it—like they haven't got the foreground or else they haven't the background. But I mean the middle, where you live.

All my stepchildren carried the burden of my fame. Sometimes they would read terrible things about me and I'd worry about whether it would hurt them. I would tell them, don't hide these things from me. I'd rather you ask me these things straight out and I'll answer all your questions. Don't be afraid to ask anything. After all I have come up from way down.

I wanted them to know of lives other than their own. I used to tell them, for instance, that I worked for 5¢ a month and I washed one hundred dishes, and my stepkids would say, "One hundred dishes!" and I said, "Not only that, I scraped and cleaned them before I washed them. I washed them and rinsed them and put them in the draining place, but," I said, "thank God I didn't have to dry them." Kids are different from grownups—you know when you get grown up you can get kind of sour, I mean that's the way it can go, but kids accept you the way you are.

I always tell them, "Don't admire somebody because they are grown up or because they say certain things—kind of observe them a little bit." I think probably that is the best advice I have given them. Just observe people for a while and then make up your own mind. And I used to tell them that about myself. I said, "See if I'm worth being a friend. That's up to you, and you figure it out after a while."

Fame to me certainly is only a temporary and a partial happiness—even for a waif and I was brought up a waif. But fame is not really for a daily diet, that's not what fulfills you. It warms you a bit but the warming is temporary. It's like caviar, you know—it's good to have caviar but not when you have it every meal and every day.

I was never used to being happy, so that wasn't something I ever took for granted. I did sort of think, you know, marriage did that. You see, I was brought up differently from the average American child because the average child is brought up expecting to be happy—that's it, successful, happy, and on time. Yet because of fame I was able to meet and marry two of the nicest men I'd ever met up to that time.

I don't think people will turn against me, at least not by themselves. I like people. The "public" scares me but people I trust. Maybe they can be impressed by the press or when a studio starts sending out all kinds of stories. But I think when people go to see a movie, they judge for themselves. We human beings are strange creatures and still reserve the right to think for ourselves.

Once I was supposed to be finished—that was the end of me. When Mr. Miller was on trial for contempt of Congress, a certain corporation executive said either he named names and I got him to name names, or I was finished. I said, "I'm proud of my husband's position and I stand behind him all the way," and the court did too. "Finished," they said. "You'll never be heard of."

It might be kind of a relief to be finished. It's sort of like I don't know what kind of a yard dash you're running, but then you're at the finish line and you sort of sigh—you've made it! But you never have—you have to start all over again. But I believe you're always as good as your potential.

I now live in my work and in a few relationships with the few people I can really count on. Fame will go by and, so long, I've had you, fame. If it goes by, I've always known it was fickle. So at least it's something I experienced, but that's not where I live.

Appendix B

Filmography

Filmography

Extensive cast and credit lists can be found in Agan, Anderson, Conway and Ricci, Hutchinson, Kobal and Robinson, Mailer, Manvell, Mellen, Shaw, and Slatzer—all of whom are cited in the bibliography. The purpose of this filmography is to put Monroe's movies in chronological order, to identify the studios and directors she worked with, and to supply plot summaries. The summaries also identify the actors and actresses who played opposite her and give some sense of her importance in the overall story of each movie. A list of important sources for certain films is listed after the plot summary and these sources are included in the bibliography. Publicity releases from 20th Century-Fox, available in the files of the Academy of Motion Picture Arts and Sciences, contain additional information on the making of Monroe's movies.

Dangerous Years

20th Century-Fox; released 12/9/47; Arthur Pierson. Eve (Monroe) is a waitress in a juke box joint. The role is incidental and provoked no comment from reviewers. The story begins with Jeff Carter (Donald Curtis) who is attempting to reform a group of adolescent delinquents under the influence of a young hood, Danny Jones (William Halop). Leo Emerson (Darryl Hickman) tries to back out of a robbery planned by Danny and tells Jeff Carter, who is murdered by Danny when he tries to prevent the crime. The rest of the film centers on Danny's upbringing in an orphanage and on startling revelations concerning the identity of his father, District Attorney Burns, who is not aware that he is prosecuting the case of his own son.

Scudda Hoo! Scudda Hay!

20th Century-Fox; released 3/4/48; F. Hugh Herbert. Only photographs reveal that Monroe appeared in this film, since her brief scene in a rowboat, was cut. She did not figure in the story of a farm boy who learns how to train two mules that have stubbornly resisted the handling of others.

Ladies of the Chorus

Columbia; released 2/49; Phil Karlson. Peggy (Monroe) becomes a successful dancer in the chorus when she takes over from Bubbles LaRue (Marjorie Hoshelle), who quits the show. Peggy falls in love with a wealthy young man, Randy Carroll (Rand Brooks), but her mother May Martin (Adele Jergins) is afraid her daughter will follow her fate by being disappointed in a marriage to a rich man. To everyone's surprise, Carroll's high society mother pretends to have had a show business background in order to put Peggy at her ease and to prevent the socialites at Peggy's engagement party from ostracizing her. Monroe sings two songs: "Every Baby Needs a Da Da Daddy" and "Anyone Can Tell I Love You." Sources: Anderson, Hirschhorn, Mailer, Mellen.

Love Happy

United Artists; released 10/10/49; David Miller. Detective Sam Grunion (Groucho Marx) is trying to solve the mystery of the missing Romanoff diamonds. In a scene that has nothing to do with the plot, a beautiful blonde (Marilyn Monroe) urgently asks for Grunion's help because "men keep following me," and saunters away from his leering presence in total control of herself.

A Ticket to Tomahawk

20th Century-Fox; released 4/21/50; Richard Sale. A drummer, Johnny Behind-the-Deuces (Dan Dailey) is forced into becoming a passenger on the Tomahawk and Western Railroad. If the train does not complete its run on time to Tomahawk, Colorado, it will not be awarded a charter, and Dawson (Mauritz Hugo) will be able to keep his stage coach line in business. Clara (Monroe) is one of the dancehall girls; she shares a dance with Johnny and sings "Oh, What a Forward Young Man You Are." Her role is very small, but she can be glimpsed in several scenes involving the train's arduous but successful trip to Tomahawk.

The Asphalt Jungle

Metro-Goldwyn-Mayer; released 5/5/50; John Huston. Angela Phinlay (Monroe) is the mistress of Alonzo D. Emmerich (Louis Calhern), who becomes involved in the planning of a jewel robbery. The thieves successfully steal the jewelry, but one of them is mortally shot, and Emmerich tries to outwit them. Instead, the thieves quickly realize they are being cheated, and Emmerich's ally is killed after he pulls a gun on them. Emmerich's other associate, Cobby (Marc Lawrence), is intimidated by the police and leads them to Emmerich, whose alibi is destroyed when Angela fails to back him up.

The Fireball

20th Century-Fox; released 8/16/50; Tay Garnett. Polly (Monroe) is one of several women attracted to Johnny Casar (Mickey Rooney) because he is a champion roller skater. Only Mary Reeves (Beverly Tyler) really cares for Johnny. He has run away from an orphanage, gotten a job in a beanery, and learned how to become a champion skater, but his success corrupts and isolates him, so that he is no longer a team player on the Bears, roller skating speedway champions. He contracts polio, is nursed back to health by Mary, and eventually learns how to help others by assisting a young team member in a big race, the International. Thus he wins the respect of his mentor Father O'Hara (Pat O'Brien) and the love of his sweetheart Mary.

All About Eve

20th Century-Fox; released 9/12/50; Joseph L. Mankiewicz. The young and dumb Miss Caswell (Monroe), the protégé of Addison DeWitt (George Sanders), a New York Drama critic, is a foil not only for DeWitt's world-weary cynicism but also for the manipulative cunning of Eve Harrington (Anne Baxter). Miss Caswell is the dumb version of Eve, the actress on the make, fooling old pros like the star actress Margo Channing (Bette Davis) into believing, for a while, in Eve's innocent desire to be a part of the theater world. One by one, Eve seduces Margo's friends into handing her the career it has been her aim all along to have. Sources: Behlmer, Brode, Mankiewicz.

Right Cross

Metro-Goldwyn-Mayer; released 10/50; John Sturges. Johnny Monterez (Ricardo Montalban) is a champion prizefighter who is sensitive about being Mexican. One of his only friends, Rick Gavery (Dick Powell), is a sports reporter in love with Pat (June Allyson), but Gavery realizes that she loves Johnny. Monroe makes only a brief appearance in a nightclub as a beautiful woman Rick has taken up with to forget about Pat. The rest of the film centers on Pat and Rick's successful efforts to convince an alienated Johnny of their friendship and love.

Hometown Story

Metro-Goldwyn-Mayer; released 5/14/51; Arthur Pierson. Monroe has a very small role as Miss Martin, who works in a newspaper office. She has scenes with Blake Washburn (Jeffrey Lynn), a state representative who returns to his home town after losing his reelection campaign, and with Slim Haskins (Alan Hale, Jr.) a reporter and Blake's friend. The movie centers on Blake's battle and reconciliation with big business.

As Young as You Feel

20th Century-Fox; released 6/13/51; Harmon Jones. Harriet (Monroe) is secretary to Louis McKinley (Albert Dekker), the president of Acme Printing Services. John Hodges (Monty Wooley) fights his enforced retirement at age sixty-five by pretending to be Cleveland, the president of Acme's parent company, Consolidated Motors. Monroe has several scenes, but her role is not integral to the story of a retiree who is successful in winning back his job and in changing company policy.

Love Nest

20th Century-Fox; released 10/15/51; Joseph Newman. Roberta Stevens (Monroe) decides to live in the apartment building owned and managed by her old army buddy Jim Scott (William Lundigan) and his wife Connie (June Haver). She raises Connie's suspicions and stimulates the wolfish behavior of Jim's friend, Ed Forbes (Jack Paar). Monroe is not important to the central story: Jim's effort to save his investment in the building which is complicated by his acceptance of a loan from Charley Patterson (Frank Fay), a con man. In an amusing twist, Charley dictates his memoirs to Jim, who is also a writer, and from his half of the profits Jim is able to renovate his building.

Let's Make It Legal

20th Century-Fox; released 10/23/51; Richard Sale. Joyce (Monroe) is a beautiful blonde dated by Hugh (MacDonald Carey), who hopes to make his divorced wife Miriam (Claudette Colbert) jealous. Joyce, on the other hand, is after the wealthy industrialist Victor Macfarland (Zachary Scott). Although Monroe makes several appearances in the film, she is a minor character, and has little significance in this story about Hugh and Miriam who become reconciled in spite of the interference of Macfarland, Miriam's suitor of twenty years before who tries to win her one more time after her divorce.

Clash by Night

RKO; released 5/16/52; Fritz Lang. Peggy (Monroe) is a fish cannery worker in love with Joe Doyle (Keith Andes), the brother of Mae Doyle (Barbara Stanwyck). Mae has returned home after many years, a disappointed and cynical woman. In spite of herself, she falls in love with the solid, dependable Jerry (Paul Douglas) and is strongly attracted to his intense friend, Earl (Robert Ryan), who is as soured on women as Mae has been on men. Monroe has the interesting role of a young woman who supports the older Mae and who challenges her bossy boyfriend Joe. While Mae is torn between a sense of responsibility to Jerry, whom she marries, and her fierce romantic pull toward Earl, with whom she has an affair, Peggy eventually succumbs to Joe, who firmly takes her in hand. Mae eventually realizes that Earl is more concerned with his sense of injury than with his love for her. Sources: Armour, Bogdanovich, Eisner.

We're Not Married

20th Century-Fox; released 7/1/52; Edmund Goulding. Annabel Norris (Monroe) and her husband Jeff (David Wayne) are one of five couples who are married by Justice of the Peace Melvin Bush (Victor Moore) a few days before his license is valid. Annabel has already won the title of Mrs. America and now is free to try for the Miss America title, to the chagrin of her husband who stays home with the baby while she diligently pursues her new title. The story ends with Jeff's reconciliation to Annabel's quest and with their second wedding.

Don't Bother to Knock

20th Century-Fox; released 7/17/52; Roy Baker. Jed Towers (Richard Widmark) is staying at a New York hotel where his girl Lyn Leslie (Anne Bancroft) is a singer. He becomes involved with a disturbed baby sitter, Nell (Monroe), who tries to incorporate Jed into her dream world. She takes him for a flyer she once loved. The film makes clear that she is a danger to herself and to others. Jed, who has had a falling out with Lyn over his insensitivity, gradually perceives the depth of Nell's disturbance and gently brings her back to reality. Now Lyn is drawn back to Jed and realizes that he does have the capacity to be compassionate, a capacity that was hidden earlier by his cynical exterior. Sources: Armstrong, Farber, Kobal and Robinson, Mellen.

Monkey Business

20th Century-Fox; 9/3/52; Howard Hawks. Dr. Barnaby Fulton (Cary Grant) is a scientific researcher working on a youth serum. By sheer accident, one of the chimpanzees gets out of his laboratory, mixes various chemicals, and pours them into the water cooler. Fulton, his boss Oxley (Charles Coburn), and his wife Edwina (Ginger Rogers) all drink from the water cooler and behave foolishly—like callow youths. Much of the energy in the film is generated by Fulton's chasing around with Miss Laurel (Monroe), Oxley's secretary, and by Oxley chasing her. Eventually the serum wears off and the adults return to normal, but Miss Laurel, the butt of many jokes, seems suspended in her juvenile world, a plaything of youth. Sources: Belton, Lucas.

O'Henry's Full House

20th Century-Fox; released 8/26/52; Henry Koster. Monroe plays a streetwalker in "The Cop and the Anthem," one of five episodes in this film. She is accosted by Soapy (Charles Laughton) who wants to be arrested so that he can spend the winter months in a warm jail. He flees when he realizes she is a woman of the street, and he even plans to reform his life, get a job, and so on when he is arrested for vagrancy and sentenced to ninety days in jail, thus ending his dream of beginning anew.

Niagara

20th Century-Fox; released 1/22/53; Henry Hathaway. Rose Loomis (Monroe) has become fed up with her neurotic husband George (Joseph Cotton). She plots with her lover Ted Patrick (Richard Allan) to murder George, but George wins in the struggle with Patrick and tracks down Rose, strangling her to death. Rose's amorality is contrasted with the normality of the honeymooning couple, Ray Cutler (Casey Adams) and Polly (Jean Peters). Source: Coursodan.

Gentlemen Prefer Blondes

20th Century-Fox; released 6/26/53; Howard Hawks. Dorothy (Jane Russell) and Lorelei (Monroe) are aboard the *Ile de France* sailing for Paris. They have a letter of credit given to Lorelei by her fiancé Gus (Tommy Noonan), who will join her in Paris for their marriage. Dorothy falls in love with Malone (Elliott Reed), a private detective hired by Gus's father to spy on Lorelei and to obtain incriminating evidence of her gold digging—a brief flirtation with Sir Francis Beekman (Charles Coburn). In Paris, Dorothy and Lorelei discover their letter of credit has been canceled, and Lorelei is accused of stealing a diamond tiara from Lady Beekman (Norma Varden). Through the strenuous efforts of Dorothy and Malone, Lorelei is exonerated, and the movie ends with a double wedding ceremony uniting Dorothy and Malone and Lorelei and Gus. Monroe and Russell sing "Two Little Girls from Little Rock," and "When Love Goes Wrong." They each sing "Bye Bye Baby." Monroe sings "Diamonds Are a Girl's Best Friend." Sources: Arbuthnot, Hirschhorn, Julia Johnson, McBride, Mast, Roud, Truffaut, Turim, Willis.

How to Marry a Millionaire

20th Century-Fox; released 11/5/53; Jean Negulesco. Three models, Pola Debevoise (Monroe), Loco Dempsey (Betty Grable), and Schatze Page (Lauren Bacall), become roommates in a luxury New York apartment in the hope of enticing millionaire husbands. Schatze is actually pursued by a wealthy businessman, Tom Brookman (Cameron Mitchell), but she mistakenly assumes that he is poor. Loco misunderstands the intentions of her already married millionaire partner, finds herself alone with him in a winter lodge in Maine, but manages to fall in love with and marry Eben (Rory Calhoun), a poor forest ranger. The nearsighted Pola, who refuses to wear glasses, takes the wrong plane but meets and marries an agreeable millionaire, Freddie Denmark (David Wayne). Schatze almost marries J. D. Hanley (William Powell), but balks at the last minute because she does not love him. With Hanley's assistance, she decides on Brookman and goes to dinner with him and the other two couples. All of them pass out when Brookman produces an enormous roll of bills to pay for their meal. Sources: Bacall, Johnson and Levanthal, Stempel, Warren.

River of No Return

20th Century-Fox; released 4/23/54; Otto Preminger. Kay (Monroe), a saloon singer, is kind to Mark, the son of Matt Calder (Robert Mitchum). Matt Calder has just been released from prison, where he had served time for killing a man who was about to murder a friend of Calder's. Calder later saves Kay and her man, the gambler Harry Weston (Rory Calhoun) by pulling their capsizing raft to shore. Weston is on his way to file a gold claim and is so eager to continue his trip that he steals Calder's only horse, leaving Kay behind. She attends to the injured Calder and his son with admirable courage, even though Weston has left all of them unarmed to confront the Indians. Kay accompanies Calder in his pursuit of Weston, and in the final confrontation between the two men she tries to fight her former lover, but he pushes her away. Calder's son Mark is forced to shoot Weston in the back to save his father's life, and thus he comes to an understanding of how his father was forced to kill. Kay and Calder, after much misunderstanding, attain a genuine appreciation of each other's characters, and Calder carries her off to start a new life. Monroe sings four songs: "The River of No Return," "I'm Gonna File My Claim," "One Silver Dollar," and "Down in the Meadow." Sources: Belton, Haskell, McGuinness, Preminger, Roud.

There's No Business Like Show Business

20th Century-Fox; released 12/8/54; Walter Lang. Vicky (Monroe) eventually becomes adopted into a show business family, the Donahues—but not before several plot complications that keep her from being accepted by the family and by her lover Tim Donahue (Donald O'Connor), who thinks (after initially being impressed by her determined efforts to improve her talent) that she has deceived him to achieve success. Tim suddenly disappears after assuming Vicky has betrayed him for the producer Lew Harris (Richard Eastham) and thus causes a family crisis. She is shunned by the family, but she is eventually able to convince Tim's mother Molly (Ethel Merman) of her sincerity, and Tim returns to reconcile with Vicky. Monroe sings "After You Get What You Want You Don't Want It," "Heat Wave," and "Lazy."

The Seven Year Itch

20th Century-Fox; released 6/3/55; Billy Wilder. Richard Sherman (Tom Ewell) has been left alone in his city apartment by his wife and son, who have gone away on a summer vacation. Almost immediately he begins to fantasize about himself as a single man and then is presented with a live possibility—The Girl (Monroe) who sublets the apartment above his. She is breezy and cool about her obvious sexual attractiveness; Sherman tries to seduce her as a suave adult lover. But his adolescent fantasies betray him, and she shrugs off his awkward advances, making clear she is interested in his air conditioner in this hot city summer. The Girl is a good sport, and she tells Sherman she does not want to be impressed by an overpowering male lover. She values his modesty and fundamental decency. But Sherman, to be on the safe side, rushes off to his family, with The Girl at the window calling after him, throwing down the shoes he has left behind in his rush to the train station. Much of the comedy between Ewell and Monroe is generated by the curious mixture of adolescence and adulthood in both of their characters. Sources: Axelrod, Brode, Dick, Julia Johnson, McBride and Wilmington, Roud, Seidman, Sinyard and Turner, Tom Wood.

Bus Stop

20th Century-Fox; released 8/15/56; Josh Logan. A callow cowboy, Bo Decker (Don Murray), latches on to a saloon singer, Cherie (Monroe) as his vision of the "angel" he must marry. Initially she is thrilled by his brash yet reverent treatment of her, but soon it is apparent that he will bully her into a marriage she is not prepared for because of her plans for a Hollywood career. In her own way, she is as unrealistic as he is. If she knows she is no virgin, she does not realize she lacks talent. She spends much of her time evading Bo's smothering embraces and running away from him. Finally, in a fight with bus driver Carl (Robert Bray), who sticks up for Cherie's right to leave Bo, the young cowboy learns a lesson in humility. Like Cherie, he is defeated by someone stronger than himself. Ironically, this is precisely the point at which Cherie and Bo can reconcile, for each has discovered the limitations and strengths of the other. Sources: Inge, Logan, Morsberger, Trebey.

The Prince and the Showgirl

Warner Brothers (Marilyn Monroe Productions); released 5/15/57; Laurence Olivier. Grand Duke Charles (Laurence Olivier), Prince Regent of Carpathia, is present in London in 1911 for the coronation of George V. The Grand Duke spots an American showgirl Elsie Marina (Monroe) at the theater and invites her to dinner at the Carpathian Embassy. He has planned the whole evening for his pleasure, yet he is curiously cold and inattentive in his presumed seduction of her. Elsie handles him rather deftly and soon is ensconced in the family counsels, becoming fast friends with the Grand Duke's son, the young King Nicholas (Jeremy Spenser) and his mother-in-law, the Queen Dowager (Sybil Thorndike). The Grand Duke never does accomplish his seduction, although Elsie realizes she has fallen in love nevertheless. Slowly, Elsie straightens out relations between father and son, wins the Grand Duke's love, and promises to wait a year and a half—when Nicholas will begin his rule—for the Grand Duke's return. Monroe sings "I Found a Dream." Sources: Cottrell, Daniels, Hirsch, Kiernan, Morley, Olivier, Rattigan.

Some Like It Hot

United Artists; released 2/25/59; Billy Wilder. Chicago, 1929: the Saint Valentine's Day Massacre. Joe (Tony Curtis) and Jerry (Jack Lemmon) are the two hapless musicians who witness it. They barely escape with their lives and are pursued by Spats Columbo (George Raft) and his gang. Joe and Jerry decide to disguise themselves as women and join a female band headed for Florida. They quickly befriend and become attracted to Sugar (Monroe) who is in flight from male bands and the saxophone players who have loved and betrayed her. Joe begins to woo Sugar by dressing up in the costume of a millionaire, and Jerry is simultaneously wooed by Osgood (Joe E. Brown), who is indeed a millionaire. Joe and Jerry's lives are again in jeopardy when Spats Columbo shows up with his gang, recognizes the musicians, and gives chase. Spats, however, is gunned down, and Joe and Sugar, Jerry and Osgood all end up in the same boat ostensibly fleeing from the violent life on shore but in fact facing each other's true identities for the first time. Monroe sings "I'm Through with Love," "I Wanna Be Loved by You," and "Running Wild." Sources: Baltake, Brode, Broeske, Farber, French, Holtzman, Kauffman, Madsen, Mast, Reitz, Sinyard and Turner, Wagner, Widener, Wilder, Zinman, Zolotow.

Let's Make Love

20th Century-Fox; released 8/24/60; George Cukor. Jean-Marc Clement (Yves Montand) is concerned about an off-Broadway revue that is planning to satirize him. He goes to the theater with his public relations director, Alex Coffman (Tony Randall), and observes Amanda Dell (Monroe) rehearsing a song. He is quite taken with her and agrees to audition for the show while being careful to conceal his true identity. Rather than trying to prevent the production, Clement decides to put money into it and works with show business professionals (Bing Crosby, Gene Kelly, and Milton Berle) to train himself for his role. He is hopelessly stiff but is successful in wooing an initially reluctant Amanda—she is upset over his deception—for she realizes she has fallen in love with him. Monroe sings "My Heart Belongs to Daddy," "Let's Make Love," "Incurably Romantic," and "Specialization." Sources: Andrews, Carey, Clarens, Hirschhorn, Kauffman, Lambert, Phillips, Roud, original sound track recording, Columbia, Stereo, ACS 8327.

The Misfits

United Artists; released 2/1/61; Huston. Roslyn Taber (Monroe) has just divorced her husband Raymond (Kevin McCarthy). She is noticed first by Guido (Eli Wallach), a mechanic who gives her a ride. Soon Guido and Gay (Clark Gable) invite her and her female friend Isabelle (Thelma Ritter) to see how they live out on the desert as rugged individualists hunting down mustangs. They are soon joined by rodeo rider Perce (Montgomery Clift). All three men appeal to Roslyn for understanding, and she soothes their troubled spirits, even though her own soul is divided and in search of the proper way to live. She opposes the roping of the mustangs, since the outcome of the brave hunt is simply to ship the horses to a cannery for dog meat. Gay tries to get her to see that she is just as inconsistent in her actions as they are, but she cannot reconcile herself to their predatory habits until Gay acknowledges that the frontier life he has prided himself on is over. Both Gay and Roslyn realize that the world they want will be built on compromise; they recognize, in the end, their interdependence. The movie ends on this note: the effort to achieve balance in human relationships. Sources: Barbaro, Bosworth, Broeske, Croce, Curtis, Garrett, Gilliatt, Huston, Jordan, Kaminsky, Kass, Kauffman, La Guardia, Madsen, Miller, Nolan, Pratley, Scagnetti, Tornabene.

Something's Got to Give

20th Century-Fox; suspended 6/62; Cukor.

Notes

The acknowledgments give complete information on my interviews (abbreviated "int." in the notes that follow). Consult the bibliography for full citations of the publications referred to in the notes by the author's name, or by name and a short title if there is more than one book by the same author. The number appearing before each note refers to a page in this book.

The chronology of Monroe's life in this biography follows both of Fred Guiles's books, *Norma Jean* and *Legend*. His dates and facts have been checked with several of the people he interviewed and against what other published accounts provide; it is abundantly clear that he is the most accurate authority. Unless otherwise noted, all factual material is taken from *My Story*, from Guiles's *Norma Jean*, and from my own interviews, and all quotations of Monroe are from Richard Meryman's *Life* interview, included in this book. Guiles has been cited in the notes only when he is directly quoted or when his facts and judgments can be fruitfully compared with other sources.

Although *My Story* was not published in book form until 1974, it was available in England in 1954 in a series of articles (May 9 through August 1) written in close collaboration with Ben Hecht for *Empire News*. The autobiography must be used with caution, since it sensationalizes several aspects of the actress's life and makes errors like identifying the University of Southern California rather than UCLA as her night school. Nevertheless, biographers, especially Guiles, have been able to authenticate many of the incidents described in *My Story*, and it is true to much of what Monroe felt about her life and expressed to the friends and associates I interviewed. Both Maurice Zolotow and Stanley Flink, friends of Ben Hecht's, testify persuasively to his intense interest in an actress whom he got to know well while helping to write the script of *Monkey Business*. Anthony Summers has interviewed Hecht's widow who remembers Monroe correcting the manuscript and expressing enthusiastic approval of the way "Benny had captured every phase of her life."

Exactly when the autobiography was written is not clear, although Erskine Johnson in the October 1954 issue of *Motion Picture* states that Hecht wrote it during the time Monroe was on suspension from Fox—in other words, in late 1953. The manuscript must have been completed in early 1954, since the last chapter is about the actress's trip to Korea shortly after her marriage to DiMaggio. Apparently DiMaggio objected to having the book published, and relations between the actress and her biographer "soured," according to Summers. Monroe left no notes or marks on the manuscript that she gave to Milton Greene for his safe-keeping, and it is not clear whether she had plans to finish it. The 1974 edition of her autobiography contains several passages that did not appear in *Empire News*, passages that could have come only from the manuscript Milton Greene briefly described to me.

1–2   Love goddesses: Thomson, *Biographical Dictionary of Film*.

  2   Avedon's photographs: *Life*, December 22, 1958.

  2   Signoret, 332.

  3   Lincoln: Eve Arnold, *The Unretouched Woman*, 89–98; Monroe, 96.

  3   Mailer, *Presidential Papers*, 38.

  3   Kennedys: Slatzer and Summers.

6–8   Flack: int.; *On Painting*, 84–89.

  6   Norma Jeane: Monroe consistently wrote her given first name this way—see Guiles, *Legend*, 16.

  8   Mailer, *Marilyn*, 18.

  9   Mortensen: Smith and Webster.

 11   Daydreaming: Monroe, 12, 16, 19.

 11   Mrs. Dewey: Guiles, *Norma Jean*, 30–31; Zolotow, *Marilyn Monroe*, 17.

 12   Orphans: Laing, *Self and Others*, 50–51, 86.

 12   Miller, 32.

 12   Laing, *The Divided Self*, 116–17, 119.

 12   Monroe, 20.

 13   Laing, *Self and Others*, 51, 137.

 15   Dougherty, 73–74.

 16   Norma Jeane's panic: see Laing, *Divided Self*, 54–57 for a case similar to Monroe's.

 16   Interim identity: Mailer, *Marilyn*, 46; Conover, *Finding Marilyn*.

17   Self-interrogation: Monroe, 31.

17   Mirrors and identity: Lacan, 1–7; Rosten, *Marilyn*, 47; Rosten, *Closeups*, 321.

17   Conover, 12.

17   De Dienes photographs: Mailer, *Marilyn*, 40, 51.

17–18   De Dienes: Hoyt, 42; Mailer, *Marilyn*, 55; Conover, 12–13.

18   Slatzer, Burnside: Summers, 24–29.

19   Modeling: Zolotow, *Marilyn Monroe*, 38, 40; Guiles, *Norma Jean*, 61–63.

19   Monroe on acting: Monroe, 39–40.

20   Changes: Zolotow, *Marilyn Monroe*, 39–40; Guiles, *Norma Jean*, 73.

20   Screen test: Zolotow, *Marilyn Monroe*, 44; Parsons, 213.

20   Publicity shots: 1946–1948: Kobal and Robinson, 38–39, 42–43, 46–49; Shaw, 133–34, 136, 138; Dougherty, photograph #24; Mailer, *Marilyn*, 66–67; Slatzer; Zolotow, *Marilyn Monroe*; Skolsky, *Marilyn*; Spada.

21   Wapner: int. Wapner; see also Winters, 91; Parsons, 214; Stack, 104; Hoyt, 65.

21   Theatrical debut: Haspiel.

21   Engstead, 195–96.

22   Schenck: Monroe, 59–66.

22   Sexual favors: int. Monroe's friends; see also Conover, 30, 38 and Summers for the most detailed account of Monroe's sex life.

22   Lytess, 2; see also Wilkie, 4–5, 172–87; Skolsky, *Marilyn*, 42, 49.

23   Karger: Monroe, 74–79.

23   *Ladies of the Chorus* reviews: *Baltimore Sun*, February 11, 1949, 12; Mellen, 63–66; Anderson, 27–29; Conway and Ricci, 29; Mailer, *Marilyn*.

24   *Stage Door*: Haspiel.

24   Stripper: Lamparski, 87.

25   Nude calendar: Guiles, *Norma Jean*, 112; Monroe, 52.

27   Johnny Hyde: Monroe, 87–94, 104–8. Guiles, *Legend*, 145; see photograph of Hyde and Monroe in Spada, 24–25.

27–28   Huston: Monroe, 88–90; Guiles, *Norma Jean*, 120–21.

32   Lytess: Guiles, *Legend*, 160.

33   Celeste Holm: Behlmer, 206.

33   Nunnally Johnson: Hoyt, 74–75.

33   Monroe, 105.

33–34   Flink and Allan: int.; see also Allan.

34   Lytess, 12.

34   Film personalities: Cavell, 27–28.

36   Skolsky, *Don't Get Me Wrong*, 124; int. Steffi Sidney.

36 Lytess, 12.

36 Mailer, *Marilyn*, 63.

36 Compare Skolsky, *Marilyn*, 42, with Mankiewicz and Carey, 222.

37 Skolsky, *Don't Get Me Wrong*, 215.

37 Different behavioral possibilities: Lembourn, 42, 49; Goffman, *The Presentation of Self*, 6, 72

37 Mankiewicz and Carey, 96–97.

37–38 Hyde: Mankiewicz and Carey, 77; Hoyt, 86; Kanin, 315–20.

41 Fraser, 52.

42 June Haver: Hoyt, 89–90.

43 Other women: Guiles, *Legend*, 178–79.

43 Acting on movie sets: int. Ellen Burstyn.

43 *Let's Make It Legal:* Conway and Ricci, 66.

43 UCLA: Monroe, 109–10.

44 Chekhov: Monroe, 133–35; Guiles, *Norma Jean*, 142; Corwin, 45; Weatherby, 57.

44–45 Chekhov, chapter 1, 22–25, 30–31, 74–83, 103.

45 Todd: int. Ralph Roberts.

46 Publicity: Zolotow, *Marilyn Monroe*, 104–8; "Marilyn 'Hurt' by Army Ban on Photo," *Los Angeles Times*, September 2, 1952, 2; Hopper, 85.

46 Mailer, *Marilyn*, 95.

49 Chekhov, 76–77.

51 Rosten: int.

51 Bancroft and Widmark: Guiles, *Legend*, 205.

52 Robinson: Kobal and Robinson, 16, 19.

52 Nunnally Johnson: Hoyt, 94; Stempel, 168–69.

54 Monroe, 121.

55 DiMaggio–Monroe relationship: Monroe, 124–30; Zolotow, *Marilyn Monroe*, 85, 120–29, 134, 146–47, 186, 195, 202–11; Guiles, *Norma Jean*, 150–51, 154–55, 163, 166–67, 171–73, 179–81; Mailer, *Marilyn*, 95–107, 111, 116–22.

56 Slatzer: Summers, 74–78, 170.

56 Winters, 308.

56 Slatzer: Summers, 76–78, 160.

59 Publicity: Williams; Muir; see clipping files of the Academy of Motion Picture Arts and Sciences.

59 Photoplay Awards dinner: Hoyt, 125–26; Zolotow, *Marilyn Monroe*, 186–88; Monroe, 113–14.

59 Kilgallen letter: Carpozi, 87–88.

59 Gretchen: Williams, "Marilyn Wants to Turn It Off."

60 Goslar: Guiles, *Legend*, 221–22, 232.

60–61 Todd, 1, 174–75, 281, 295.

63 Monroe as put-on: Brackman, 19; Mailer, *Marilyn*, 106.

63 Truffaut, 72.

65 Johnson: Stempel, 170.

65 Bacall, 208.

66 Negulesco: Zolotow, *Marilyn Monroe*, 191–93.

66 Negulesco, 227.

66 Johnson: Hoyt, 116–17.

66 Winters, 450–54; Preminger, 128.

69–71 Korea: Monroe, 141–43; Jennings; Guiles, *Norma Jean*, 180–82; Skolsky, *Marilyn*, 82.

73 Monroe's coworkers: int. Wapner.

75 Monroe's costume: 20th Century-Fox publicity release in files of American Academy of Motion Picture Arts and Sciences.

75 Monroe's illness: Zolotow, *Marilyn Monroe*, 218–19; Hoyt, 140–41; Carpozi, 106; int. Wapner.

75–76 Pills, fears of insanity, Schaefer: Summers, 85, 109–12.

76 Strasberg, 41.

76 Wapner: int.

76 Strasberg, 41.

80–82 DiMaggio–Monroe breakup: Guiles, *Norma Jean*, 186–91; Zolotow, *Marilyn Monroe*, 222–25; Skolsky, *Don't Get Me Wrong*, 224.

82 Winters: Funke and Booth, 156.

82 Ken Darby: Hoyt, 135.

83 The Beatles: Lahr.

85–88 Milton Greene: int. Milton Greene, Rupert Allan, and Steffi Sidney; Guiles, *Norma Jean*, 195.

86 Strasberg and Guiles: tape-recorded int. (January 15, 1967).

86 Black and white sequence: Mailer, *Of Women and Their Elegance*, 218–30.

88 Amy Greene: Bolstad; Mailer, *Of Women and Their Elegance*, 72–74, 79–84, 88–89, 284; Summers, 123, Pepitone, 75–76.

88 Monroe's child: Summers, 123; Pepitone, 75–76.

88 Dr. Siegal: Summers, 123.

88 Greenson: Summers, 188.

89–90 *Person-to-Person*: Mailer, *Of Women and Their Elegance*, 99–112; Slatzer, 213.

90 Chronology of events leading to meeting with Strasberg: Zolotow, *Marilyn Monroe*, 244–45; Mailer, *Marilyn*, 145; Guiles, *Norma Jean*, 206.

91   Reading Stanislavsky: Hoyt, 152; Zolotow, *Marilyn Monroe*, 257; Martin, 56.

91   Strasberg: int. Fred Guiles. Easty, 159.

91   Easty, 159.

91   James Dean: Dalton, 92.

92   Stella Adler: Adams, 178.

92   Ellen Burstyn: int.

92   Helen Hayes: Funke and Booth, 71.

92   Miller, *Theatre Essays*, 274.

92   Zolotow, *Marilyn Monroe*, 246.

93   John Springer: int.

93   Wilder: Zolotow, *Marilyn Monroe*, 259–60, 321.

93   Strasberg: int. Fred Guiles.

93   Strasberg with a student: Adams, 210.

94   Strasberg: Hethmon, 5.

94–95   Strasberg: Hethmon, 30.

94–95   Strasberg's classes: Zolotow, *Marilyn Monroe*, 247; Guiles, *Norma Jean*, 208.

95   Steinem, 36.

95   One observer: Easty, 159.

95   Kitten: Adams, 255.

95   Classic Stanislavsky exercise: Stanislavsky, *An Actor Prepares*, 86.

96   Stanislavsky's approach: Stanislavsky, *Building a Character*, 279.

96   Character embodiment: Stanislavsky, *An Actor Prepares*, 96.

96   Sing a popular song: Zolotow, *Marilyn Monroe*, 248; Hethmon, 224–26, 242.

96   Gestureless moments: Pudovkin, 334.

96   Clurman: introduction to Odets, *Golden Boy*, ix–xii.

97   Meryman and Flink: int.

97–98   Easty, 161.

99   Strasberg: int. Fred Guiles.

99–100   Stanislavsky: Adams, 107; Stanislavsky, *An Actor Prepares*, 49, 242; Stanislavsky, *Building a Character*, 108, 114.

100   Strasberg: int. Fred Guiles

100   One male studio member: Adams, 261.

100   Kim Stanley: int. Kobal.

100   Cheryl Crawford: Adams, 261–62.

100–101   Maureen Stapleton: Summers, 145.

101   Monroe's reaction: Adams, 261–62.

101 Milton Greene, Rupert Allan, Susan Strasberg: int.

101 Fred Stewart: Guiles, *Legend*, 272.

101 Ralph Roberts, John Springer: int.

101 One reporter: recorded on *Marilyn Monroe: Rare Recordings*.

102 Logan, 43, 46; Zolotow, *Marilyn Monroe*, 275.

102–3 Logan, 43–45, 55–56.

103 Susan Strasberg: int.

103 Lee Strasberg: int. Fred Guiles.

103–4 Logan, 47–48, 52.

104 Murray: Trebey, 20–21.

104 Rupert Allan: int.

104 Logan, 55.

104–5 Stanislavsky's legacy: Easty, 49.

105 Strasberg: int. Fred Guiles.

105 Rupert Allan: int.

105 Markel: Summers, 218–19.

105–6 Stanislavsky, *Building a Character*, chapter 2.

106 Strasberg: int. Fred Guiles.

106 James Dean: Dalton, 101.

106 Filming: Guiles, *Norma Jean*, 230.

106 Logan, 57–59.

107 Zolotow, *Marilyn Monroe*, 287.

107 Logan, 61.

108 Mellen, 112, 114–16, 118–19, 121.

108 Flink: int.

108 Stanislavsky, *An Actor Prepares*, 289.

112 Logan, 55.

112 Strasberg: Hethmon, 255.

112 Anne Bancroft: Funke and Booth, 196.

113 *Focus:* Skolsky, *Marilyn*, 60.

114 Snapshot of Miller: Cook, 4M.

114 Lytess: Joyce, 98.

114 Skolsky, *Don't Get Me Wrong*, 213.

114 Strasberg: Adams, 259.

115 Odets, "To Whom It May Concern," 136.

115 Alan Levy: Wagenknecht, 18.

115   Stanislavsky, *An Actor Prepares*, 294–95.

115   Ralph Roberts: int.

115–16 Miller and the Rostens: int. Norman and Hedda Rosten.

116   Miller's impressions of Monroe: Hamilton, 110.

116   Miller's ebullience: Cook, 4M.

116   Monroe's surprise: Rosten, *Marilyn*, 34; int. Rupert Allan.

116–17 Miller's testimony: Bentley.

117   Levy: Wagenknecht, 19.

117   Monroe's identification with Miller: Rauh, 15–16.

117   Rupert Allan: int.

118   Monroe's conversion: Rosten, *Marilyn*, 38.

118   Hoyt, 178.

119   Guiles, *Norma Jean*, 240–41.

119   Paula Strasberg: Quoted in "Marilyn," *Look*, May 29, 1956, 74.

119   Miller in 1969: Guiles, "Marilyn Monroe," 7.

119   Laing, *The Divided Self*, 37.

119   Rosten, *Marilyn Monroe*, 36–38.

121   Monroe's uncertain reception: Manning, 98.

121   Meeting Olivier: Earl Wilson, "The Things She Said to Me!," 84; Winters, 313.

121   Accounts of the planning and production of *The Prince and the Showgirl*: Guiles, *Norma Jean*, 253–64; Guiles, *Legend*, 319–24; Zolotow, *Marilyn Monroe*, 296–311; Mailer, *Marilyn*, 160–66; Mailer, *Of Women and Their Elegance*, 178–206; Hoyt, 179–86; Carpozi, 139–45; Martin, 116–22; Rosten, *Marilyn*, 42–45; Olivier, 205–13.

122   Vivian Leigh: Cottrell, 281–82.

122   Olivier's first meeting with Monroe: Olivier, 205.

122   The press conference: Martin, 120.

124   Schizoid: Olivier, 205; Greene: int.; Laing, *The Divided Self*, 17.

124   Hutchinson, 69.

124–25 Rosten, *Marilyn*, 43.

125   Olivier and the Method: Olivier, 207.

125   Winters: Funke and Booth, 147–48.

125   Olivier's honesty: Daniels, 136.

126   Hedda Rosten: int.

126   Paula Strasberg: Strasberg, 67.

126   Milton Greene: Summers, 166–67.

126   Rosten, *Marilyn*, 45.

127   Logan, 67.

127   Conflicting evidence of Olivier's behavior: Cottrell, 282–84; Korda, 447; Hirsch, 114.

127   Olivier's pride: Cottrell, 284.

127   Eyewitness account: Kiernan, 257.

127   Hedda Rosten: int.

127   Resistance to acting: Cottrell, 280.

128   Thorndyke: Quoted in Mailer, *Marilyn*, 164.

132   Critics: Mellen, 123; Welsch, 202; Hirsch, 116–17.

134   Chaplin: Welsch, 201–2; Logan, 56.

134   Mellen, 123.

134   Hirsch, 113–17.

135   Logan, 66–67.

138   Rosten, *Marilyn*, 70–71.

139   Rosten, *Marilyn*, 73–74.

139   Monroe's nightmare: Wagenknecht, 32.

139   Guiles, *Norma Jean*, 266.

139   Rosten, *Marilyn*, 47.

140   Rosten, *Marilyn*, 45–46.

140   Abortions: Mailer, *Marilyn*, 171; Summers, 148, 285–86.

140   Karger: Monroe, 78.

140–41   Suicide: Rosten, *Marilyn*, 75; Summers, 6, 23–24, 48–49, 193, 197.

141   Rosten, *Marilyn*, 55.

141–42   Strasberg, 51.

141   Rosten: int.

142–43   Shaw, 129.

142   Psychiatrist: int. Rosten.

142   Fan mail: int. Rosten.

143   Rosten, *Marilyn*, 11–12.

143–44   Pepitone and Stadiem, 25.

143–44   Pepitone and Stadiem, 14–16.

144   Mirrors: Pepitone and Stadiem, 23, 25, 27, 30, 64–65, 80, 84, 89.

144   Capote, *Music For Chameleons*, 238.

144   Pepitone and Stadiem, 64.

145   Laing, *The Divided Self*, 42–43.

147   Epigraph: *The American Weekly*, May 1, 1960 and Zolotow, *Marilyn Monroe*, 332.

147 Wilder: see Zolotow, *Billy Wilder in Hollywood*, for the fullest account of the director's point of view on the making of *Some Like It Hot*.

148 Rupert Allan: int.

148 Lemmon: Wagner, 303.

148 Ralph Roberts, John Springer, Rupert Allan: int.

148 Pepitone and Stadiem, 114–16, 129.

148 Miller: Guiles, *Legend*, 355.

149 Lemmon: Widener, 170.

150 Strasberg: int. Fred Guiles.

150 Lemmon: Widener, 170.

151 Farber, 370–71.

153 French, 147.

156 Sinyard and Turner, 220–21.

156 Critics: Mast, *The Comic Mind*, 278; Dick, 235.

158 Wilder: Guiles, *Norma Jean*, 287.

158–59 Miller and Wilder: Zolotow, *Billy Wilder in Hollywood*, 265–67.

159 Guiles, *Norma Jean*, 294.

160 Audrey Wilder: Zolotow, *Billy Wilder in Hollywood*, 271.

160 Wilder in 1968: Zolotow, *Billy Wilder in Hollywood*, 272.

160 Rosten, *Marilyn*, 78.

160–61 Pepitone and Stadiema, 108.

161 Estelle Parsons: Adams, 210.

161 Ralph Roberts: int.

161 Lembourn, 177.

161 Ellen Burstyn: int.

162 Ralph Roberts: int.

162 Miller: Guiles, "Marilyn Monroe," 7.

164 Signoret, 335.

164 A recent article: Hodgson, 14.

164 Skolsky, *Don't Get Me Wrong*, 228.

165–66 Greenson: Summers, 188–89, 205–6.

166 The press: "Walk Like This, Marilyn," 104.

167–68 Signoret, 336–39.

168 Guiles, *Legend*, 324.

168 Freud, 42.

168 Greenson: Summers, 205–6.

169   Taylor: Goode, 17. See Goode for the most complete account of the filming of *The Misfits*.

170   Wallach, Ritter, Clift: Goode, 66–67, 86–87, 95.

170   Clift: Goode, 94.

170   Miller: La Guardia, 211.

170   Monroe's doubts about Roslyn: Rosten, *Marilyn*, 85–86; Conover, 140.

170   Lee Strasberg: int. Fred Guiles.

172–73   Sam Shaw's photograph: Mailer, *Marilyn*, 156.

173   "To the Weeping Willow": Rosten, *Marilyn*, 59–60.

174   Goode, 200.

175   Huston, 325.

175   Ritter: Goode, 86.

177   Huston, 323.

178   Setbacks: Whitcomb, 53.

178   Retakes of rodeo scene: McIntyre, 76.

178   Clift: Weatherby, 67.

178   Taylor: Bosworth, 352.

178   La Guardia, 310.

179   Goode, 93, 141–44.

179   Clift: La Guardia, 215.

179   Lemmon: Widener, 170; Wagner, 304.

179   Guiles, *Norma Jean*, 329.

180   Roslyn's hysteria: Mailer, *Marilyn*, 204–6.

181   Monroe's double bind: for more comment on this scene, see Oppenheimer, 80.

181   Revisions of *The Misfits*: Goode; 215–16, 306; Weatherby, 33; Guiles, *Norma Jean*, 338. Garrett, Hardison, and Golfman, *Film Scripts*, 202–382, contains an early version of the movie.

181–82   Gable: Goode, 206.

181–82   Miller: Goode, 75.

182   *Some Like It Hot*: Wagenknecht, 33.

182   Huston: Barris and Wilson.

182   Newcomb and Allan: int. Rupert Allan.

182–83   The Strasbergs: int. Susan Strasberg.

183   Rupert Allan: int.

183   Weatherby, 73–75.

183   Kennedy: Summers, 206, 215–16.

185   Epigraph: Tennyson, "The Lady of Shalott." See also Murray, 152.

185–86 Weatherby, 125, 143–51, 166–70, 175, 182–89.

186 Rosten, *Marilyn*, 90–92.

186 Dr. Kris and Ralph Roberts: int. Ralph Roberts. Dr. Kris, described as a "pioneer psychoanalyst and teacher," specialized in the treatment of children, and was "founder and first president of the International Association for Child Psychoanalysis." See her obituary in the *New York Times*, November 25, 1980, D23.

186 Meryman, "Behind the Myth," 54.

186–87 Monroe's letter to the Strasbergs: reprinted in Speriglio, 248–49.

187 Rosten, *Marilyn*, 92.

187 Levy: Wagenknecht, 27.

187 Another friend: Slatzer, 227.

187 Newcomb: Guiles, *Norma Jean*, 346.

187 Rosten: Allen, 203.

188 March 9: *Detroit News* photograph.

188 Skolsky, *Don't Get Me Wrong*, 230.

188 Rupert Allan: int.

188 Kay Gable: "Shocked Disbelief; Spada and Zeno, 176.

188 Greenson: Summers, 189, 231–32.

188–89 Signs of aging: Pepitone and Stadiema, 180–81; Slatzer, 28.

189 Marjorie Stengel: Mailer, *Marilyn*, 216.

189 Murray, 13–14, 16.

189 Rosten: int.

189 Slatzer: int. Allan.

189 Summers, 242.

190 Fred Field: Summers, 254.

190 Rosten, *Marilyn*, 100–101.

190–91 Greenson to Zolotow: Zolotow, "Marilyn Monroe's Psychiatrist," 2.

190–92 Greenson, 115–16, 118–23, 126–31.

192 Greenson wrote to a colleague: Summers, 189.

192–93 Johnson and Levanthal, 206–8.

193 Nunnally Johnson: Stempel, 173.

193 Bernstein, 105–8.

193 Guiles, *Norma Jean*, 360.

194 Murray, 101–2.

194 Ralph Roberts: int.

194–95 John Kennedy: Wills, 22–26, 28–30, 34–35. For accounts of Monroe and the Kennedys, see: Martin, *A Hero of Our Time*; Skolsky, *Don't Get Me Wrong*;

Wilson, *Show Business Laid Bare*; Schlesinger, *Robert Kennedy and His Times*; Summers.

195   Cukor: Bernstein.

195   Rosten, *Marilyn*, 112–14.

195   Greenson's correspondence: Summers, 242–43.

195   Lowen, 47, 62, 186.

195–96   Greenson: Summers, 269.

196   Bernstein.

196   Rupert Allan: int.

196–97   Weatherby, 210.

197   George Barris' photographs: Mailer, *Marilyn*, 241, 243, 245–46.

197–98   Stern, *The Last Sitting*, 10–11, 14–16, 19, 23, 41, 55–59, 61–69, 71, 88, 146, 186. See a related sequence of photographs in *Eros*, Autumn 1962, 6–7, where the more casual, middle range of Monroe's emotions fills out the calm, almost stately ones in Stern's book.

197   Greenson: Summers, 189.

198   Meryman: int.

198–99   Meryman: Summers, 276.

199   Death by accident: Summers, 324.

199   Farber, 61, 66–70, 79, 117, 197.

200   Leary: Summers, 280.

200   Homosexuality: Summers, 242; Monroe, 76.

200–201   Greenson: Summers, 308.

201   Collier and Garbo: Capote, *Music for Chameleons*, 140.

201   Henri Cartier-Bresson: Goode, 101.

201   John Huston: Madsen, *John Huston*, 228.

201   "Find me, find me / complete this form": lines from Julie Suk's poem, reprinted in Oppenheimer, 55.

Bibliography

Adams, Cindy. *Lee Strasberg: The Imperfect Genius of the Actors Studio*. New York: Double-day, 1980.

Agan, Patrick. *The Decline and Fall of the Love Goddesses*. Los Angeles: Pinnacle, 1979. Photographs. Filmography.

Allan, Rupert. "Marilyn Monroe: A Serious Blonde Who Can Act." *Look*, October 23, 1951.

Allen, Maury. *Where Have You Gone, Joe Di Maggio: The Story of America's Last Hero*. New York: Dutton, 1975.

Alvarez, A. *The Savage God: A Study of Suicide*. New York: Bantam, 1973.

Anderson, Janice. *Marilyn Monroe*. New York: Crescent, 1983. Photographs.

Andrews, Matthew. *Let's Make Love*. New York: Bantam, 1960.

Ansbacher, Walter. "Alfred Adler, Individual Psychology." *Psychology Today*, February 1970.

"Apprentice Goddesses." *Life*, January 1951.

Arbuthnot, Lucie, and Gail Seneca. "Pre-Text and Text in *Gentlemen Prefer Blondes*." *Film Reader*, Volume 5.

Armour, Robert A. *Fritz Lang*. Boston: Twayne, 1977.

Armstrong, Charlotte. *The Charlotte Armstrong Treasury*. New York: Coward, McCann, and Geoghegan, 1972. Contains *Mischief*, the novel on which *Don't Bother To Knock* is based.

Arnold, Eve. *Flashback! The 50's*. New York: Knopf, 1978. Photographs.

————. *The Unretouched Woman*. New York: Knopf, 1976. Photographs.

Asbury, Edith Evans. "Marianne Kris, a Psychoanalyst, Specialized in Treating Children." *New York Times*, November 25, 1980, p. D23.

Avedon, Richard. *Portraits*. New York: Noonday, 1976.

Axelrod, George. *The Seven Year Itch*. New York: Bantam, 1955.

Bacall, Lauren. *By Myself*. New York: Knopf, 1979.

Baltake, Joe. *The Films of Jack Lemmon*. Secaucus, N.J.: Citadel, 1977.

Barbaro, Nick. "*The Misfits*." *Program Notes*. *Cinema Texas*, May 4, 1976.

Barris, George, and Theo Wilson. "Marilyn Speaks." *Philadelphia Daily News*, August 20–25, 1962.

Behlmer, Rudy. *America's Favorite Movies: Behind the Scenes*. New York: Frederick Ungar, 1982.

Belton, John. "*Monkey Business*." *Film Heritage*, Volume 6, 1970–71, pp. 19–26.

————. *Robert Mitchum*. New York: Pyramid, 1976.

Benjamin, Walter. *Illuminations*. New York: Schocken, 1969.

Bentley, Eric, ed. *Thirty Years of Treason: Excerpts from Hearings Before the House Committee on Un-American Activities, 1938–1968*. New York: Viking, 1971.

Bernstein, Walter. "Monroe's Last Picture Show." *Esquire*, July 1973.

The Best of Playboy, Number Four. Chicago: Playboy Press, 1970. Reminiscences of Monroe.

Bogdanovich, Peter. *Fritz Lang in America.* New York: Praeger, 1969.

Bolstad, Helen. "Marilyn in the House." *Photoplay,* September 1955.

Bosworth, Patricia. *Montgomery Clift.* New York: Bantam, 1979.

Brackman, Jacob. *The Put-on.* New York: Bantam, 1972.

Brode, Douglas. *The Film of the Fifties.* Secaucus, N.J.: Citadel, 1976. Photographs.

Broeske, Pat H. "The Misfits." *Magill's Survey of Cinema. English Language Films.* Volume 3. Englewood Cliffs, N.J.: Salem Press, 1980.

————. "Some Like It Hot." *Magill's Survey of Cinema. English Language Films.* Volume 4. Englewood Cliffs, N.J.: Salem Press, 1980.

Cahn, Robert. "1951 Model Blonde." *Collier's,* September 8, 1951.

Capote, Truman. *The Dogs Bark: Public People and Private Places.* New York: Random House, 1973.

————. *Music for Chameleons.* New York: Random House, 1980.

Carey, Gary. *Cukor & Co.: The Films of George Cukor and His Collaborators.* New York: Museum of Modern Art, 1971.

Carpozi, George. *Marilyn Monroe—Her Own Story.* London: World Distributors, 1961.

Carroll, Ronald H. (Assistant District Attorney), and Alan B. Tomich (Investigator). *The Death of Marilyn Monroe: Report to the District Attorney,* December 1982.

Cavell, Stanley. *The World Viewed: Reflections on the Ontology of Film.* New York: Viking, 1971.

Chaikin, Joseph. *The Presence of the Actor.* New York: Atheneum, 1972.

Chekhov, Michael. *To The Actor: On the Technique of Acting.* New York: Harper & Row, 1953.

Clarens, Carlos. *George Cukor.* London: Secker and Warburg, 1976.

Conover, David. *Finding Marilyn.* New York: Grosset and Dunlap, 1981. Photographs.

Conway, Michael, and Mark Ricci. *The Films of Marilyn Monroe.* Secaucus, N.J.: Citadel, 1964. Photographs.

Cook, Jim. "Marilyn and Her Man." *New York Post,* July 8, 1956.

Corwin, Jane. "Orphan in Ermine." *Photoplay,* March 1954.

Cottrell, John. *Laurence Olivier.* Englewood Cliffs, N.J.: Prentice-Hall, 1975.

Coursodan, Jean-Pierre, with Pierre Sauvage. *American Directors.* Volume 1. New York: McGraw-Hill, 1983.

Croce, Arlene. "The Misfits." *Sight & Sound,* Volume 30, 1961.

Crowther, Bosley. "The Prince and the Showgirl." *New York Times,* July 15, 1957.

Curtis, Mark. "Memories of 'The Misfits' in Nevada: The Last Sunset of Reno's Frontier." *Gazette Journal* (Reno Nevada), October 23, 1977, p. 1.

Dalton, David. *James Dean: The Mutant King.* San Francisco: Straight Arrow Books, 1974.

Daniels, Robert L. *Laurence Olivier: Theater and Cinema.* New York: Barnes, 1980.

Dick, Bernard F. *Billy Wilder.* Boston: Twayne, 1980.

Dostoevsky, Fyodor. *The Brothers Karamazov.* New York: Bantam, 1981.

Dougherty, James E. *The Secret Happiness of Marilyn Monroe.* Chicago: Playboy Press, 1976. Photographs.

Easty, Dwight. *On Method Acting.* Orlando, Fla.: House of Collectibles, 1980.

Eisner, Lotte. *Fritz Lang.* New York: Oxford University Press, 1977.

Engstead, John, *Star Shots: Fifty Years of Pictures and Stories by One of Hollywood's Greatest Photographers.* New York: Dutton, 1978.

Farber, Leslie. *Lying, Despair, Jealousy, Envy, Sex, Suicide, Drugs, and The Good Life.* New York: Basic Books, 1973.

Farber, Stephen. "The Films of Billy Wilder." *Film Comment,* Volume 7, 1971–72.

Farrell, James T. "Waif to Woman." *Coronet*, January 1957.

Flack, Audrey. *On Painting*. New York: Abrams, 1981.

Fraser, Kennedy. "On and Off the Avenue (Feminine Fashions)." *New Yorker*, November 9, 1981.

French, Brandon. *On the Verge of Revolt: Women in American Films of the Fifties*. New York: Frederick Ungar, 1978.

Freud, Sigmund. *Beyond the Pleasure Principle*. New York: Bantam, 1967[1920].

Funke, Lewis, and John E. Booth, eds. *Actors Talk about Acting: Fourteen Intimate Interviews*. New York: Avon, 1963.

Garrett, George P., O. B. Hardison, Jr., and Jane R. Gelfman, eds. *Film Scripts Three*. New York: Merideth, 1972. Contains an early version of *The Misfits*.

Gilliatt, Penelope. *Unholy Fools: Wits, Comics, Disturbers of the Peace: Film and Theater*. New York: Viking, 1973.

Goffman, Erving. *Frame Analysis: An Essay on the Organization of Experience*. New York: Harper Colophon, 1974.

_____. *Gender Advertisements*. Cambridge, Mass.: Harvard University Press, 1979.

_____. *The Presentation of Self in Everyday Life*. Garden City, N.Y.: Anchor, 1959.

Goode, James. *The Story of The Misfits*. New York: Bobbs-Merrill, 1963.

Greenson, Ralph. *Explorations in Psychoanalysis*. New York: International University Press, 1978.

"The Growing Cult of Marilyn." *Life*, January 25, 1963. Paintings and poems.

Guiles, Fred. *Legend: The Life and Death of Marilyn Monroe*. York: Stein and Day, 1984. Photographs.

_____. "Marilyn Monroe." *This Week*, March 2, 1969.

_____. *Norma Jean: The Life of Marilyn Monroe*. New York: Bantam, 1970. Photographs.

Hamilton, Jack. "Marilyn's New Life," *Look*, October 1, 1957.

Haskell, Molly. *From Reverence to Rape: The Treatment of Women in the Movies*. New York: Holt, Rinehart and Winston, 1974.

Haspiel, James Robert. "Marilyn Monroe: The Starlet Days." *Films in Review*, January–June, 1975.

Hethmon, Robert H., ed. *Strasberg at The Actors Studio*. New York: Viking, 1983.

Hirsch, Foster. *Laurence Olivier*. Boston: Twayne, 1979.

Hirschhorn, Clive. *The Hollywood Musical*. New York: Crown, 1981.

Hodgson, Moira. "Yves Montand—From the Musical Hall to the Met." *New York Times*, Arts and Leisure, September 5, 1982, pp. 1, 14.

Holtzman, Will. *Jack Lemmon*. New York: Pyramid, 1977.

Hopper, Hedda. "Marilyn Tells the Truth to Hedda Hopper." *Photoplay*, January 1953.

Hoyt, Edwin P. *Marilyn: The Tragic Venus*. London: Robert Hale, 1967. Photographs.

Huston, John. *An Open Book*. New York: Ballantine, 1982.

Hutchinson, Tom. *Marilyn Monroe*. New York: Exeter, 1982. Photographs.

Inge, William. *Bus Stop*. New York: Bantam, 1956.

Jennings, C. Robert. "The Strange Case of Marilyn Monroe vs. the U.S. Army: A Reminiscence," *Los Angeles*, August 1966.

Johnson, Dorris, and Ellen Levanthal. *The Letters of Nunnally Johnson*. New York: Knopf, 1981.

Johnson, Julia. "Gentlemen Prefer Blondes." *Magill's Survey of Cinema. English Language Films*. Volume 2. Englewood Cliffs, N.J.: Salem Press, 1980.

_____. "The Seven Year Itch." *Magill's Survey of Cinema. English Language Films*. Volume 4. Englewood Cliffs, N.J.: Salem Press, 1980.

Jordan, Rene. *Clark Gable*. New York: Pyramid, 1973.

Joyce, Alex. "Marilyn at the Crossroads." *Photoplay*, July 1957.

Kaminsky, Stuart. *John Huston: Maker of Magic*. Boston: Houghton Mifflin, 1978.

Kanin, Garson. *Hollywood*. New York: Viking, 1974.

Kass, Judith M. *The Films of Montgomery Clift*. Secaucus, N.J.: Citadel, 1979.

Kauffman, Stanley. *A World on Film: Criticism & Comment*. New York: Dell, 1966.

_____. *Living Images: Film Criticism & Comment*. New York: Harper & Row, 1975.

Kierkegaard, Soren. *Repetition: An Essay in Experimental Psychology*. New York: Harper Torchbooks, 1964.

Kiernan, Thomas. *Sir Larry: The Life of Laurence Olivier*. New York: Times Books, 1981.

Knight, Arthur. "Speaking of Artists." *Saturday Review*, September 15, 1956.

Kobal, John. "Dialogue on Film: Kim Stanley." *American Film*, June 1983.

_____, ed. *Movie-Star Portraits of the Forties*. New York: Dover, 1977.

_____, ed. *Film-Star Portraits of the Fifties*. New York: Dover, 1980.

Kobal, John, and David Robinson. *Marilyn Monroe: A Life on Film*. New York: Hamlyn, 1974.

Korda, Michael. *Charmed Lives: A Family Romance*. New York: Random House, 1979.

La Guardia, Robert. *Monty: A Biography of Montgomery Clift*. New York: Arbor House, 1977.

Lacan, Jacques. *Ecrits: A Selection*, translated from the French by Alan Sheridan. New York: Norton, 1977.

Lahr, John. "The Beatles Considered." *The New Republic*, December 2, 1981.

Laing, R. D. *The Divided Self*. Baltimore: Pelican, 1965.

_____. *Self and Others*. Baltimore: Penguin, 1971.

Lambert, Gavin. *On Cukor*. New York: Putnam's, 1972.

Lamparski, Richard. *Hidden Hollywood, Where the Stars Lived, Loved and Died*. New York: Simon and Schuster, 1981.

Lembourn, Hans. *Diary of a Lover of Marilyn Monroe*. New York: Bantam, 1979.

Lewis, Robert. *Method or Madness*. New York: Samuel French, 1958.

Logan, Josh. *Movie Stars, Real People, and Me*. New York: Delacorte, 1978.

Lowen, Alexander. *Fear of Life*. New York: Macmillan, 1980.

Lowry, Ed. "*Monkey Business*." *Program Notes*. Cinema Texas, April 22, 1976.

Lucas, Blake, "*Monkey Business*." *Magill's Survey of Cinema. English Language Films*. Volume 3. Englewood Cliffs, N.J.: Salem Press, 1980.

Luce, Claire Booth. "The 'Love Goddess' Who Never Found Any Love." *Life*, August 7, 1964, pp. 70–76.

Lytess, Natasha. *My Years with Marilyn*. 28-page manuscript deposited in the Maurice Zolotow collection, Humanities Research, University of Texas at Austin.

McBride, Joseph., ed. *Hawks on Hawks*. Berkeley: University of California Press, 1982.

_____, ed. *Focus on Howard Hawks*. Englewood Cliffs, N.J.: Prentice-Hall, 1972.

McBride, Joseph, and Michael Wilmington. "The Private Life of Billy Wilder." *Film Quarterly*, Volume 23, 1970.

McGuiness, Richard. "On River of No Return." *Film Comment*, September 1972.

McIntyre, Alice T. "Waiting for Monroe or Notes from Olympus." *Esquire*, March 1961.

Maddow, Ben, and John Huston. *The Asphalt Jungle: A Screenplay*. Carbondale: Southern Illinois University Press, 1980.

Madsen, Axel. *Billy Wilder*. London: Secker and Warburg, 1968.

_____. *John Huston: A Biography*. New York: Doubleday, 1978.

Mailer, Norman. *Marilyn: A Biography*. New York: Grosset and Dunlap, 1973.

_____. *Of Women and Their Elegance*. Photographs by Milton Greene. New York: Simon and Schuster, 1980.

_____. *Presidential Papers*. New York: Putnam's, 1963.

Malcolm, Janet. "The Impossible Profession." *New Yorker*, November 24 and December 1, 1980.

Mankiewicz, Joseph L., and Gary Carey. *More About All About Eve*. New York: Random House, 1972. Contains screenplay and commentary on Monroe.

Manning, Dorothy. "The Woman and the Legend." *Photoplay*, October 1956.

Manvell, Roger. *Love Goddesses of the Movies*. New York: Crescent, n.d. Photographs. Filmography. Bibliography.

Marilyn Monroe: Rare Recordings, 1948–1962. Sandy Hook Records, 1979.

Martin, Pete. *Will Acting Spoil Marilyn Monroe?* Garden City, N.Y.: Doubleday, 1956. Photographs.

Mast, Gerald. *The Comic Mind: Comedy and the Movies*. Indianapolis: Bobbs-Merrill, 1978.

_____. *Howard Hawks, Storyteller*. New York: Oxford University Press, 1982.

Melamed, Elissa. *Mirror Mirror: The Terror of Not Being Young*. New York: Linden Press, 1983.

Mellen, Joan. *Marilyn Monroe*. New York: Pyramid, 1973. Photographs. Filmography. Bibliography.

"The Merger of Two Worlds." *Life*, January 25, 1954.

Meryman, Richard. "Behind the Myth of Norma Jean." *Life*, November 4, 1966.

_____. " 'Fame May Go By . . .': An Interview." *Life*, August 3, 1962.

Miller, Alice. *Prisoners of Childhood*. New York: Basic Books, 1981.

Miller, Arthur. *Collected Plays*, Volume II. New York: Viking, 1971.

_____. *Death of a Salesman*. In *The Portable Arthur Miller*. New York, 1971.

_____. *Focus*. New York: Penguin, 1978.

_____. *I Don't Need You Any More: Stories*. New York: Viking, 1967.

_____. "My Wife Marilyn." *Life*, December 22, 1958.

_____. *The Theater Essays of Arthur Miller*. Robert A. Martin, ed. New York: Penguin, 1978.

_____. "With Respect for Her Agony but with Love." *Life*, February 7, 1964.

"Monroe Magic." *After Dark*, August/September 1981. Photographs.

Monroe, Marilyn. *My Story*. New York: Stein and Day, 1974. Written by Ben Hecht.

Morley, Margaret. *The Films of Laurence Olivier*. Secaucus, N.J.: Citadel, 1978.

Morsberger, Katherine M. "Bus Stop." *Magill's Survey of Cinema: English Language Films*. Volume 1. Englewood Cliffs, N.J.: Salem Press, 1980.

Muir, Florabel. "Reporting." *The Mirror*, February 10, 1953.

Murray, Eunice. *Marilyn: The Last Months*. New York: Pyramid, 1975. Photographs.

Negulesco, Jean. *Things I Did . . . and Things I Think I Did*. New York: Linden Press/Simon and Schuster, 1984. Photographs and drawings.

Nolan, William F. *John Huston: King Rebel*. Los Angeles: Sherbourne Press, 1965.

Odets, Clifford. *Golden Boy: A Play in Three Acts*. New York: Random House, 1937.

_____. "To Whom It May Concern: Marilyn Monroe." *Show*, October 1962.

Olivier, Laurence. *Confessions of an Actor: An Autobiography*. New York: Simon and Schuster, 1982.

O'Neill, Eugene. *Anna Christie*. *The Plays of Eugene O'Neill*. Volume 3. New York: Random House, 1956.

Oppenheimer, Joel. *Marilyn Lives!* New York: Delilah, 1981. Photographs.

Parrish, James Robert. *The Fox Girls*. New Rochelle, N.Y.: Arlington House, 1971.

Parsons, Louella. *Tell It to Louella*. New York: Putnam's, 1961.

Patrick, Bob, ed. *Marilyn*. New York: O'Quinn Studios, 1980. Photographs.

Pepitone, Lena, and William Stadiem. *Marilyn Monroe Confidential.* New York: Pocket Books, 1980. Photographs.

Phillips, Gene D. *George Cukor.* Boston: Twayne, 1982.

Pratley, Gerald. *The Cinema of John Huston.* Cranbury, N.J.: Barnes, 1977.

Preminger, Otto. *Preminger: An Autobiography.* New York: Doubleday, 1977.

Pudovkin, V. I. *Film Technique and Film Acting.* New York: Grove Press, 1976.

Rattigan, Terrence. *The Sleeping Prince.* London: Hamish Hamilton, 1954.

Rauh, Olie, and Joe Rauh, as told to Harriet Lyons. "The Time Marilyn Monroe Hid Out at Our House." *Ms.,* August 1, 1983.

Reitz, Carolyn. *"Some Like It Hot." Program Notes. Cinema Texas,* April 21, 1975.

Rollyson Jr., Carl E. *"Marilyn*: Mailer's Novel Biography." *Biography,* Volume 1, 1978.

Roman, Robert C. "Marilyn Monroe: Her Tragedy Was Allowing Herself to Be Misled Intellectually." *Films in Review,* October 1962, pp. 449–68. Filmography.

Rosten, Norman. *Marilyn: An Untold Story.* New York: Signet Books, 1973. Photographs. Documents.

_____. *Selected Poems.* New York: George Braziller, 1979.

Rosten, Patricia. "Patricia Rosten on Marilyn Monroe." *Closeups.* Danny Peary, ed. New York: Workman, 1978.

Roud, Richard. *Cinema: A Critical Dictionary.* Volumes 1 and 2. Norwich, England: Secker and Warburg, 1980.

Sayre, Nora. "Screen: Monroe Myths." *New York Times,* February 1, 1974, p. 14C.

Scagnetti, Jack. *The Life & Loves of Gable.* Middle Village, N.Y.: Jonathan David, 1976.

Schjeldahl, Peter. "Marilyn: Still Being Exploited?" *New York Times,* December 17, 1967, p. 40D.

Schlesinger Jr., Arthur M. *Robert Kennedy and His Times.* Boston: Houghton Mifflin, 1978.

Seidman, Steve. *The Film Career of Billy Wilder.* Boston: G. K. Hall, 1977.

Shaw, Sam. *In the Camera Eye.* New York: Hamlyn, 1979.

"Shocked Disbelief is Hollywood Reaction to Marilyn's Death." *Philadelphia Daily News,* August 7, 1962.

Signoret, Simone. *Nostalgia Isn't What It Used To Be.* New York: Penguin, 1979.

Sinyard, Neil, and Adrian Turner. *Journey Down Sunset Boulevard: The Films of Billy Wilder.* Ryde, Isle of Wight: BCW Publishing, 1979.

Sklar, Robert. "Marilyn Monroe." *Notable American Women: A Biographical Dictionary.* Barbara Sickerman, Carol Hurd Green, Ilene Kantrov, with Harriet Walker, eds. Boston: Harvard University Press, 1980.

Skolsky, Sidney. *Don't Get Me Wrong—I Love Hollywood.* New York: Putnam's, 1975.

_____. *Marilyn.* New York: Dell, 1954. Photographs.

Slatzer, Robert. *The Curious Death of Marilyn Monroe.* New York: Pinnacle, 1974. Photographs. Documents. Filmography.

Smith, Ronnie, and Bob Webster. "Dead Man's Papers Shed Light on Marilyn Mystery." *Riverside Press Enterprise,* February 22, 1981, p B5.

Sontag, Susan. *On Photography.* New York: Farrar, Straus and Giroux, 1977.

Spada, James, and George Zeno. *Monroe: Her Life in Pictures.* Garden City, N.Y.: Doubleday, 1982.

Speriglio, *Marilyn Monroe: Murder Coverup.* Van Nuys, Calif.: Seville Publishing, 1982.

Stack, Robert. *Straight Shooting.* New York: Berkeley, 1981.

Stanislavsky, Constantin. *An Actor Prepares.* New York: Theatre Arts, 1942.

_____.*Building a Character.* New York: Theatre Arts, 1949.

Steinem, Gloria. "Growing Up With Marilyn." *Ms.,* August 1972.

Stempel, Tom. *Screenwriter: The Life and Times of Nunnally Johnson.* New York: Barnes, 1980.

Stern, Bert. Untitled photographic layout. *Eros*, Autumn 1962.

_____. *The Last Sitting*. New York: William Morrow, 1982.

Strasberg, Susan. *Bittersweet*. New York: Putnam's, 1980.

Summers, Anthony. *Goddess: The Secret Lives of Marilyn Monroe* New York: Macmillan, 1985.

Taylor, Roger, ed. *Marilyn in Art*. Salem, N.H.: Salem House, 1984.

Thomson, David. *America in the Dark: Hollywood and the Gift of Unreality*. New York: William Morrow, 1977.

_____. "Baby Go Boom!" *Film Comment*, September–October 1982.

_____. *A Biographical Dictionary of Film*. 2nd ed. revised. New York: William Morrow, 1981.

_____. *Movie Man*. New York: Stein and Day, 1967.

Todd, Mabel Elsworth. *The Thinking Body: A Study of the Balancing Force of Dynamic Man*. New York: Paul B. Hoeber, 1937.

Tornabene, Lyn. *Long Live the King: A Biography of Clark Gable*. New York: Putnam's, 1976.

Trebey, Guy. "Don Murray." *Inter/view*, Volume 37, 1973.

Trent, Paul, and Richard Lawton. *The Image Makers: Sixty Years of Hollywood Glamour*. New York: Crescent, 1972. Photographs.

Truffaut, François. *The Films in My Life*. New York: Simon and Schuster, 1975.

Turim, Maureen. "Gentlemen Consume Blondes." *Wide Angle*, Volume 1, 1979.

Wagenknecht, Edward, ed. *Marilyn Monroe: A Composite View*. Philadelphia: Chilton, 1969. Contains her last two interviews; memories by Hollis Alpert, Flora Rheta Schreiber, Edith Sitwell, several of her photographers, Adele Whitely Fletcher, and Norman Rosten; reflections by Cecil Beaton, Lee Strasberg, Lincoln Kirstein, Diana Trilling, David Robinson, Alexander Walker, and Wagenknecht. Photographs.

Wagner, Walter. *You Must Remember This*. New York: Putnam's, 1975. Interview with Jack Lemmon.

"Walk Like This, Marilyn." *Life*, April 20, 1959.

Warren, Doug. *Betty Grable: The Reluctant Movie Queen*. New York: St. Martin's Press, 1974.

Waters, Harry. "Taking a New Look at MM." *Newsweek*, October 16, 1972.

Weatherby, W. J. *Conversations with Marilyn*. New York: Mason Charter, 1976.

Welsch, Janice R. *Film Archetypes: Sisters, Mistresses, Mothers, and Daughters*. New York: Arno Press, 1978.

Whitcomb, Jon. "Marilyn Monroe—The Sex Symbol versus the Good Wife." *Cosmopolitan*, December 1960.

Widener, Don. *Lemmon: A Biography*. London: Allen, 1977.

Wilder, Billy, and I. A. L. Diamond. *Some Like It Hot*. New York: Signet, 1959. Not the screenplay but an accurate transcription of dialogue.

Wilkie, Jane. *Confessions of an Ex-Fan Magazine Writer*. Garden City: N.Y.: Doubleday, 1981.

Williams, Dick. "Should Marilyn Tone It Down?" *The Mirror*, February 13, 1953.

_____. "Marilyn Wants to Turn It Off." *The Mirror*, March 10, 1953.

Williams, Tennessee. *A Streetcar Named Desire*. New York: Signet, n. d.

Willis, Donald. *The Films of Howard Hawks*. Metuchen, N.J.: Scarecrow Press, 1975.

Wills, Gary. *The Kennedy Imprisonment*. Boston: Little Brown, 1982.

Wilshire, Bruce. *Role Playing and Identity: The Limits of Theatre Metaphor*. Bloomington: Indiana University Press, 1982.

Wilson, Earl. *Show Business Laid Bare*. New York: Signet, 1975.

_____. "The Things She Said to Me!" *Photoplay*, May 1956.

Wilson, William. "A Lethal Slice of the American Pie." *Los Angeles Times*, June 9, 1972.

Winters, Shelley. *Shelley*. New York: William Morrow, 1980.

Wood, Michael. *America in the Movies*. New York: Basic Books, 1975.

Wood, Tom. *The Bright Side of Billy Wilder, Primarily*. New York: Doubleday, 1970.

Zinman, David. *50 from the 50s: Vintage Films from America's Mid-Century*. New Rochelle, N.Y.: Arlington House, 1979.

Zolotow, Maurice. *Billy Wilder in Hollywood*. New York: Putnam's, 1977.

_____. "Joe & Marilyn: The Ultimate L.A. Love Story." *Los Angeles*, February 1979, pp. 138, 140, 238–47.

_____. *Marilyn Monroe*. New York: Bantam, 1961. Photographs.

_____. "Marilyn Monroe's Psychiatrist: Trying to Untarnish Her Memory." *Chicago Tribune*, Section 5, September 16, 1973.

Index